Penguin Education
**The Psychology of Learning**

Robert Borger and A. E. M. Seaborne

140-147

Robert Borger and A.E.M. Seaborne

# The Psychology of Learning

Second Edition

Penguin Books

Penguin Books Ltd, Harmondsworth, Middlesex, England
Penguin Books, 625 Madison Avenue, New York, New York 10022, U.S.A.
Penguin Books Australia Ltd, Ringwood, Victoria, Australia
Penguin Books Canada Ltd, 2801 John Street, Markham, Ontario, Canada L3R 1B4
Penguin Books (N.Z.) Ltd, 182–190 Wairau Road, Auckland 10, New Zealand

First published in Penguin Books 1966
Reprinted 1967, 1969, 1970, 1971 (twice), 1973, 1974, 1976, 1977
Second Edition published in Penguin Education 1982

Made and printed in Great Britain by
Richard Clay (The Chaucer Press) Ltd, Bungay, Suffolk
Set in Monophoto Times

# Contents

Acknowledgements 7

1 Introduction 9

2 An Analysis of Simple Learning Situations 22

3 Learning and Evolution 49

4 Learning Theory 74

5 Language 104

6 Memory 131

7 Skill 156

8 Human Development 184

9 Mental Illness and Behaviour Therapy 205

10 Learning Theory and Education 231

11 The Application of Psychological Knowledge 256

References 265

Further Reading 273

Index 275

*Acknowledgements*   We would like to express our gratitude to the many colleagues who have over the years made helpful comments and suggestions, both on the original edition and on the current revision – especially to Dr John Odling-Smee; also to Catherine Woodgate at the London School of Economics and to the whole secretarial staff of the Brunel Psychology Department, for typing seemingly innumerable drafts.

# 1. Introduction

At most times during their lives people are engaged in some learning activity or other – learning to ride a bicycle or speak a foreign language, to swim, cook or play a new card game, to handle a pneumatic drill, manage a shop or administer a government department. For each person a selection of such experiences, especially the universal one of school, goes to make up his* idea of what learning involves and what sorts of questions about learning it might be interesting and useful to have answered. Interests and expectations of this kind no doubt played a part in the decision to buy a copy of this book. So we should ask at the very beginning: how do the reader's questions and problems about learning compare with those that psychologists try to answer? To what extent do they mean the same thing by 'learning'?

From the examples given above it will be apparent that learning occurs throughout the whole range of human activity. How can one deal with such a varied and complex field?

Consider two very different approaches. On the one hand we can concentrate on 'real' practical situations, in which people learn mathematics, or languages, or a particular skill, and try to determine for each case the circumstances and methods most effective for achieving success. This approach has been characteristic of much educational research and literature, produced by people with extensive experience of trying to generate learning

---

* It is no longer possible to use the masculine pronoun in this comprehensive way without attracting accusations of sexism. The authors wish it to be known that the usage in this book was determined by tossing a coin – once for the entire book rather than for each separate occasion.

in others. It has the advantage of being expressed in terms that are readily translated into application; also, since its problems, purposes and methods relate to situations that are familiar to most people, they make good sense and are assimilated without undue difficulties.

The other approach is an attempt to understand learning *as such*, in a more fundamental way. This involves a search for underlying processes and structures, for general principles that will answer questions about learning without specifying in detail the particular content, situation or type of learner. Since we do, after all, use the same term 'learning' in so many different types of instances, we may be tempted to suppose that this reflects the existence of some basic features of the learning processes, common to them all. If this is the case, a series of simplified and controlled experimental situations could help us to investigate the nature of learning in a systematic way. This, on the whole, has been the approach of experimental psychology, and has led to an interest in many problems that may seem a long way removed from the classroom, library or training school.

It is the object of this book to present, in outline, the problems of learning from a psychological point of view, the different experimental approaches and their underlying rationale. But although the immediate purposes of the learner, the teacher and the scientist are undoubtedly different in many ways, it is also in their mutual interest that they should not lose sight of each other; accordingly space is given to the interaction between theory emerging from the laboratory, and everyday practical experiences of learning.

## A working definition

Let us begin by looking for a provisional, working definition of learning. One way of doing this would be to take a wide variety of situations in which we *talk* about learning, and try to identify the features that are essential for our description to apply. If, for example, we think about learning history or algebra, learning to drive a car, operate a lathe or play chess, learning to recognize a faulty paint finish, a superior vintage or a case of Legionnaire's disease, what is it about all these that makes us use the word 'learning' in every case? The procedures, the time scale, the nature of the achievement involved, are very different. The only obvious common feature would seem to be that in each case someone *changes*, according to criteria specific to the situation; and it must be a change not just from one moment to the next, but something relatively stable. Thus we would look out for the history student talking or writing about the events leading up to the outbreak of the First World War, when at a previous time he could not; for the young chess player beating his father with increasing frequency; for the L-driver finally passing his test.

All these are changes of behaviour. Is this an essential part of learning? Well, let us say that these are the sorts of observations we would use in deciding whether learning had taken place or not. If we were challenged, or asked to explain what we meant by saying that someone had learned something, it would be such changes of behaviour that we would point to.

The examples we have used have other, perhaps less apparent features in common. They are of a kind in which the learner usually recognizes some objective that he wishes to attain; often there are specially created institutions, like schools or training schemes, to help him do it. Since we spend a large part of our lives learning in such explicit ways, these provide the most immediate examples. But does learning *have* to be explicit, does it have to involve intention, or, indeed, awareness? We would certainly accept that children, especially, learn a great many things without it being in any way deliberate on their part. And there need not be intention on anyone else's part either – no stage-managing is necessary for the proverbial child learning to avoid fires. While an element of deliberation, of conscious purpose, undoubtedly influences the course that learning takes, it is not really an essential component. The point about circumstances that have been *designed* for learning is that the relevant aspects are readily labelled – perhaps too readily. When learning takes place in a context that has not been arranged by anyone, or has been arranged with some quite different end in view, the structure of the learning process will be less apparent, and may at first be difficult to recognize at all. Still, such cases ought to be included in our analysis, and covered by any generalizations or explanations we eventually come up with.

Again, our original examples involved recognizable *achievements* as stages or end-points in learning. There are many cases of stable behaviour changes which are not usually thought of as accomplishments, or even as behavioural entities: acquiring the habit of taking a particular route to work, wearing certain kinds of clothes, smoking, speaking with a particular accent, refusing certain foods, associating with certain people. We might not immediately think of the development of a food preference as a learning phenomenon, but the important role of cultural influences in this respect, or the fact that we talk about 'acquired tastes', should persuade us to include it. Similar considerations argue for the inclusion of the other examples.

The reference to smoking raises an interesting question. Most of the examples of learning that we have given involved changes that were in some way advantageous for the learner, enabling him to do or recognize things, generally to cope more effectively with his situation: they were adaptive. When people behave in a way that is damaging, either to their health or to their social relationships, sometimes quite disastrously, are we prepared to regard *that* as the result of learning? Often such maladaptive behaviour is thought of rather as a *failure* to learn, perhaps the result of some defect in the individual concerned – though we do of course talk about people 'picking up' bad habits. If it could be shown that a behaviour pattern, though damaging, was systematically related to particular kinds of experience, we might be more ready to think of it as learned, or at least as being 'a reaction to' the experiences in question. There is of course always the possibility that behaviour might be adaptive in one context and not in another, or adaptive to begin with and not later on. Such considerations suggest that learning processes might be involved in, or at least relevant to, behaviour classified as 'pathological' – a topic to which a later chapter is devoted.

Are there any kinds of behaviour change that we would definitely *not* want to include under the heading of learning? As children grow larger, they are able to lift heavier weights and open doors whose handles they were previously unable to reach. Old people tend to get out of breath more easily and do things more slowly. Paralysis has profound behavioural consequences. Such changes are not regarded as examples of learning, either because they are seen as by-products of 'built-in' maturational processes, or because they involve some relatively crude, and usually damaging, interference with the functioning of the body. Our idea of learning seems to require that it should be the result of interaction with the environment, more specifically an interaction mediated by the senses: the direct consequence of an injury, say the amputation of a leg, would not qualify.

Let us now try out a working definition of learning – a definition, that is, which will identify for us, provisionally at any rate, the events or phenomena that a study of learning should encompass: learning is *any change in an individual that expresses itself in a relatively stable form of behaviour, and which is the result of an interaction with the environment, mediated by the senses*. It is perhaps a little cumbersome, and certainly not wholly adequate, but it provides a beginning. It includes all the instances of learning that we have considered, and extends to any conceivable aspect of behaviour, important or trivial, simple or complex, deliberately contrived or brought about by accident. It also extends to animals, although our examples so far have been confined to human beings. This broadening of scope is quite consistent with ordinary usage – there are many changes in animal behaviour that come about under the influence of the environment, which we would normally classify as learning. Indeed we might expect *some* capacity to change, in response to the properties of the external world, to be present in most living organisms. Making suitable allowances for differences between species, this opens up the possibility of investigating learning processes in dogs, cats, chimpanzees and a whole range of others – including of course the notorious white rat.

Our search for a working definition has resulted in enlarging an already vast range of situations to be dealt with. But there are compensations. Our attempt to specify the nature of the phenomena to be studied provides a lead to what we might look for in the first instance: systematic relationships between variables indicated in the definition – i.e. between variables describing the behaviour of an individual, the change of behaviour, and the impact of the environment. There are advantages also in extending the scope to animals in general. It makes possible the use of experimental procedures, degrees of control and forms of measurement which ethical considerations, as well as sheer inconvenience, would rule out in the case of human beings. One might even hope that carefully controlled and comparatively simple experiments could serve as prototypes for whole ranges of learning situations; that from these an explanatory framework could be built up, in terms of which even the most complicated case could be analysed and understood.

It was this perhaps somewhat optimistic belief that inspired the bulk of learning research up to about 1960. Add to this the fact that many people just like working with, or are specifically interested in, animals, and it accounts for the very large volume of animal research carried out by psychologists concerned with learning. Some important principles have emerged from this work, and have found at least limited application to human beings.

Needless to say, there has always been a great deal of *direct* work on human learning also. While some experimental procedures are ruled out, many others are *only* possible with people – all those involving verbal material, for example. In fact, whatever human behaviour is being studied, there is always some verbal communication between subject and experimenter; and, quite apart from any instructions or explanations that might have been given to them, people inevitably bring a vast conceptual and interpretive framework to bear on any situation in which they find themselves. Despite such apparent gaps between animal and even the simplest human learning, many psychologists believed – and some still continue to believe – that the differences are essentially quantitative, that they have their origins in the variability of the environment, and that provided sufficient detail is taken into account, a single set of basic principles can explain all instances of learning, from the most primitive to the most complex.

Before looking at some possible misgivings about such an approach, let us briefly recapitulate. We started off with a look at what learning might mean to most people who are not in fact professionally concerned with it. We pointed out that psychologists were primarily interested in the search for common processes and underlying principles. Trying to look for characteristic features of learning situations led to a provisional definition: learning involves a relatively permanent change of behaviour in response to sensory interaction with the environment. This allowed for the inclusion of various situations that are not readily thought of in connection with learning. It also allowed for the inclusion of animal behaviour as a relevant subject for study, without sharp distinctions being made between different species, including man. A great deal of research has been carried out in rigorously controlled and comparatively simple situations, in the hope that such 'pure' instances would systematically reveal principles applicable to all learning.

The reader may well have doubts about two aspects of what has been said so far. First, there is the emphasis on *behaviour*: this might be suitable for animals, or perhaps for the learning of physical skills, but is not the learning of history, or of mathematics, concerned with the growth of knowledge and understanding, rather than with the acquisition of new behaviour? Secondly, can a belief in a common set of processes across so many species, and so many situations, really be justified? Is it plausible? What if we do classify all these different cases as 'learning' – horses and motor cars may be classified together as forms of transport, but we don't expect a study of horses to further our understanding of the internal combustion engine.

Let us examine this distinction between behaviour and knowledge or understanding. To find out what progress is being made in learning to drive a car, we look at some aspects of performance, at something that the learner *does*, and we compare present with past achievement. And what happens in the case of, say, mathematics? Unless the learner does something, in writing or speaking or by giving some other kind of sign, we will be unable to establish how he is getting on. Our judgement of whether any learning has taken place must ultimately rest on making some sort of observation on the learner's behaviour, no matter what he is learning. And if we are pressed to explain what we mean by saying that someone *understands* a given mathematical theorem, ultimately we must do so in terms of various things he can *do* – reproduce it, explain it, apply it correctly in different situations, etc.

There are differences between this last case and one involving some routine manual task. One is in the *type* of behaviour that is relevant – speaking or writing words, as compared to making relatively straightforward movements. Another is a difference in flexibility. But we can contrast 'understanding' with 'rote learning' both in mathematics and in the use of a tool or machine. Judged from the point of view of criteria it amounts to contrasting a wide and variable range of behaviour with a much more limited one.

These are important differences and any comprehensive account of learning will have to deal with them – but, as far as the basic *data* of any investigation are concerned, they are differences in behaviour. Perhaps now that it has been said, it may seem an obvious point, but it needs to be made. We cannot study even the most profound and abstract knowledge, except by making observations on the behaviour that it produces. In fact, it is because we observe particular sorts of behaviour that we start talking about knowledge in the first place.

## Behaviourism

The emphasis on the observation of behaviour as the necessary starting point for a study of learning – or of any psychological problem – is one of the hallmarks of *behaviourism*: a psychological movement gaining its original impetus from Watson (1919), as a reaction to the strong speculative and philosophical element in the psychology of the time. But behaviourism in its various manifestations went a great deal beyond insisting that psychology should have a firm empirical basis. Partly to drive the message home, it tended to concentrate on very simple observations, and never to stray very far from them in its theorizing: in extreme cases it took the form of denying the usefulness of ever talking about anything that could not be directly observed.

The fact that we need to observe changes of behaviour to *demonstrate* the results of learning does not mean, however, that we should therefore regard them as identical. To be considered an expert on the French Revolution, a man need not be talking about it all the time, and the concert pianist is not regarded as having lost his competence while he is eating or reading a newspaper. The change which learning has brought about in these people is a change in *disposition*, or an *ability* to behave in certain ways. To say that a man is able to recognize different kinds and vintages of wine is, in one sense, another way of saying that if you put a glass of wine in front of him, he *does* as a rule make the correct judgement. However, the person who can and the one who cannot must be different in some way even at a moment when neither is demonstrating his ability.

The same point can of course be made with respect to animals. It is the distinction between competence and performance. What is it that makes performance possible at different times, and that endures between-times? We have a variety of terms like competence, disposition, knowledge and understanding, which have proved valuable for communicating with others: they say something about the individuals to whom they are applied, and lead us to expect certain kinds of behaviour from them. They do not in themselves *explain* what it is that makes the behaviour possible, but they do draw attention to something that needs to be explained. Increasingly, in more recent times, psychologists have been prepared to face the full complexity of what is conveyed by some of these terms, and to accept that some basic behaviourist assumptions fail to do justice, not only to mathematicians, but to rats as well. The latter also 'know' and 'understand', if in a somewhat more modest sense.

But how, over and above using such words, *could* one do them justice? Take the analogy of a weight-lifter: his competence *manifests* itself in lifting weights; it is *brought about* by training sessions, eating certain foods and perhaps steroid drugs; but if we want to know what mediates between the training and its intermittent behavioural expression, then a general account of muscle physiology, changes of bulk and efficiency of operation with repeated use, will go some way towards explaining how the ability to lift is represented or embodied within the lifter. Is it reasonable to search for that kind of explanation with respect to other, more complex kinds of competence?

There have been very great advances within disciplines such as physiology, neurology, biochemistry and molecular biology, in providing a picture of structure and function beneath the skin. Living organisms, even the simplest, are very complex indeed when compared with existing man-made machines, and we are some way from being able to relate such observations on the micro-structure systematically to any but comparatively gross aspects of behaviour. Nevertheless, some limited correspondences between neurological and what might be considered 'mental' events are being established. What is perhaps more important, artificial systems that we are now able to construct are capable of increasingly complex performances – the kind for which one might feel tempted to invoke terms like understanding. As a result, mental or cognitive processes have become a much more respectable subject of study. We still have to rely on behaviour, in the widest sense, as the source of data, but it is now possible to talk much more freely and plausibly about structures underlying that behaviour.

## Learning and maturation

Before going on to the second question – the credibility of a single set of explanatory principles for all learning – let us return to another distinction referred to earlier: changes due to learning, as compared to maturational changes. Bodily growth or the sexual changes at puberty are referred to as maturational, to emphasize that they are controlled by factors within the individual, and are relatively independent of the environment. Many of the more obvious physical characteristics of people and animals are genetically determined – eye and hair colour are well-known examples, and of course that elaborate combination of characteristics we tend to take for granted, which makes the offspring of people into *people*, rather than into chimpanzees or polar bears. These characteristics appear and develop in a way that is (always within limits) unaffected by the circumstances in which the individual matures. It is as though there is in the organism, right from the moment of its conception, a blue-print or program that lays down the course of development of the characteristics in question.

Such programs also affect behaviour. An animal's anatomy will determine the kind of movements it can make and its sensitivity to aspects of its surroundings. Apart from such general and indirect influences, there are quite complex and detailed patterns of behaviour that appear to be specified by genetic factors. Such behaviour is called 'innate', and develops within wide limits irrespective of the animal's experience.

We will consider later in some more detail the interrelationship between innate and environmental factors in bringing about changes of behaviour. While, strictly speaking, we can never entirely separate hereditary and environmental influences, it remains convenient to distinguish those aspects of behaviour that can best be elucidated by paying attention to the individual's environment from those that are characteristic of the species, and *relatively* independent of particular experiences. Yet even in those cases that are properly instances of learning in the above sense, where interaction with the environment plays a predominant part in determining the course that behavioural change will take, innate factors are found to affect the situation more indirectly. In the course of evolution, species have come to differ from each other, not only in structure and behaviour, but also in the way and extent to which they are able to adapt to their environment during individual lifetimes. The capacity to learn must itself be regarded as a product of evolution, developed by a given species in the context of its own particular and changing problems. There is now much accumulated evidence that learning is rather more variable, more species- and also more situation-specific than had at one time been supposed.

What are the implications of all this for 'a psychology of learning', and especially for the relevance of the large body of animal research to human behaviour? With the greater awareness of variation there is now also an increased readiness to examine different learning phenomena in their own terms. The recognition that human learning in particular has some very distinctive features will probably not come as a surprise to the reader; it has, however, had something of a liberating effect on theory and research in that area and there have been substantial recent developments, especially relating to language. Yet the same biological perspective, that has shown up and provided a rationale for differences in learning, also points to a continuity between species – and to the common theme of successful reproduction as the filter through which surviving species, with all their component mechanisms, have repeatedly passed. There is always hope that what are now seen as exceptions and special cases will eventually be revealed as instances of a more sophisticated pattern.

The psychology of learning has, until comparatively recently, been dominated by a number of general and powerful ideas that provided the driving force for much of the research during this century, but which have inevitably proved inadequate and stultifying in the long run. At present the field has some resemblance to the aftermath of a crumbled empire. Interest has become more local, more parochial. The old laws are no longer in force, but they have not yet been replaced by an equally comprehensive set, and their influence lingers on, in many indirect and subtle ways. Thus they provide a background and orientation for appreciating newer developments. The course we have adopted in the second edition of this book is to take the pervasive 'old order' as a point of departure for introducing some of the different directions being taken by more recent work on learning.

The chapters that follow can be thought of as grouped into sets of three. Chapters 2 to 4 show something of the rationale, the difficulties and the decline of 'behaviourist' learning theories: Chapter 2 presents the attempt to understand learning by concentrating on the structure of the *situations* in which it takes place, while playing down the characteristics of the learner, either as an individual or as a member of a species; Chapter 3 considers some of the evidence on variety and limitation in the learning process, and attempts to set it in a wider biological and evolutionary context; Chapter 4 looks at changing ideas about what may be going on inside the learner and at the prospects for a future synthesis. Chapters 5 to 7 deal with specifically human accomplishments: Chapter 5 with the acquisition of language and its role in learning more generally; Chapter 6 with verbal memory; Chapter 7 with motor skills. Chapters 8 to 10 share a concern with learning as a more long-term, cumulative phenomenon. Thus Chapter 8 looks at human development, and at some of the problems of trying to disentangle maturational and environmental influences. In Chapters 9 and 10 we outline some of the ways in which ideas based on learning theories have been applied in therapy and in education. Finally Chapter 11, as a postscript, takes up some of the general issues that are raised by a scientific approach to human learning and behaviour, and by the idea of *applying* the results.

# 2. An Analysis of Simple Learning Situations

One of the authors has a cat* that scratches at the kitchen window to be let in – not through the window itself but through a door some distance away. The sequence of events usually runs something like this: cat scratches window – runs to door and waits – door is opened (sometimes) – cat comes in. From here on things are more variable; she may head straight for a comfortable chair, or hang around her plate on the floor, or just sit down and wash.

This cat has another, equally unremarkable characteristic: anyone handling a newspaper is likely to be followed around with much miaowing, purring and rubbing against legs. Quite often the newspaper is subsequently put down on the floor with a plate of food on top of it.

This sort of thing will be familiar to anyone who has ever had a domestic animal. Dogs, even more noticeably than cats, will, over time, develop patterns of behaviour that are in various ways adapted to how things work in their particular surroundings: from 'begging' for biscuits to fetching leads or walking sticks as a preliminary to going for a walk. How do we explain this sort of behaviour?

Suppose that a visitor who has just opened the *Guardian* asks, 'Why is your cat getting so excited?'. If we tell him that the paper frequently serves as a kind of feeding mat, he is likely to be quite satisfied with this explanation. Clearly the cat thinks

* This particular animal has, alas, died between editions. We have resurrected her for the purposes of exposition.

she is going to be fed. What puzzles the visitor is not the general and very familiar fact that repeated experience gives rise to expectations, or that expectations lead to various forms of appropriate behaviour, but simply the way this particular animal is behaving. For this purpose, and in this context, the explanation given is perfectly adequate. But if we are making a study of learning, we may want to ask questions precisely about those familiar facts and relationships in terms of which we just explained the individual case, and which we normally – quite rightly – take for granted. *How* does experience lead to expectation, or expectation to behaviour? And just what is expectation? Since, especially in the case of a cat, expectations may be difficult to identify in their own right, can we perhaps dispense with such an intermediary stage altogether, and simply investigate the relationship between experience and behaviour?

These are general questions, and just to ask them in this form leads very naturally to setting up the inquiry in a corresponding way. Thus we may try to identify and arrange a number of prototypical learning situations, intended to represent and emphasize features that are common to a wide variety of individual cases – hoping (or assuming) that their study will provide general insights into the 'nature of learning'. Consider two well-known early experiments on animal learning.

## Conditioning

The Russian physiologist Pavlov, in the course of investigations on the digestive system in dogs, decided to examine in detail the 'anticipatory' behaviour of his animals. He had noticed that some features of their behaviour which at first occurred only when the dogs were being fed, began to make their appearance when they were *about to be* fed, apparently in response to the feeding preparations. Instead of taking this familiar phenomenon as self-evident and simply labelling it 'expectation of food', he set about a detailed examination of what this expectation amounted to, and on what features of the situation it depended.

Dogs were placed in a harness, in a sound-proof room with

constant temperature and constant illumination. The reason for taking these precautions was to ensure that accidental variations of position, noise, etc. would not affect the course of the experiment. A small operation made it possible to tap one of the salivary ducts in the dog's mouth and to obtain an accurate measure of the amount of saliva being secreted. Salivation is one aspect of an animal's eating behaviour and Pavlov singled it out for scrutiny because it was comparatively easy to quantify.

When the animals had acclimatized themselves to the experimental situation, the following sequence of events was introduced. A bell was sounded, and after a short interval, with the bell still sounding, a small measured quantity of dry food was delivered to the animal. The bell–food sequence was presented over and over again. Gradually the amount of saliva produced began to increase as soon as the bell sounded, anticipating the arrival of the food. The animal could now be said to salivate in response to the bell, whereas at the start of the experiment it had not done so.

Pavlov called the presentation of the food the *unconditioned stimulus* (UCS) and the salivation which it evoked the *unconditioned response* (UCR). The repeated pairing of the bell with food turned the originally 'neutral' stimulus into a *conditioned stimulus* (CS) which now evoked salivation as a *conditioned response* (CR). The whole process was called conditioning, now usually known as *classical or respondent conditioning*. The essence of conditioning came to be seen as the gradual *transfer* of responses, which at the outset occurred only in conjunction with one stimulus – the UCS – to another, originally neutral, stimulus – the CS;* Pavlov and his students examined in great detail the effects of such CS–UCS pairings on experimental subjects, using different conditioned and unconditioned stimuli, varying the relative time of occurrence, duration, intensity, etc. Changes in the animal's response pattern were observed, but normally did not affect the course of stimulus presentation.

* Or as the *substitution* of the CS for the UCS in eliciting the responses.

## Instrumental conditioning

At about the same time, E. S. Thorndike in America used cats in another simple, though differently structured, learning experiment. He put a hungry cat into a cage, food being available outside and visible through the bars. The cage was so constructed that a given operation, such as the pulling of a loop of wire hanging from the top, or the pressing of a lever, would open the door of the cage. At first the animal would struggle against the sides of the cage, reaching out paws towards the food, biting the bars – i.e. it would behave in a way that we call 'trying to get out', 'trying to get at the food'. In the course of its activity the cat would sooner or later work the escape mechanism 'by accident', leave the cage and eat.

After an interval, the cat was put back into the cage, escaped, and so on. Thorndike observed that as time went on, the animal's general activity shifted increasingly towards the vicinity of the 'door latch', and that the period between arriving in the cage and getting out got progressively shorter. After a large number of trials the cat would operate the escape mechanism as soon as it was put in the box, struggling, reaching, etc., having completely stopped.

A more modern version of Thorndike's experimental situation is provided by a 'Skinner box', a flexible type of laboratory device named after Harvard psychologist B. F. Skinner who first developed it. Such a box is constructed so that we can arrange for a selected piece of behaviour (pressing a lever, pushing a door open, pecking at a key) to be followed by a consequence (such as the delivery of a food pellet, access to water, the turning on or off of lights, sounds, etc.). Usually it also incorporates a provision for the automatic and timed recording of any stimuli that are presented, of responses made and of their consequences. While the overall way in which the box works is of course arranged by the experimenter, it is a characteristic feature of this type of experimental situation that the animal's activity forms an integral link in the sequence of events which it experiences.

Thorndike expressed the results of his experiments in terms of his 'Law of Effect': 'Acts followed by a state of affairs which the individual does not avoid, and which he often tries to preserve or attain, are selected or fixated.' He called such desirable states of affairs *satisfiers* and the learning process *trial-and-error learning*. The term *reinforcer* is now normally used, corresponding to Thorndike's satisfier, and *instrumental* or *operant conditioning* replaces trial-and-error learning.

Many of the subsequent developments in learning theory rest on these two types of experiment, and the way in which they represent learning as taking place; it will be useful therefore from the outset to have some appreciation of their similarities and differences, as well as of the particular features of our interaction with the world to which they draw attention. In this chapter we will be concerned with these basic models, some of their later elaborations, and the way they have been applied to analyse both artificial and naturally occurring learning situations. There has also been much controversy about whether classical and instrumental conditioning involve different learning *processes*, and not just different experimental procedures; whether there are one, two, or indeed more basic learning processes. There will be some reference to these issues in Chapter 4, though their detailed discussion lies outside the scope of this book.

## Classical and instrumental conditioning compared

Both classical and instrumental conditioning experiments essentially present the subject with an environment in which there is a simple relationship between two events, A and B. In the examples that we have considered, the occurrence of B depends on the (slightly) earlier occurrence of A. Typically the second event B is chosen to be 'of significance' to the subject – i.e. it is an event, like the presentation of food to an animal, to which there tends to be a definite response. The object of the experiment is to examine in detail the changes in the subject's behaviour as a result of being exposed to this relationship, or *contingency*.

In the case of classical conditioning, both events are initiated outside and independently of the subject: the sound of a bell is followed by food, a loud noise follows the turning on of a light, a buzzer is paired with shock. Whatever the changes that occur in the subject's behaviour, they do not affect the course of A–B presentations; they may be thought of as potential indicators of what *is going to happen*.

In instrumental conditioning event B again depends on the occurrence of event A; but this time A is something that the subject himself must do or bring about, an operation on the environment, with B as its consequence. The situation provides an opportunity for the subject to *determine what does happen*.

We may thus think of classical conditioning experiments as examining the bases of *prediction*, while instrumental conditioning is similarly concerned with the achievement of *control*.

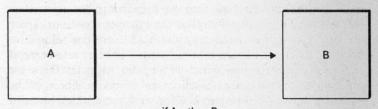

if A – then B

(i) The classical conditioning situation: A is an (externally initiated) event, here called the CS, followed by another event B (such as the presentation of food) called the UCS.

(ii) The instrumental (or operant) conditioning situation: A is an action (operant) carried out by the subject, followed by an event B (such as the presentation of food) called a reinforcer.

## Change of behaviour and the UCS/reinforcer

There is a good reason for choosing something 'significant' as the second event – we are more likely to be affected by a sequence of happenings, or by an action and its consequence, if the final outcome is in some way interesting or important. In the case of animals, we can regard an event as being important if it evokes some well-established response. The presentation of food has been one of the favourite choices, as being of obvious importance in this sense, and has been used in both classical and instrumental conditioning. However, the role that it is regarded as playing is very different in the two cases.

As we noted earlier, the original view of what took place in classical conditioning was a transfer of responses from a UCS (such as food) to a CS (such as a bell). It was quickly apparent that the anticipatory responses making their appearance as a result of repeated CS–UCS pairings were not identical to those that occurred in the presence of the UCS. (Such differences are particularly noticeable if – unlike the usual practice in Pavlov's experiments – the animal is not restrained during the experimental session. Under such 'free-range' conditions, a dog is likely to hover around the source of the CS, bark at it, perhaps lick it, and after the stimulus has come on, run over to the place where food is about to be provided.) But there are some parts or aspects of the UCR that *do* frequently reappear in the conditioned response – reactions like salivation, changes of heart rate or pupillary size, that we would normally, at least when talking about human beings, describe as 'involuntary'. It was reactions of this kind that Pavlov had singled out for study, and which provided the basis of his model of the learning process.

Compare this to an instrumental experiment in which the presentation of food is used as the reinforcing consequence of some selected action. *Now* all the interest is focused on what happens to the response that secures the reinforcement – changes in its frequency, intensity or other modifications. The only aspect of the *consequence* that we are here concerned with is whether it promotes or inhibits the behaviour that preceded it – i.e. whether it is what we ordinarily call 'pleasant' for the animal (a reward), or 'unpleasant' (a punishment). Apart from that, the reinforcer is typically not regarded as having any bearing on the nature of the instrumental response to be learned. This is determined quite independently by the experimenter, or by other factors outside the learner. (*Note*: it will be important to distinguish between the *required* response, the condition on which the presentation of the reinforcer depends, and the actual behaviour that eventually develops. The former can be selected quite arbitrarily, but there are clearly restrictions on what a given animal can do or learn – restrictions that have turned out to be rather more extensive than had been supposed.)

*To summarize*: Classical and instrumental conditioning experiments investigate the behaviour changes that result when a subject is exposed to a contingent relationship between events in its environment: classical conditioning focuses attention on the effects of 'announcing' something important, while instrumental conditioning examines what happens when a subject is provided with different kinds of opportunity for bringing about (or avoiding) some important event. In classical conditioning, if it is food (as UCS) that is signalled in advance by the CS, the experimenter is usually on the lookout for some anticipatory occurrence of reactions *to* food. By contrast, if food is used as the reinforcer in instrumental conditioning, generally there is little interest in the detailed reactions to the food itself (and hence in any similarity that this might have to the 'instrumental' behaviour that eventually develops); instead, we follow the animal's progress in meeting the (arbitrary) conditions which must be met before food is provided. This also means that the *kinds* of responses that are highlighted in the two types of experiment are different: 'involuntary' reactions in classical conditioning, actions, operations on the environment, in instrumental learning. This difference is reflected in the Skinnerian terms 'respondent' and 'operant' in place of 'classical' and 'instrumental' conditioning.

## Applying the learning models

Let us now see how we can use these models to describe the case of the domestic cat with which we started this chapter. The development of the window-scratching habit looks like a case of instrumental conditioning. The opening of the door, and the opportunities that this presents, are the consequences of the animal's behaviour and we may therefore suppose that the habit has developed because of this relationship. On the other hand, the circumstances leading up to the cat's excited reaction to paper-rustling have the structure of classical conditioning: over a period of time, this kind of sound has been followed (though not invariably) by the provision of food, and this sequence has (to the best of our knowledge) been unaffected by the cat's behaviour during the interval between the two events.

We can, however, in this last situation, also find features that fit an instrumental pattern. Although feeding does not *in fact* depend on the cat's reactions and behaviour after she has heard the sound of paper, it does nevertheless usually follow, and, from the cat's point of view, this may be indistinguishable from a 'real' consequence. The animal is affected by the arrival of food in a particular context, not by someone's intention that it should be a reinforcer, unconditioned stimulus, or whatever. Again, in the window-scratching–door-opening sequence we have to remember that the response that came to be reinforced, i.e. scratching, was in the first instance provided by the cat, it was something she did 'spontaneously', and this suggests that it could be something like an unconditioned response made to an obstacle.

Earlier we drew attention to the fact that the *types* of response that are usually given prominence in the two kinds of experiment are different: movements, operations in one case, reactions like salivation or sweating in the other. These types of response are also differentiated by some of their physiological characteristics, and for a long time it was thought that each was modified exclusively by the corresponding kind of learning contingency. More recently it has become clear that there is overlap: heart rate, for example, can be influenced by its consequences – this is the basis of the therapeutic use of *bio-feedback* (see Chapter 9); on the other hand, movement-type responses do occur purely as a result of CS–UCS sequences, as will be discussed in the next chapter. Meanwhile, in our domestic example, although the first analysis probably isolates the dominant learning influences we are left with some uncertainties. For example, is the excited miaowing before being fed like the anticipatory salivation in Pavlov's experiments, or more like the operation of a lever in a Skinner box? Clearly in such naturally occurring circumstances there are going to be complexities and ambiguities which a traditionally designed classical or instrumental experiment might avoid or conceal.

We have been looking at just a few among the very many, more or less stable features that characterize the world as it affects one particular cat. In the world of most infants we would find that raising their arms was often followed by their being picked up, and that the sound of the mother's voice occurred in frequent conjunction with particular kinds of visual and tactual experiences. For every one of us, whether human or animal, the environment provides a whole network of such experiential patterns. Many of the relationships involved are complicated; they overlap, interact, and will often be a great deal more variable than any described so far – but they are not chaotic. If learning is a process of adaptation to the environment, then we should find clues to the learning process by paying attention to the *structure* of the environment in which a given individual lives – more precisely, to the way in which that environment impinges on him. We could even approach the study of learning by concentrating *exclusively* on the relationships and pattern of events in the environment of the learner, and try to explain any variations in the course of behaviour by reference to corresponding differences in these patterns.

This has been the very influential, and, within limits, successful approach associated with Skinner, sometimes called the Experimental Analysis of Behaviour. It is an analysis based on classical and instrumental conditioning, although it gives a great deal more prominence to the latter – to operant conditioning, in Skinner's terminology. It deliberately avoids any reference to what may be going on inside the learner – either in terms of mental or cognitive events, or of physiological processes – and for this reason it has sometimes been referred to as the 'psychology of the empty organism'. Skinner does not of course deny that there are internal stages and happenings, but he believes that because they simply mediate between the impact of the environment and behavioural output, to consider them does not add anything to an account that tries to relate behaviour directly to the environment.

We shall try to show later on that this view is mistaken and severely limits the kinds of relationship that can be dealt with. But quite apart from this, for most people, a description of how behaviour is, and can be, modified by its consequences – whatever its predictive power and usefulness for devising special learning situations – does not by itself amount to an explanation. In Chapter 4 we will turn to learning theories that attempt in various ways to include the learner in the model. But for the moment we will stay 'on the outside', to see, in particular, how far an analysis along Skinnerian lines will take us. Let us begin by looking in a little more detail at some of the basic features of conditioning.

## Timing

We have been talking about the relationship between events, between actions and their consequences, in terms of their following each other with some regularity. How does the interval that separates related events affect the rate and extent to which behaviour is modified?

If we tried to train a dog to 'beg' by arranging to feed him every time he got onto his hind legs, but postponed the actual presentation of food until, say, a quarter of an hour after the selected response had occurred, we would not anticipate much progress. We may have made 'food follows begging' an invariable rule of the animal's environment, but if the time gap is too large, the relationship fails to make an impact on behaviour. People become aware of the connection between two happenings much more readily if they follow each other closely than if they occur at widely different times. Pavlov found that best results were achieved when the conditioned and unconditioned stimuli were separated by about half a second. In instrumental learning also the rate of learning falls off rapidly if anything but a very short period intervenes between the response to be learned and the presentation of a reinforcer. To maintain this rule we will have to introduce some qualification of the idea of a reinforcer (see below); but there are also some more fundamental exceptions to be discussed in Chapter 3.

## Primary and secondary reinforcers

Often when we want to reward a child for something that he has done, we promise there and then to give him something that he likes. Although the reward itself may be some way off, the promise alone produces an effect at the moment at which it is made, anticipating the impact of the reward itself. We are here dealing with the use of language and an altogether more complex situation than the sort of thing we have been considering, but there is an analogous phenomenon at a more primitive level.

The food delivery mechanism in a Skinner box usually makes a click as it operates. If the experimenter operates it repeatedly, the animal will be exposed to a classical (or respondent) conditioning situation in which a click is followed by the presentation of food. This conditioning can produce an effect which does not show up within the normal classical conditioning procedure: if at this stage we arrange things in such a way that some operation, like pressing a lever, is followed by a click and *nothing else*, there is some limited learning of the bar-pressing response, much as when food is actually presented. The click is thus acting as a reinforcer – a *secondary* or *conditioned* reinforcer, as distinct from a *primary* reinforcer like food. A primary reinforcer is one that requires no special learning to make it effective. A secondary reinforcer – and it is assumed that this could be any event whatever – acquires its special property through being repeatedly followed by a primary reinforcer.

Obviously we do not want to draw too close a parallel between promises and clicks. They are similar only in the (important) sense of deriving their power from their relationship to another and more fundamental event which they announce. Clicks, like promises, lose their effectiveness if they repeatedly fail to be honoured.

We can see now that the instrumental learning situation inevitably involves secondary as well as primary reinforcers – for example, the sight of food is a secondary reinforcer, even though this property will have been developed outside the experimental situation. We can also make deliberate use of secondary reinforcement by pairing a suitable signal with food presentation. The advantage of this is that a signal, like a click, can be made to follow a desired response immediately, whereas there is inevitably some delay before the presented pellet of food is seized and eaten. It is in this kind of context, rather than on its own, that the phenomenon of secondary reinforcement is best observed – helping to bridge the time gap between action and primary reinforcement.

## Extinction

What happens if learning takes place under a given set of conditions, and there is then a change, so that particular relationships cease to hold? Suppose for example that we have established a conditioned salivary response, and now change the situation so that the CS is no longer followed by food. Since salivation has come to *precede* the arrival of food, it will obviously occur to an undiminished extent the first time the bell sounds under the new rules. As we repeat the presentation of bell without food – CS without UCS – the conditioned response continues to occur, but to a decreasing extent, until it eventually disappears. Like the impact of the original rule, the impact of the changed rule is gradual in its effect. The process is called *extinction*, and has a counterpart in instrumental conditioning, when a response established by reinforcement eventually ceases after repeated non-reinforcement. In both cases, a response comes about gradually when B repeatedly follows A, and ceases gradually when this is no longer the case.

We should not, however, think of extinction as a simple reversal or undoing of the original learning. Although the response may appear to have ceased, it will tend to start off again after an interval such as that separating two experimental sessions. This recurrence is called *spontaneous recovery*. It is only if the extinction procedure is repeated several times that spontaneous recovery finally fails to occur. Even then we do not have a return to the animal's original state, in that the time taken to re-establish the response, if the A–B rule comes once more into operation, tends to be less than on the first occasion.

## Continuous and partial reinforcement

Extinction is a gradual process. If a reinforcement is again provided before extinction is complete, this will keep the behaviour going for a while longer, and in this way we can change from an arrangement in which every response is reinforced – *continuous* reinforcement (CRF) – to one in which only some are reinforced – partial reinforcement (PRF). This will maintain the response, paradoxically with increased vigour and at an increased rate. Partially reinforced behaviour is also more resistant to extinction, in the sense that the number of responses made after the cessation of all reinforcement is greater than in the continuously reinforced case.

There is no close parallel to this phenomenon in classical conditioning, where the CR is generally *weaker* when CS and UCS are *partially* coupled. If, anticipating the discussion of the next chapter, we reflect on the evolutionary *utility* of such an arrangement, we see that it makes good sense: when reinforcement is partial, increased effort is likely to pay off; nothing is achieved if an animal salivates more in response to an unreliable predictor of food than to a reliable one.

## Schedules of reinforcement

When reinforcement is partial, it follows the instrumental response intermittently. The rules which describe just when it does occur define a *schedule* of reinforcement. We may arrange, for example, that there will be a reinforcement after a fixed number of responses have been made – say after every fifth response. This is a *fixed ratio* schedule (FR), and such schedules can produce very high rates of response. Ratios of one reinforcement to a thousand pecks have been maintained with pigeons. On the other hand, we may arrange that after every reinforcement there is a pause of fixed duration during which no reinforcement is given, whether the animal responds or not. This is a *fixed interval* (FI) schedule, producing response pauses after every reinforcement, with a build-up in the response rate as the interval draws to a close. *Variable ratio* (VR) schedules maintain a given average ratio between responses and reinforcements, but the number of responses required to earn a reinforcement varies; similarly, with *variable interval* (VI) schedules, the interval during which no reinforcement is available changes from occasion to occasion, while maintaining a given average value. Both produce a very steady rate of responding, the rate being much higher for VR schedules than for VI schedules. VR schedules are particularly resistant to extinction. Skinner has pointed out that the reinforcement conditions under which gamblers operate are essentially of this kind. Although we may suspect that there are many factors that enter into the behaviour of roulette players which do not apply to pigeons, it is nevertheless interesting to note that their notorious persistence is predicted by their reinforcement schedule.

There are many other types of schedule – their potential number is after all only limited by the experimenter's ingenuity in devising functional relationships between action and consequence – whose effects on behaviour have been studied in detail. Skinner has claimed that even the most complex behaviour is generated and maintained by the interaction of the many schedules into which real life can be analysed – indeed if we cannot account for behaviour in a given instance, this must be because the analysis has not gone far enough. Be that as it may, the deliberate use of this approach has been very successful in developing, maintaining and controlling comparatively simple animal behaviour, suggesting that it is an appropriate analysis at least for this purpose and at this level.

## Generalization and discrimination

What happens when we look at behaviour in situations which are different in various ways from those in which the original learning took place? This is obviously an issue of considerable importance, since in 'real life' situations rarely repeat themselves exactly. We normally expect that the effects of a learning experience will not be limited too precisely by the conditions in which it took place – indeed, judging by the great contrast which usually exists between the setting and content of formal education and the circumstances in which we hope to benefit from it, we appear to have great faith in the possibility of a very general extension of learning to new situations, at least when we are dealing with human beings. Are there any parallels to this at a more primitive level?

Although our cat is normally fed on the *Guardian*, it will get just as excited by a tabloid and probably by brown wrapping paper – no exact tests have been carried out. There are in fact a whole variety of events which produce greater or lesser effects that look like anticipation of food, and this is probably because there have been, over the years, a variety of antecedents to feeding, in constantly changing combinations. But even if we establish a conditioned response in controlled conditions, and to a precisely defined stimulus – say, to a particular tone of constant pitch – if we now present a tone of a different frequency, there will still be a response, though usually at a lower intensity. The phenomenon is called *stimulus generalization* and has been extensively investigated. There are of course many dimensions along which stimuli can differ, especially when the original CS is at all complex. Some important work involving *compound stimuli* will be discussed in Chapter 4.

Generalization occurs also in instrumental learning, but before considering this we must take another look at our model. We have represented the instrumental learning situation as one in which a particular response A is followed by an event B, i.e. an animal is exposed to circumstances in which this rule holds. These circumstances, however, have other characteristics also – reinforcement follows a given action in a particular setting, be it Skinner box or classroom, and this setting must, strictly speaking, enter into a description of the conditions involved in bringing about the final behaviour. If we train an animal to press a lever in one sort of box, will it do so in another?

Boxes (not to mention classrooms) are very complex settings and can differ from each other in an enormous number of ways. We might expect that differences that are more salient, more pronounced, will have a more disrupting effect on a learned performance than those that are less so. In part this will depend on the kind of animal that we are dealing with – smells, for example, are likely to affect dogs more than pigeons, and generally different species tend to be susceptible to different aspects of the environment. But quite apart from this, the 'relevance' of a stimulus change can be influenced by learning.

Suppose for example that a pigeon has learned to peck at an illuminated key by repeated reinforcement. A change in the colour of the light will not normally make much difference to this behaviour once it has become established. If, however, we arrange that pecking the key is reinforced only when the light is green, and never when it is red, then the response becomes strongly established in the first, and extinguished in the second situation – i.e. the colour of the key becomes a critical factor in the occurrence of the response. The environmental rule has now become: 'Response A is followed by reinforcement B, in the presence of stimulus 1, but not in the presence of stimulus 2.' Skinner uses the symbol $S^D$ to denote a stimulus that signals the occasion for reinforcement, and $S^\Delta$ for one that announces non-reinforcement. By means of this sort of *differential* reinforcement we can produce *discrimination* where there would otherwise be a greater degree of generalization.

## Stimulus control

Discrimination involves *stimulus control* – in the sense that presenting the $S^D$, the stimulus associated with reinforcement, brings about the appropriate responses, whereas $S^\Delta$ inhibits it. Children learn to recognize the occasions on which requests of different kinds are likely to be met. Our cat, observed from another room, will lie quietly on the kitchen-window ledge, and will begin to 'ask' for admission only when someone enters the kitchen. More generally, discriminative stimuli can mark the transition from one reinforcement schedule to another and in this way produce an appropriate switch of behaviour. Like most of the phenomena in this section, stimulus control is not so much a discovery, as a more explicit recognition of a principle, claimed to have universal application. For Skinner all behaviour sooner or later comes under stimulus control (though usually we don't know what the controlling stimuli are). While this last claim is open to serious objection, the phenomenon of stimulus control undoubtedly *plays a part* in the regulation of behaviour, and can be deliberately utilized in the design of training procedures. Equally, the identification of controlling stimuli can help in the treatment of unwanted – e.g. compulsive or addictive – behaviour.

## Response chains

When a stimulus like the green light in the previous example becomes an $S^D$ it is at the same time increasingly paired with reinforcement. This is because the animal comes to respond regularly in its presence, and these responses are reinforced. A stimulus thus becomes a secondary reinforcer at the same time as becoming an $S^D$. We can now arrange that the green light – which announces that response A will henceforth be reinforced – will itself be turned on if some other response A′ is first made. In this way we can establish a short *chain* of behaviour: pecking one key, say, turns the light from red to green, which provides the go-ahead for the next response, which leads to reinforcement. Actually the chain is already longer than this. The sound made by the food dispenser, itself a secondary reinforcement for the immediately previous response, has become an $S^D$ for the response of looking in the food tray, where the sight of food reinforces looking, and provides an $S^D$ for pecking and eating. This illustrates the way in which the concepts of secondary reinforcement and stimulus control *can* be used, not only in the deliberate regulation of behaviour but also, by extension, in the description of what takes place 'naturally', without human intervention. Whether such an extension to behaviour regulation in general is justified is another matter.

## Shaping

We have mentioned reinforcement schedules involving one reinforcement to a thousand responses. Obviously we cannot arrive at such a performance at one go. If we simply put a pigeon into a situation arranged in such a way that the thousandth peck at a key will produce a grain of food, key pecking will never get established, let alone at a high rate. Nor can we change directly from the continuous reinforcement which is most effective in developing the response, to this sort of ratio. However, it can be achieved by a gradual increase in the response–reinforcement ratio; a gradual shift, that is, in the exact conditions for earning a reward. As this ratio increases, so does the number of un-reinforced responses emitted before extinction. The gradual increase in the ratio thus ensures that the behaviour will not extinguish at any stage of the process, and we are able to arrive at a level of performance far removed from the original one.

In this particular example, the change in conditions involved the number of responses required to secure reinforcement. What happens when we change the conditions relating to the *kind* of behaviour that is required?

Skinner has described the process of training two pigeons to play a modified form of table-tennis. This is important, not because there is any particular demand for birds with this sort of skill, but because it illustrates the efficacy of the principles on which the training process is based in a rather dramatic way. The pigeon version of the game involves the two birds standing at the ends of a low table each attempting to propel a ball past its opponent and off the table. Such behaviour is quite a long way removed from what we ordinarily associate with pigeons, and it may at first be difficult to see how the principles of operant conditioning may be used to achieve this sort of result. Since they involve the reinforcement of the behaviour to be learned, the behaviour must occur, before it can be reinforced. If, given a pair of novice pigeons, we simply impose on them the condition that engaging in a fully fledged game will be reinforced, it is unlikely that either of them will even as much as show interest in a ping-pong ball.

Operant conditioning must necessarily utilize such existing behaviour as has a reasonable probability of occurring. Although at the start of training the final achievement aimed at may be quite certain not to occur spontaneously, the animals' 'behavioural repertoire' will contain some components which lie in the direction of this achievement. Thus, if we start with one pigeon wandering about in the presence of a ping-pong ball, it will sometimes be close to, at other times farther away. If we reinforce 'closeness to ball' we soon get a situation in which most of the bird's activity takes place in this area. Under these new circumstances, there is a much better chance than at the beginning that the pigeon will peck at the ball. We can now begin to restrict reinforcement to these occasions – setting at first comparatively loose criteria for what constitutes a peck, but as soon as this behaviour has become established, tightening conditions so as to reinforce only pecks that move the ball in a specified direction. When the process has been repeated with the other animal, we are obviously a great deal nearer the desired end result and can start on selective reinforcement in the competitive situation. Needless to say, a secondary reinforcer such as a click is used to make possible the very precise timing on which success depends.

This process of 'edging' an animal's behaviour towards a goal, by using a gradual change in the conditions for reinforcement, is known as *shaping*. It involves the selection, at consecutive stages, of modified criteria for success, such that they move the behavioural spectrum towards the goal, and at the same time have a good chance of being met. The concept of shaping makes explicit a principle that is used implicitly in many teaching procedures.

When we can, in advance, map the 'space' between the start and the end point of a learning sequence into a number of over-lapping reinforcement conditions, such a sequence of conditions constitutes a *learning program* and will be discussed in Chapter 10.

### Painful stimulation

In considering the effects of various kinds of A–B relationships to which an animal might be exposed, we have so far concentrated primarily on cases where B – the 'significant' event – was essentially pleasant, something liable to be approached, a reward. What if B is a noxious, an *aversive* stimulus? In the case of classical conditioning, we might expect that, again, some portion of the unconditioned response to the stimulus itself would come to occur earlier, following the 'warning signal'; and that in the instrumental case, the use of an aversive stimulus as consequence for some response – like a punishment – might be thought simply to reverse the learning effects produced by reinforcement, to undo them. This is what Thorndike believed at first; a section within his account of the 'Law of Effect' stated that 'acts followed by states of affairs which the individual avoids or attempts to change, are eliminated'. But things turned out to be more complicated, and that part of the Law had to be abandoned. Skinner also found it difficult to assimilate aversive events within his scheme and tended to minimize their influence in his account of behaviour. Let us consider a few of the more salient observations.

In animals, painful stimulation, depending on its severity, usually gives rise to various forms of intense activity and to a complex of physiological changes, including for example an increase in heart rate, which facilitate it. When such a stimulus – say, electric shock – is used as the UCS in classical conditioning, results are obtained that are difficult to reconcile with any idea of response transfer or stimulus substitution. The typical *conditioned* response is *freezing* – keeping absolutely still. In human subjects, as in animals, one reaction to electric shock is cardiac acceleration; but the corresponding *conditioned* response is *deceleration*, the exact opposite. It may seem perfectly reasonable that a response made in anticipation of an event should be different from the reaction to the event itself – the trouble is that the proposed account of what happens in classical conditioning will not cope with it. We will postpone further discussion of this difficulty to Chapter 4, which is more explicitly concerned with *mechanisms*.

## Punishment

One form of instrumental conditioning with an aversive stimulus, like its rewarding counterpart, involves making the stimulus contingent on a particular response – the response is *punished*. This is only possible of course with a response that occurs with reasonable regularity, otherwise the effects of the procedure cannot be adequately observed. As an example, consider regular lever pressing in a Skinner box that has been maintained by a variable interval schedule. If these responses are now closely followed a given number of times by some unpleasant consequence, there is, as we might expect, a drop in the response rate; and indeed, responding might stop altogether. But with moderate levels of punishment, the suppression of behaviour is temporary and will pick up again, often as though the aversive consequences had not occurred. In certain circumstances, mild punishment can even enhance the rate and vigour of concurrently rewarded activity. It becomes very important to specify the conditions exactly, the delay between response and punishment, the nature of the stimulus used, its intensity, the animal's previous experience with the stimulus, the amount of previous positive reinforcement of the punished response, and indeed the species we are dealing with. It is not really surprising that Skinner, concerned with finding very general laws of behaviour, should have come to regard punishment as an *unreliable* factor. That does not mean, however, that unpleasant consequences – whether they are deliberately introduced or occur naturally – do not exercise an important influence on behaviour, and we will return to the subject in Chapter 4.

## Escape

Another way in which unpleasant stimulation can form part of a learning experience is as an existing condition which is *terminated* by some action. The selected response now has, as a consequence, the removal of aversive stimulation, which is a rewarding or reinforcing event – and there have been attempts to identify *all* cases of reinforcement as the termination of some unpleasant condition, however produced. There are, however, sufficient differences between a condition like hunger, and the presence of electric shock, say, for a special term *negative* reinforcement to be applied to the effect of terminating or reducing aversive stimulation. (It is a somewhat confusing usage – *both* positive and negative reinforcement are rewarding.) The process is called *escape learning*, and, perhaps not surprisingly, actual physical escape from the whole situation in which the unpleasant stimulus has occurred is most easily 'learned' under such circumstances – in fact, very little learning may be involved. Other responses however are sometimes much more difficult to establish in this way, even though they may present no problem when rewards are used. This is an issue that will be taken up in the next chapter.

*Avoidance learning*

This phenomenon has produced a great deal of controversy and theoretical difficulty – although, as in so many cases, it is something with which we are quite familiar. Suppose that an unpleasant event is preceded by a 'warning signal' – it might be an actual signal, like a buzzer, or it might simply involve being in a place where the event has previously occurred; and suppose further that a particular response, like 'getting away', not only terminates the event, but, provided it happens in time, avoids it altogether. Such avoidance responses are often maintained for a very long time. The problem is that there appears to be no reinforcement, since the shock, or whatever, is completely avoided. The 'danger' might in fact no longer exist. But without reinforcement, why does the behaviour not extinguish, as all good responses should under such conditions? One favourite explanation has been in terms of two separate processes: one, which establishes a conditioned response of *fear* to the buzzer or situation, which thus itself becomes aversive; and a second, which involves escape from the now aversive *conditioned* stimulus – it is the latter which continues to provide the reinforcement. There are many difficulties with this solution, due originally to Mowrer (1947). Why, for example, since there is no more shock, does the warning signal continue to arouse fear? And indeed there is evidence to suggest that after a time it doesn't. We will come back to this problem also in Chapter 4. In the meantime it may help to think of the situation as involving exposure to two consecutive 'rules' of the environment: (1) stimulus is followed by shock; (2) stimulus-plus-response is not followed by shock. The second rule continues to be confirmed. If confirmation of a rule can maintain behaviour – and these are all ideas which do not fit too easily into the framework that we have presented so far – then we can see that it helps to insulate the individual from certain critical aspects of the environment. As long as avoidance behaviour continues, the *original* rule, which caused all the trouble, is not tested, and continues to hold *for the learner*, even though it may no longer do so in fact.

### Active and passive avoidance

The avoidance of aversive stimulation may depend on *omitting* a response (i.e. when the response is singled out for punishment) – this is sometimes called *passive* avoidance; or it may depend on *carrying out* a particular response – running away, performing some designated operation – which is *active* avoidance. The learning involved in passive avoidance appears to be a very basic capability of animals, even very primitive ones. On the other hand, active avoidance, learning to do something specific to avoid danger, presents much greater difficulties, unless the required response happens to resemble one which comes spontaneously in such circumstances.

At least part of the explanation for this difference probably depends on the fact that animals, especially the more primitive ones, have well established, unconditioned reactions to pain and to danger (which can, as we saw earlier, be different). These will interfere with existing patterns of behaviour (producing passive avoidance) and with the establishment of new behaviour (hindering active avoidance). All that is required for passive avoidance therefore is that an animal should be capable of learning to recognize danger (by classical conditioning) and the suppression of behaviour will automatically be taken care of. This is another instance of a learning situation that looks instrumental, but may be accounted for in terms of classical conditioning, coupled with responses that are 'built in'.

## Helplessness

When an aversive event occurs repeatedly irrespective of what the individual does (as is the case in classical conditioning) this can produce a condition, sometimes prolonged, which prevents the subsequent learning of escape and avoidance responses, even when these have become clearly effective. Sometimes this also generalizes widely to quite unconnected learning situations. It is as though the individual has learned from the first experience that responding does not work, that control is not possible. Seligman (1975) has given the name *helplessness* to the condition, and has used it as a central concept in a theory about depression to which we will return in Chapter 9. In the present context it furnishes an important example of how specification of the 'environmental contingencies' alone may provide a misleading account of the learner's effective experience.

## Frustration

The counterpart to the avoidance of a punishment is the omission of a reward. We have come across the effect of this when talking about extinction, which might have been seen simply as an instance of previously established learning 'fading away'. But just as the avoidance of punishment produces rewarding effects, so the witholding of a reward has predominantly aversive consequences. These have been labelled *frustration*, and their *immediate* expression usually takes the form of responding even more vigorously. (It is a phenomenon that has no doubt contributed to the devastation of many telephone kiosks.) Frustration has raised the same problems as avoidance learning: effects produced by something *not* happening, by a 'non event'. If we want to *explain* what is going on here, it is clearly again going to be difficult if we are confined to talking about the environment only.

*Punishment and human behaviour*

We have indicated a few of the complexities in the behaviour changes that are brought about by aversive stimulation, based on comparatively simple animal experiments. Clearly there is an enormous gap between this and the way in which various punishments are used in human societies, and we do not really need this evidence to realize that simple reliance on 'bigger and better' punishments is unlikely to make our penal system more effective in controlling crime. We can see, however, how such a belief comes about. Punishment *is* very effective in stopping whatever is going on at the moment at which it is applied, and as the *users* of punishment, in one form or another, we have all, from childhood onwards, been promptly reinforced by its success in (temporarily) getting rid of the annoying activities of others. This frequent experience probably contributes towards the idea that punishment is in some way intrinsically appropriate to wrong-doing.

But if this view is simplistic, so is the notion that punishment 'just doesn't work'. Any species that was incapable of adjusting its behaviour to unpleasant as well as pleasant consequences would be extinct. If a society really wants to influence the behaviour of some of its members, it must start by taking a more comprehensive look at the whole context of reinforcements and punishments (and values) within which the undesirable behaviour occurs, and on this basis devise procedures *with the explicit objective of changing it*. Since our penal system has not been designed with this aim in view, its poor showing in this respect should not be surprising.

This chapter has been about a way of looking at 'simple' learning situations. In its later stages, the idea that we could give an adequate account of learning, even a purely descriptive one, without involving the learner, has become increasingly implausible. Terms like stimulus, response, reinforcement, etc. can be used with comparatively little ambiguity in experimental situations specially designed to avoid embarrassing decisions about what response has in fact been made, or whether the stimulus that was delivered is the same as that which was received. It is possible to derive useful procedures for the regulation of behaviour from such situations, and to extend them, tentatively, to others. But we must not try too hard to explain behaviour and learning generally in terms of such restricted concepts, in case we are driven to ignore (or even deny) whole ranges of 'troublesome' phenomena. The next chapter will be concerned with more of these.

# 3. Learning
# and Evolution

'Little Albert' is one of the legendary figures of early learning theory. In 1920, Watson and Rayner showed this infant a white rat, and when he reached out to touch it they produced a loud and startling noise by striking a metal bar with a hammer. After only very few such pairings of rat and noise, Albert had developed a persistent fear of the rat, which generalized to rabbits and other furry objects. The case of little Albert became a standard example of the way in which classical conditioning could produce aversive reactions, providing a plausible alternative to other more fanciful explanations for the common phobias. It also implied an alternative approach to treatment. If fear of a particular object or situation was acquired as a result of an ordinary learning process, then it could presumably be modified or extinguished in the same way as other learned responses.

In the years following the Watson and Rayner experiment, a number of other investigators used the same technique in an attempt to produce similar fear reactions to a variety of familiar objects, such as blocks or wooden ducks, but they failed. Either it was difficult to establish conditioned fear at all, even after many trials, or it extinguished comparatively readily. It seemed that it was easier for children to become frightened of some things than of others, even with the same conditioning procedures; in some way, the Albert experiment was a special case. However, such discrepant findings became submerged under a growing tide of research that emphasized similarities in conditioning rather than differences.

More recently, Garcia and Koelling (1966) carried out what has become another signpost in the conditioning literature. They first trained two groups of rats to drink water from a tube – one (the 'audio-visual') group drank plain water to the accompaniment of clicks and flashes of light, triggered by the act of licking; the other ('gustatory') group drank saccharine-flavoured water under normal undisturbed conditions. When drinking under these circumstances was well established, they divided each group into two; one half of each group now received a brief shock to the feet shortly after beginning to drink, just sufficient to interrupt drinking; the other group was given a dose of X-ray radiation, producing no immediate effect but eventual nausea. Thus, there were four conditioning sequences: (1) drink bright–noisy water → shock; (2) drink bright–noisy water → nausea; (3) drink flavoured water → shock; (4) drink flavoured water → nausea. When the animals were tested some days later, the results were quite clear-cut. Among the rats receiving shock, those for whom it was preceded by bright–noisy water had learned to avoid it, but those who had drunk flavoured water continued to drink. Among the rats that had been made ill, the consequences were the other way round: they had learned to avoid the flavoured water, but not the bright–noisy water.

Because of the carefully balanced design, these differences could not be attributed to any of the conditions – light–noise, taste, shock or sickness – considered independently. Nor could they be due to any differences of timing or frequency of reinforcement because these had been kept the same for both stimulus conditions. What the results showed was that rats must in some way be *predisposed* to associate nausea with ingested flavours but not with visual or auditory stimuli – and to associate the latter kind of stimuli with external pain, but not with the onset of nausea.

The following experiment neatly demonstrates that such relative learning predispositions and difficulties are specific to species, and are not universal characteristics. Wilcoxon, Dragoin and Kral (1971) trained rats and quail to drink water that was both blue and sour. Both groups of animals were then made ill, with the result that rats learned to avoid sour but not blue water, and quail learned to avoid blue but not sour water. Quail, and other birds that feed during the daytime, are much more guided by visual cues in their eating than are rats, who tend to depend on taste and smell. The different selective associations that each species forms with sickness, thus clearly have survival value for rats and for quail, respectively.

That some things are learned more easily or more permanently than others, and that species vary in what (and probably how) they learn, is not perhaps very startling. In particular, the tendency to associate nausea, even after considerable delays, with something one has eaten, especially something unfamiliar, rather than with other features of the situation (e.g. one's eating companions) is well known, as is the readiness with which rats become 'bait-shy'. Even in human beings, the making of this link cannot entirely be put down to 'understanding', since the aversion for the implicated food frequently survives the discovery that sickness was in fact the result of some coincidental and independent cause (as indeed it was in all the quoted aversion experiments). It is as if many animals are especially ready and 'tuned' to make this particular connection. Anyone having some familiarity with animals will be aware of other examples of impressive learning abilities which appear to be specialized in such a way as to match the characteristics, life-style and normal habitat of the animal in question. Such specialization and diversity of learning is, however, difficult to reconcile with some of the underlying assumptions in the approach we described in the last chapter, and generally with the mainstream of learning theory, as it developed from the work of Pavlov and Thorndike, during most of this century.

Most psychologists who studied learning had been searching for very general laws that would hold across different situations and across different species. Obviously, account had to be taken of gross differences in sensory or motor capacity – moles could be expected to be poor at visual discrimination problems, and Skinner, in training pigeons to play 'table tennis' prudently, did not aspire to getting them to hold bats. Skinner also recognized that reinforcers had to be discovered and defined separately for different types of animal – what is sauce for the goose might well be sauce for the gander, but does not necessarily impress a rat or rabbit. However, once such allowances had been made, once we were dealing with stimuli that the animal could discriminate, responses that it could perform, and consequences that were significant, it was assumed that the course of learning could be understood in terms of conjunction and timing only, without reference to the particular components of the learning situation, or indeed to the animal involved. Skinner (1956) expressed this as follows:

Pigeon, rat, monkey, which is which? It doesn't matter. Of course, these species have behavioral repertoires which are as different as their anatomies. But once you have allowed for the differences in the ways in which they make contact with the environment, and in the ways in which they act upon the environment, what remains of their behavior shows astonishingly similar properties.

What Skinner was not prepared to allow for was that the differences between species might extend beyond the *forms* of transaction with the environment, to the *consequences* of these transactions, i.e. to some aspects of the learning process itself – an assumption arguably appropriate as a first approximation. But the 'astonishing similarities' he refers to tended to emerge in rather specialized and restricted experimental circumstances, the preference for which was in turn justified by the belief that these situations could be regarded as representative of a potentially much wider range. In this way, the risk of astonishment by *dis*-similar results was kept to a minimum, and any that did show up were treated as anomalies that a more detailed examination of timing and dependencies could be expected to resolve.

If evidence of species and specific situation differences were a nuisance for learning-psychologists, learning phenomena tended to be avoided or ignored by those coming to the study of animal behaviour from a biological background: *ethologists*, like Lorenz and Tinbergen, concentrated in their earlier work on the given, innate, or instinctive characteristics of many different species, studied as far as possible in a great variety of natural conditions. Each specialist group regarded the findings of the other as relatively unimportant distractions from their own preoccupations.

This situation has now substantially changed. In the early 1970s anthologies like *Biological Boundaries of Learning* (Seligman and Hager, 1972) and *Constraints on Learning* (Hinde and

Stevenson-Hinde, 1973) presented in a systematic way the evidence that had been accumulating, especially during the previous decade, placing the study of learning firmly within a biological context. Although the titles of these books seem to emphasize the biological limitations of learning, the idea that there is biological *facilitation* of different learning processes is simply the reverse side of the same coin.

Seligman in particular has proposed the concept of *preparedness*, as an alternative, or at least as a qualification, to the reigning assumption of *general processes* in learning theory. Animals do not confront potential learning opportunities 'from scratch', but from a position that has been prepared by the process of natural selection, in the context of environmental pressures peculiar to the species. Measures of preparedness can be obtained by comparing the relative ease or difficulty in establishing different responses in different situations. This can be expressed as the number of trials required, the amount of permissible delay, etc.; and similarly the consequences of learning can be compared in terms of the frequency or the probability of the response, its strength, its resistance to extinction, and so on. These various measures will not necessarily go together, and the investigation of their relationships would constitute a more detailed exploration of what preparedness consists of in different cases. Seligman's proposal draws attention and gives a name to an important and previously neglected aspect of learning; it does not, by itself, furnish an explanation. Recognizing, illustrating and measuring a phenomenon is nevertheless an important step in that direction.

Let us consider some additional examples of preparedness. An interesting counterpart to the aversions generated by eating → sickness sequences is the establishment of flavour preferences brought about by their association with recovery from illness. It has been shown for several species, including rats, that if animals suffering from specific vitamin or mineral deficiencies are fed on an appropriate restorative diet, they develop a stable preference for the flavours associated with it. Together with the aversion that develops for the taste of the deficient diet (which has made them ill), this specialized taste-learning may be the basis for the apparent ability of many animals to balance their food intake, the so-called 'wisdom of the body'. What makes this learning specialized is the considerable delay that can occur between ingestion and the onset of malaise or recovery, as well as the fact that very few experiences – often only a single one – are needed to establish a relatively long-lasting effect. The familiarity–novelty dimension also plays an important role. It is very difficult, for example, to produce aversions to familiar foods, and when there is a mixture of relatively familiar and unfamiliar flavours preceding illness, it is the unfamiliar tastes that become selectively aversive.

The above examples have been concerned with facilitation or difficulty in classical conditioning. There are many similar cases involving instrumental learning. Thus it turns out to be no accident that the great majority of pigeon studies involving a food or drink reward have required the animals to learn a pecking response. Pigeons can do other things; they preen, for example, but it is comparatively difficult to condition preening. Seligman has drawn attention to one of Thorndike's puzzle-box experiments which is seldom quoted. In one such experiment, the door of the box was opened by the experimenter whenever the cat licked or scratched itself. Although under these circumstances licking and scratching did gradually become more frequent, this took much longer to establish than string pulling or button pushing. Preening, or grooming, although they are clearly part of the animals' repertoire, somehow do not 'belong' to food-getting or to escape situations. Pecking in pigeons, on the other hand, clearly does belong to feeding, in a way that throws an interesting light on many instances of successful operant conditioning. When pigeons are presented with food *unconditionally*, following the brief illumination of a disc, they will begin to peck at the disc, even though this response is not in fact instrumental in securing the reward. The presentation of food simply has the effect of making pigeons peck, not only at the food itself, but also in an anticipatory, classically conditioned way. The phenomenon has been called 'auto shaping'. If pecking is now also *required* by the experimenter to secure food – food delivery being made conditional on a peck in a given place or on a given colour, say – then this arrangement further reinforces a response that is already made spontaneously in that situation, mimicking what must be a common occurrence in a pigeon's normal habitat. The relationship between pecking and the nature of the reinforcer used is further illustrated in an experiment comparing the effects of food and water as reinforcers. By taking detailed high speed photographs, Moore (1973) showed that instrumental pecking in the two situations closely resembles the characteristic ways that pigeons use their beaks when they are eating and drinking, respectively. Pigeons 'eat' the key that leads to food, and 'drink' the key reinforced with water.

It is in fact very difficult to *stop* pigeons pecking when food is involved, even if the experimenter has capriciously decreed that food will only be provided on condition that the pigeon has *not* pecked for a prescribed period. It is also difficult to train pigeons to avoid shock by pecking, and rats do not easily learn bar-pressing as an avoidance response. The most suitable 'operants' for this kind of situation are running, jumping or standing absolutely still ('freezing') – again responses that animals make spontaneously when shocked or otherwise startled. One implication of all this is that if you want to train an animal, it is advisable to build your requirements around responses that the animal is in any case likely to make in the chosen situation, or at least to avoid requirements for which it is in some sense 'counter-prepared'. What can happen if you don't is recounted by Breland and Breland (1961) in an article entitled 'The Misbehavior of Organisms'.

The Brelands had set up professionally to utilize operant conditioning principles for training a great variety of animals for theatrical and other commercial purposes. Amidst considerable success, they had some instructive failures, usually involving the persistent intrusion of unwanted 'instinctive' behaviour patterns into the act. Thus racoons and pigs, trained for some obscure reason to deposit a succession of coins into a 'piggy-bank', using a shaping procedure with food reward, gradually developed patterns of 'misbehaviour' which increasingly interfered with the required performance – despite the fact that this self-indulgence greatly postponed and reduced their reward. The racoons began to 'wash' their coins, rubbing them together and dipping them into the container without letting go – washing is something they often do with their food under natural conditions. Pigs spent more and more time 'rooting' and tossing their coins, and this behaviour became more pronounced the hungrier they got. The Brelands named this phenomenon 'instinctive drift' and together with many similar examples it convinced them of the inadequacy of operant conditioning theory for explaining many aspects of animal learning and behaviour.

We will take up some of the theoretical implications of this work in the next chapter. For the moment, let us simply note that these results do not do away with the need for careful and controlled analyses of the circumstances in which learning occurs, nor do they imply a need to abandon what is after all a very fundamental characteristic of all scientific enterprise – the search for generality and order. One thing they do illustrate is the everpresent danger for theory and experiment to enter into a kind of collusion with each other – experiments being designed in such a way that they cannot help but reflect and confirm the very order and regularity that was 'discovered' at an earlier stage. We must continue to look for general processes in learning, even while remaining alert to evidence that might challenge or qualify their generality. One may hope that this could also lead to the emergence of *new* forms of order. The interaction of biological and psychological approaches to behaviour, as well as showing up much idiosyncratic variation, could well point towards greater simplicity and synthesis in other directions. The rest of this chapter will be concerned with explorations of this possibility.

Many animals, especially animals that have short lives and confront the full complexity of their environment from the very beginning, have built-in reactions which guide them towards food and keep them out of harm's way, to an extent sufficient to ensure the survival of their kind. They are, in these respects, *adapted* to the particular world in which their species lives. Other animals have fewer ready-made response patterns, but instead are able to develop appropriate behaviour as a consequence of experience: they are able to learn, to *become* adapted. To think of learning in this way helps to bring out *the essential similarity between what is achieved by learning on the one hand, and by natural selection on the other:* both processes, in different ways, produce animals whose characteristics reflect and take.account of relevant aspects of their world, a more or less permanent, more or less flexible matching of organism to environment. Indeed, the potential for learning, the particular form that it takes in any given species, must *itself* be regarded as an evolutionary development, extending the capacity of the selection process to cope with environmental pressures. This continuity between natural selection and learning is further underlined by the earlier examples of 'preparedness' – a kind of innately provided, partial adaptation, which receives its finishing touches within the individual animal, through experience of its own, particular environment. Before going on to a more detailed examination of the many forms that this continuity can take, it may be helpful to look briefly at the mechanisms of the evolutionary process, as it is currently understood.

**Sexual reproduction**

Sexually reproducing animals start their existence as single cells from which the complete animal grows through repeated cell division. The nucleus of each cell contains long strands of complex molecules – deoxyribonucleic acid or DNA – with the capacity to synthesize from the surrounding material the constituents required for the two daughter cells, including a duplication of themselves. The separate strands are called *chromosomes*, and they are made up of a large number of functional units called *genes*. These in turn consist of different sequences of smaller units (*nucleotides*). Although there are only four kinds of nucleotide, the number of different *sequences* that can be generated clearly becomes very large as the length of the chain increases. (A chain of N units can be arranged in $4^N$ different ways.) This is the basis of the very large amount of 'information' carried by the genes.

Chromosomes are arranged in matched pairs, one member of

each pair deriving from each of the parents. They are matched in the sense that corresponding genes are of the same type, though not necessarily identical. (The matching rule does not apply to the pair determining the sex of the individual.) Since, in each cell division, chromosomes make duplicates of themselves, nearly all types of cell contain an identical set, carrying the same manufacturing 'instructions'. The exceptions are *gametes* – the reproductive cells, when these are eventually formed. These contain only *one* chromosome from each chromosome pair. Such a set of single unpaired chromosomes contains a mixture of contributions derived from each parent, and the mixture varies from gamete to gamete.

The genetic program that makes its first appearance as a distinct entity in the fertilized cell must be thought of as *guiding*, rather than as *determining*, the characteristics of the developing individual at all stages. In some respects, this guidance restricts the course of development quite narrowly, with species identity at an extreme end: we take it for granted that if a human fertilized cell grows into anything at all, it will be a human being and not a chimpanzee or chicken. Similarly, a great many structural features that may vary among different members of the species will depend fairly closely on the individual genetic inheritance. In the case of many other – including many behavioural – characteristics, there is a varying amount of leeway for possible developmental paths, depending on differences in the environment.

A given set of genetic instructions can thus give rise to a more or less restricted *range* of end products, and at the same time, again depending on the developmental setting, different genetic endowments can converge to produce similar results. This interaction between genetic instructions, and the context within which they are executed, is the basis of the important distinction between *genotype* and *phenotype*: the genotype being defined by the particular set of instructions, as embodied in the inherited genes, the phenotype being the form taken by their eventual realization in the grown animal.

When the animal reproduces, it passes to each of its offspring one of a variety of genetic packages, all of which are derived from the gene-complex that guided the animal's own development. The greater the number of viable offspring an individual produces, the greater will be his or her genetic contribution to the next generation, and hence the potential contribution to the generation after that. If we focus attention not only on animals, but also on the genes they carry, on the gene-population or *gene-pool*, we can summarize the mechanism of natural selection as follows:

Any combination of genes that tends to confer, for whatever reason, a relative reproductive advantage (or disadvantage) on the corresponding phenotype, will have a relatively greater (or lesser) representation in the gene-pool of the next generation.

So, if there is a gene pattern that favours the development of some characteristic X in the grown animal, and if animals with this characteristic tend to produce more offspring than those without, then there will be a relative increase in the frequency of these genes in the next generation, available for the subsequent reproductive round.

### Novelty: mutation and genetic recombination

There are basically two ways in which novelty arises within this system. One is a kind of absolute novelty: *mutations* are random 'mistakes' in the duplication process, breaking the sequence of copies, and continuing henceforth with copies of the mutant gene. While the great majority of such accidental changes is disadvantageous – i.e. the corresponding phenotype is not viable at all, or else less capable, for one reason or another, of reproduction – every now and then mutant animals are produced that can hold their own among the rest of the species, and, occasionally, some that have a reproductive advantage. These will begin to contribute their modified genetic program to the 'pool' where, as the generations succeed each other, it will either attain some stable equilibrium with other forms, or, if there is a pronounced advantage, replace them.

The other source of novelty arises from a complication in the special kind of cell division – called *meiosis* – which makes reproductive cells, or gametes. We mentioned earlier that these cells contained only *one* chromosome from each pair. It is not normally, however, a chromosome that corresponds in its entirety to either of the pair from which it came – i.e. it does not derive wholly from either the father or the mother of the individual that produced it. In the course of meiosis, parts of each chromosome pair change places – they *cross over*. If we think of the paired chromosomes as tapes, what happens is equivalent to cutting the members of the pair at corresponding points, exchanging the parts, and resplicing them. The 'cut' can occur anywhere along the length of the chromosome, and there is normally just one such cut per pair. The gamete which becomes available for reproduction thus contains a reassembled version of the chromosomes of its immediate ancestor, and is in this sense wholly unique. Since genes achieve their effects to some extent in interaction with their neighbours, the new genetic 'neighbourhoods', that are in this way constantly produced by crossing over, make a second important contribution to variety in the reproducing population, and so to the evolutionary process. This area has for some years been the focus of intensive research and controversy (see, e.g. G. C. Williams, 1975).

## The selection of 'fitness'

The situation is rather different from the somewhat literal interpretation that is often given to the phrase 'survival of the fittest'. Firstly, while it is the fitness of the animal, of the *phenotype*, that is important, the survival that is selectively promoted is that of *genes*. Secondly, the kind of fitness that is ultimately critical for selection is *fitness to produce viable offspring*, when *all* contributory circumstances and factors are taken into account. It is the animals that go into the environmental firing line, but their success is measured in terms of the genes that come back. Individual survival to maturity is obviously necessary if reproduction is to take place at all, and this will require the ability to cope in a whole variety of ways. But beyond this, the characteristics required to achieve a *reproductive* advantage will depend on the environment in yet other ways, in particular on the social environment. Ability to drive off the competition may help to secure a mate, but so may relative attractiveness to potential partners. And since it is the number of offspring reaching maturity that matters, factors that influence behaviour towards the young can become very important. Thus, to take an extreme example, a hereditary disposition to protect them is likely to be passed on more frequently than a taste for eating them. The causal networks through which some particular characteristic eventually confers a resultant reproductive gain or loss can, however, be a great deal more complex and indirect. This helps to explain the enormous variety of evolved forms, both structural and behavioural, many of which do not have any immediately obvious bearing on fitness or survival in the narrower senses of those terms.

*To summarize*: Natural selection produces adaptive changes in the characteristics of species. Its operation is best understood by concentrating on the composition of the 'gene-pool'. The pool is constantly but randomly 'refreshed' by mutation and genetic recombination; the relative reproductive success of the animals generated by different genetic programs is then directly expressed as a matching contribution towards the gene-pool of the next generation. In this way the characteristics of species come to reflect relevant properties of their environment; in this way also, but only within limits, a species can progressively adapt to, or 'track', a changing environment.

We can now return to the relationship between natural selection and learning, their similar and complementary function, and their interdependence. The relevance of *environmental change* to evolution and the emergence of learning is the central topic of a recent paper by Plotkin and Odling-Smee (1979). They stress that, while natural selection and learning both achieve a kind of transfer of 'information' from environment to organism, they do so by operating on different systems, and following different time-scales. The adaptive effect of selection can only be understood by considering *populations*, while learning involves changes

that take place, and remain, within the *individual*:* the paper
talks about the different *referents* of selection and learning, respectively. Natural selection is regarded as the basic or primary
method whereby a species 'gains information' and maintains
itself in the face of a changing environment. But it is a slow
process, with a whole generation as the irreducible unit of time.
There comes a point where the rate of environmental change
puts a premium on the capacity of organisms to adapt within
their individual lifetimes. If such a capacity, specialized in those
particular respects where it confers an advantage, emerges
through mutation, this will pass into the gene-pool; but the information gained during the individual's lifetime – what he has
learned – will not. Plotkin and Odling-Smee make the assumption that a capacity to learn will only emerge and establish itself
if natural selection cannot otherwise cope, since there is a price
to be paid for *adaptability*: that of not being *already adapted*. To
the extent to which you have to *learn* what the world is like, you
are ignorant and ill-equipped to begin with.

This inverse relationship has a number of evolutionary implications. One is that the capacity to learn should emerge spar-
ingly where it is necessary, building upon and augmenting existing forms of adaption. Another is that the period during which
the most important information is acquired will have to be 'protected' to some extent, if the individual is to survive, benefit
from his capacity, and pass it on. There should therefore be a
tendency for increased adaptability to appear side by side with
other characteristics that favour such protective arrangements.
Like most evolutionary hypotheses, these predictions are difficult
to test directly. There is, however, no shortage in the ethological
literature of examples that illustrate this kind of parsimony, and
the interdependent emergence of different behavioural systems.
Consider the following.

Many birds and rodents build nests of complex and standard
designs. However, their competence to do this is often only partly

* This is not wholly true, of course, in any species that has a *culture*, which
can serve as a vehicle for the transmission of learning, and which contributes
towards the context in which both learning and selection occur. But see also the
postscript to this chapter.

'built in'. A variety of behaviour fragments, called Fixed Action Patterns (FAPs) may be provided ready-made, in the sense that they will make their appearance irrespective of experience; there will also normally be a disposition to collect suitable kinds of material, although again there are considerable differences between species in this respect; and there will be a sense of time and a sense of place for the whole operation. But the full, accomplished behaviour pattern develops in many species only after a certain amount of 'practice', changing from an assembly of relatively unco-ordinated movements to a smooth and accurate sequence.

How does the change come about? It looks as though different stages of manufacture can provide highly specific 'reinforcements' for successful completion. Lorenz (1977) describes the trembling movement (an FAP) with which jackdaws insert twigs into the growing nest. As the twig becomes more and more firmly lodged, so the trembling works up to a kind of 'orgasmic climax' after which the bird abandons the twig, and temporarily loses interest in the nest. Lorenz's description is, as usual, highly evocative and involves a lot of interpretation, but certainly the firmly-lodged object constitutes some kind of 'goal' for the jackdaw – not simply an endpoint, at which behaviour changes because it cannot continue as before, but an event that is in some way rewarding. This is demonstrated further by the developing preference for objects like twigs that *can* be firmly entangled – in jackdaws such a preference does not exist to begin with, and they will start by using whatever materials 'come to beak'. The combination of FAPs and comparatively simple intermediate goals is enough to produce a nest of sorts, but also serves as the basis for the eventual, much more skilled performance. There is no indication that jackdaws possess the goal of 'nest' in any more finished and functional sense: thus pieces of twisted wire will, if available, be preferred to twigs, presumably because they get entangled even more effectively: but they are unsuitable in other ways, e.g. from the point of view of thermal insulation.

The study of bird song provides another example of the way in which existing structures are utilized, and of learning constrained to operate within precise limits. Different species have

characteristic calls and songs that are transmitted virtually un-
changed from generation to generation. While some birds appear
to be genetically provided with the finished article, others depend
on experience in various ways, and accoustic analysis has made
it possible to examine this dependence in considerable detail.
Marler (1970) has described a series of such studies on the male
white-crowned sparrow. These birds, which are to be found all
over North America, have a species-specific song, with local
variations or 'dialects'. By rearing birds in acoustic isolation
during different periods of their lives and exposing them to recordings of different sparrow dialects, as well as to songs of
other species, Marler was able to show that they need to hear an
appropriate song if they are to develop the normal singing pattern. Birds kept in acoustic isolation produced typical fragments, but in rudimentary and abnormal arrangements.

There are, however, strict limitations on what is 'appropriate'
for this purpose: any white-crown dialect will do, and is matched
by the 'trainee'; but exposure to the songs of other species
produces the same effect as isolation. Marler also found that, to
be most effective, exposure has to occur between ten and fifty
days after hatching. Between fifty and a hundred days there is a
limited effect; earlier and later, no effect at all.

It had previously been shown that in many species song development is in fact a two-stage process. If birds are made deaf
at any time before they come into full song – in the case of the
white-crowned sparrow this is between two and six months *after*
the critical period for exposure – they develop a song that is
even more rudimentary than that of birds kept in isolation. But
if they are deafened after the full song has developed, they
continue to sing normally.

These results suggest the following model for the development
of song in this particular species.

(i) The birds are provided genetically with a variety of song fragments; and also with some sort of rough *sensory representation* –
a kind of 'template' – of the species song.

(ii) This template acquires a more detailed, specific form if the
bird hears appropriate songs at the right time. Songs that do not

match the outline of the species' pattern, as expressed in the template, remain ineffective.

(iii) Birds learn to *produce* the correct song provided they can hear themselves during the formative period. They come to match their output to the internal representation which has been completed some months beforehand.

(iv) Once the song has been developed, its production is subsequently controlled by non-auditory factors.

There is evidence also that the females, although they do not sing themselves, learn to recognize and prefer a particular dialect in a similar way. This favours inbreeding within relatively closed local communities, which in turn facilitates the development of other forms of adaptation to the local terrain.

In one sense these examples are highly specific, highly individual. For each species the interaction between what is given, and what has to be acquired, takes on a unique form that can usually be understood in terms of the species' other characteristics, its habitat, its evolutionary history. But there are a number of themes which emerge repeatedly from the study of such individual cases.

One is the existence of built-in 'targets' or 'values' in different species which are not necessarily related to individual survival, but help to further, in one way or another, the total reproductive cycle.* They can be instrumental in learning, but often their effectiveness is concentrated in a particular behavioural area. Another is the assembly, from predesigned components, of larger behavioural sequences, which subsequently function as stable, organized units. This subject will be taken up in the chapter on skill. Yet another is the acquisition, or elaboration, of 'perceptual templates', providing the basis for 'recognition', and guiding subsequent behaviour in a whole variety of ways. Typically they are built up during a prescribed period of an animal's life and

* It is important to appreciate the limited nature of such targets, and to distinguish them from the more comprehensive ends which they in *fact* promote, but which do not constitute a goal for the individual animal. This is especially true with respect to reproduction, which for species other than man is always an *outcome* rather than a goal.

have great stability thereafter. We turn next to a particularly striking and much investigated example of such template formation.

## Imprinting

Many animals achieve independent existence before they are fully equipped to fend for themselves. They consequently need protection and support during the period in which the necessary physical maturation and/or learning takes place, and usually this is provided by one or both of the parents. One factor clearly useful for helping to keep the young reasonably close to the parents is an ability to recognize them. However, given the flexible relationship between genotype and phenotype, such an ability may be difficult to build in. Individual recognition is much more efficiently handled by 'gaining information' directly from the finished phenotype itself. Where the young are relatively immobile for a long period, this can be achieved through gradual learning processes; but if they move about quite early on, then there is clearly an advantage if the process can be speeded up. Immediate recognition needs to be good enough to maintain proximity, and this provides the opportunity for acquiring more detailed recognition later, if this is necessary. *Imprinting* is such a process, one of the first to be recognized as inconsistent with 'general process' views of learning.

Many readers may have seen a photograph of Konrad Lorenz, walking away and followed at a little distance by some half dozen goslings in single file. Lorenz first described how several species of ground-dwelling birds, notably certain ducks and geese, will tend to follow moving objects to which they are exposed shortly after hatching, especially if they are about the right size and move at about the right pace. It also helps if they make an appropriate noise, but that is not necessary. After a relatively brief period – sometimes only a matter of hours – a selective preference develops for the moving object, and this can have fundamental repercussions for the animals' subsequent social and sexual behaviour.

The object that is normally around and meets all the requirements is of course the mother, and so on an evolutionary scale the system works perfectly well. But if mother is replaced by a moving box or crouching ethologist, then these are followed instead, and come to be preferred. Not only will the substitute be followed, but as time proceeds, the birds will attempt to direct towards it other responses that are usually reserved for members of the species. One imprinted jackdaw persistently tried to feed Lorenz with freshly caught worms, which is typical courtship behaviour. Imprinting appears not only to produce recognition of 'mother' but also to provide the basis for the eventual recognition of 'another member of my species'.

The phenomenon has been studied extensively since Lorenz drew attention to it and several interesting additional features have emerged. One that is important in the present context is that the process is not quite as irreversible as was at first thought. The object of imprinting *can* be changed, but only in the direction from substitute to appropriate animal, not the other way round. We have therefore another instance of a situation that is highly 'prepared', in respect of time and a whole variety of other parameters, to favour the occurrence of a particular kind of learning. What is also important is the diversity of behaviour that is *subsequently* directed at the imprinted object. The imprinting experience sets up a selective sensitivity for a particular complex stimulus, which later elicits and attracts a whole variety of responses.

It is the very dramatic and concentrated quality of the phenomenon in some birds that has led to its early recognition and separate designation. It seems certain, however, that in most animals there are periods of longer or shorter duration when there is a heightened readiness to acquire certain relatively general dispositions; and that these serve as preconditions, constraints or signposts for much subsequent learning. Both sensory and motor experience can be involved. If, for example, young female rats are prevented from licking themselves – this was done in one experiment by fitting them with collars – they subsequently fail to look after their young, and frequently eat them. Early 'enriched' or 'impoverished' environments – judged by the amount of perceptual variety and opportunity for manipulation – have been shown to produce significant differences in the adult learning and problem solving capacity of several species. Early, non-specific experience with a variety of materials often turns out to be a condition of their effective use in nest-building at a much later stage. In animals whose learning is more complex and prolonged, the effects of early experience are often not readily identifiable, because there is no simple one-to-one relationship between particular kinds of experience and particular later consequences; also, in the case of human beings, the kind of drastic experimental intervention which brought to light the importance of early experience in a variety of animals, is obviously unacceptable. Nevertheless, we should expect that here too the effects of learning at any stage provide the foundations for the next, and that in particular the events of infancy and childhood have an important influence on later tastes, inclinations and interests. This topic will be taken further in the chapter on human development.

### The 'innate' and the 'acquired'

We have at various times in this chapter referred to characteristics as 'innate' or 'genetically determined' in contrast to 'learned' or 'acquired', although we warned earlier that this is not the simple and sharp distinction that it is sometimes taken to be: indeed the whole of this chapter has been about the complex interaction of genetic and environmental influences in producing phenotypic characteristics. It is a convenient and tempting, if potentially misleading, shorthand for distinguishing between adaptations that have been achieved largely by natural selection, and those where a substantial amount of information has still to be obtained from the environment during each individual's lifetime. Since arguments contrasting 'heredity and environment', 'instinct and learning', 'nature and nurture' have a perennial appeal, and often generate a lot of heat and confusion, we will give some more space to this issue.

The only wholly 'genetic' contribution that an individual

receives from his parents is, in fact, his genes: inheriting the family nose is nothing like getting the family portraits. All characteristics are a developmental outcome of continuous organism–environment interaction, and there is nothing that is wholly independent of either the genetic instructions or the environment within which they are worked out. There are those cases, however, where the environmental contribution within the lifetime of the individual is limited to *permitting* a specified development to take place – in the extreme case, a given feature, usually something structural, will emerge in a prescribed form, provided only that the animal survives. At the other extreme there are characteristics, which depend in a detailed and flexible way on the individual's particular environment, and these we call learned, even though their acquisition inevitably presupposes some appropriate genetic basis. Whether a child grows up speaking English or Italian depends directly on the language to which it is exposed. Such exposure or opportunity does little, however, for English or Italian dogs, who may learn to respond to a limited number of utterances in the appropriate language, but appear incapable of learning to *use* either, whatever the circumstances. The capacity for learning and using language will be discussed further in Chapter 5. For the moment we simply want to underline that the achievement of speaking some language fluently is the result of *prepared learning* – the appropriateness of stressing the learning or the genetic preparation depends on the kind of comparison that is being made.

Difficulties arise when the comparison does not point so clearly to corresponding genetic or environmental differences. Some dogs can round up sheep, and some cannot. Clearly, whether or not they have been appropriately trained has a lot to do with it. The fact that competence in this skill is usually found among dogs of certain types may simply reflect a conventional human preference for training these breeds; given patience and the right approach, retrievers can probably be taught to handle sheep, and sheepdogs to retrieve. On the other hand, sheepdogs and retrievers do seem to have a decided flair for picking up the respective skills from which they derive their names, and this is not surprising when we consider that these varieties are the result of a great deal of selective breeding, in which successful performance of the appropriate skill has been one of the criteria.

So – is sheep-handling a matter of genetics or of learning? It is not possible to give any simple answer if the question is put in that form. If we ask on the other hand, 'does it take more training effort to get some types of dog to achieve a given level of performance than it does others?', then the answer is straightforward; and there are probably some breeds which, for one reason or another, do not take to this kind of activity at all. The notion of preparedness conveniently encapsulates these differences. If required, careful observation and experimentation should make it possible to document in greater detail the particular features of preparedness in any given case.

There are of course differences between individuals from the *same* breed, and indeed from the same litter. There will generally be genetic differences, though it may often be difficult to label them, and there are bound to be some environmental differences also. Sometimes the learning situation to which an animal is exposed will depend on its initial characteristics: for example, the response to early stages of training may have direct or indirect consequences for later training, including its discontinuation. In various ways genetic and environmental characteristics will combine and interact to produce behavioural differences at every stage. But we are in difficulties as soon as we attempt an assessment of the relative 'contributions' of these influences. If, for example, there are differences in environment that *result from* early behaviour, leading in turn to different kinds of learning, to what extent should we then regard the final outcome as a consequence of the initial predisposition? Our questions will require very careful formulation if we are to avoid misleading answers.

## Human differences

It is when we come to human beings that the situation becomes really complicated and emotionally charged. People are capable of a much greater range of behaviour than other animals; a great deal of early learning takes place at home, which means that the parents' genetic contribution towards their children's capacities is accompanied by an environment that the same parents have helped to create, and which therefore reflects the many other, environmental influences that contributed towards the *parents'* characteristics; learning is much more prolonged, so that the cumulative effects are more complex; there is restriction, modification or enhancement of opportunities by a whole variety of social factors, which in part respond to the characteristics of the individual at various stages – and at the same time, each person influences the nature of his own learning opportunities more directly through his habits, interests, tastes, friends, heroes, etc. Any attempt to disentangle differences in human behaviour or competence into genetic and environmental 'components' thus becomes meaningless. It is only by the use of indirect methods, such as the comparison of similarities and differences of achievement in identical and fraternal twins that we can estimate the relevance of genetic differences in the development of this or that behavioural characteristic: and even here we cannot be *entirely* certain how to interpret results, since it can always be argued that differences between people tend to create corresponding differences in their environments, thus ultimately confounding the genetic and the experiential.

The idea of preparedness was of considerable interest and importance when considering the process of learning in different species. Is there any point in dwelling on it when we are trying to account for differences *within* a species, especially in the human case, given the impossibility of separating out genetic and environmental influences? The whole issue has become very sensitive in recent times because the very notion of genetic differences is seen as an affront to the political ideal of universal equality; and people are liable to accusations of racism, sexism or elitism if they as much as contemplate the possibility. Certainly even the acceptance of initial differences in no way implies any absolute limits to what might be achieved by some appropriate design of the learning environment. In purely practical terms, however, we find that individuals differ, for whatever mixture of reasons, in the facility with which they acquire different kinds of skill, knowledge or intellectual competence. With limited resources it becomes a question of our social and political values how we apportion them between the objectives of enhancing strengths, and overcoming weaknesses.

## Postscript

The brief account of evolution that we gave earlier is the orthodox and most widely accepted version, usually referred to as neo-Darwinism. Its characteristic feature is that the ultimate source of variation, of new structures and also of new innate behaviour is random mutation. On this view all genetically based adaptation has to await the chance occurrence of the appropriate 'mistake', or more likely, the coincidence of a whole variety of accidental modifications in the genes, while an enormous number of non-viable or disadvantageous ones are eliminated. Although the periods of time that are available for these evolutionary changes are admittedly immense, some biologists have felt that, nevertheless, many observed adaptations, especially the behavioural ones, are too precise and improbable if we assume a purely random origin. One of the earliest and best-known proposals for coping with this problem was that of Lamarck, involving the inheritance of acquired characteristics. On this theory, adaptive modifications, including learned behavioural changes achieved by individuals, would over a number of generations pass directly into the genetic structure: eventually members of a species would be provided, *ab initio*, with information that their ancestors had to acquire through experience. The evidence against such a *direct* transfer is overwhelming, but there have been a number of other more plausible suggestions that would at least tend to channel genetic changes into the specific areas where they were 'needed'. A recent proposal comes from Jean Piaget whose name is primarily identified with a monumental work on child development, spanning most of this century. In *Behaviour and Evolution* (1979) he puts forward the view that in addition to random mutation, there is an organizational source of change in evolution, and that 'behaviour is its motor'.

Piaget's proposal is based on Weiss's ideas of the organism as a hierarchically organized, self-regulatory 'open system' (cf. Weiss, 1969). It is an *open* system in the sense that its constituents are constantly being replaced through transactions with the environment: yet such are the characteristics of organisms that their organizational structure, their identity, remains intact throughout these transactions. Change consists in the gradual adjustment or accommodation of relevant aspects of this structure through interaction with the environment – and this would of course include the behavioural interactions that lead to learning. The genetic 'program' of an organism, represented in all its cells and intimately involved in its constant regeneration, is part of this overall dynamic. Piaget's suggestion is that the regulatory influences between genes and their immediate context are not purely in one direction. New relationships with the external environment produce internal adjustments which work their way back through the organizational hierarchy, leading to changes in the environment of the genetic program. Even the most limited capacity for change on the part of the genome would make a profound difference to the mechanism of evolutionary change – Piaget suggests that it might respond to the 'strains' produced by the modified environment simply by generating variants. At this point, the processes of selection, first by the internal environment, and eventually by the external, would take over, retaining the variations that worked. But the variations themselves, in so far as they occurred in response to the essentially *goal-directed* behaviour and functioning of the organism, would no longer be quite random, but to some extent integrated into the processes of self-regulation and maintenance.

This brief outline can do no more than to convey the flavour of Piaget's theoretical proposals; for a fuller account the reader is referred to Piaget's monograph, as well as to C. H. Waddington's *The Evolution of an Evolutionist* (1975) for related ideas. Although explicitly speculative, we have included this account because it has for us a high degree of plausibility; and any such integration of behaviour, organic functioning and genetic change would make the relationship between learning and evolution into an even more reciprocal affair than has emerged from the discussions in the rest of the chapter.

# 4. Learning Theory

In Chapter 2 we described attempts to express the rules of learning purely in terms of relationships between behaviour and environmental events. Learning was presented as adaptive behavioural change to current circumstances, with the implication that a careful analysis of the learner's environment should account for the changes involved. This was followed in the last chapter by a more general discussion of adaptation, in which learning was seen both as a product and an extension of a prior and more basic process of adaptation – natural selection. This emphasis on evolutionary function, while suggesting the possibility of greater variety in the forms taken by learning in different species, also held out the promise – as yet unrealized – of providing some new unifying principles. Leaving aside speculations like those of Piaget just presented, neither of these approaches was explicitly concerned with changes *in* the learner, providing a basis for the (intermittent) occurrence of learned behaviour. To know something about the way experience leads to, say, avoidance of poisoned food, or about the processes of selection that would account for the existence of animals with appropriate learning mechanisms, still leaves unexplored questions about the *nature* of those mechanisms. It is to questions of this kind that we now turn.

The most straightforward approach to the problem of what happens in the learner would seem to be taking a *look*. This is the way we would go about discovering how a machine worked, after we had found out all we could from the outside: the definitive explanation would be given by the arrangement of connecting gears, circuits and other parts. By analogy, we might expect that regularities of behaviour and its relationship to stimulation could properly be accounted for only in terms of the intervening 'stuff' – its anatomy, physiology, biochemistry, etc. It certainly seems reasonable to assume that there is some systematic connection, and in the course of this chapter we will consider some observations and hypotheses that link behaviour and its 'substrate'. But the analogy to examining a man-made machine is misleading in an important respect. Even if we were looking at something quite new and revolutionary, built let us say by a rival firm or foreign power, still the components, and the principles underlying their arrangement, would be basically familiar. It is for this reason that examining the structure of a machine seems to *reveal* the explanation of how it works. But consider the investigation of some device of totally alien, extra-terrestrial origin. In such a case, an important contribution to understanding the nature of the parts and the significance of their organization would have to come from studying the behaviour of the entire system – it might not even be at all clear where one 'component' ended and the next began. Making sense of the whole and of the parts would be very much a mutually supportive process. It is this kind of situation that confronts us when we try to understand the working of living organisms, in particular the involvement of their nervous systems in behaviour. Although we can to some extent take them apart and study the properties of various sub-units and 'preparations', they do not necessarily behave in the same way as part of the intact animal. A very brief outline of the structure of nervous systems will help to illustrate the difficulty, and also prepare the ground for examples of psychophysiological experiments.

Nervous systems are made up of large numbers of interconnected nerve cells, or *neurons*. In human beings the number is estimated to be around ten thousand million. Like other living cells, each neuron has a *cell body*, which houses the genetic material on which the cell's internal manufacturing processes depend. The cell body has two kinds of extensions: *dendrites*, which are involved in the receipt of excitation from other cells; and an *axon*, which may be extensively branched, and which is concerned with the outward transmission of excitation. The axon terminals of any one cell are in contact with the cell bodies and dendrites of several others, up to many thousands; in turn, each cell receives the terminals of others, again varying from a few to thousands. The points of contact, where the membranes of two cells are separated by a microscopic gap, are called *synapses*.

When suitably stimulated – and sometimes spontaneously – a neuron will 'discharge' – i.e. an electrochemical disturbance will travel from the cell body along the axon to all its terminals, where it is in synaptic contact with other neurons. At the synapse the arrival of this disturbance or pulse has the effect of releasing a minute quantity of *transmitter substance* (there are several kinds) which travels across the gap separating neurons and sets up a local disturbance in the receiving cell. Synapses are of two kinds: *excitatory* and *inhibitory*. At the receiving end of any neuron there will therefore be, at any one time, a pattern of such disturbances. If the combination of these – the process is not fully understood, but is more complex than simple summation – exceeds some threshold level, the receiving neuron will 'fire', and in turn 'transmit' excitation to many others. Rates of firing can reach up to about eight hundred per second. The interaction of received pulses extends over time as well as space, so that pulses which arrive in rapid succession at the same synapse are to some extent cumulative in their effect, facilitating (or inhibiting) responses in the receiving neuron. It is important to understand, however, that a pulse in a given neuron does not simply *pass on* a signal received from a single source, but usually reflects a pattern of signals from many sources.

A part of the network consists of cells that are specialized for translating stimulus energies of different kinds – such as light, vibration of the air, temperature changes – into the standard form of activity within the nervous system. These are *sensory neurons*, located in the various sense organs, as well as in the skin, muscles, joints and other parts of the body. Yet other cells, *effector neurons*, terminate in muscles and glands, where their activity produces graded contractions, secretions, etc. There are some relatively simple circuits, especially in organisms with more primitive nervous systems, which connect sensory neurons to particular muscle groups. In most cases, however, the immediate result of a stimulus input impinges on a complex and *active* network, so that its eventual 'effect' is a function also of the anatomy of this network and of what is going on within it at the time. Any temptation to think of the nervous system as an elaborate telephone exchange, routing incoming messages to selected output stations, is therefore quite misleading (notwithstanding the increasing tendency of telephone networks towards autonomy and unpredictability).

The physiological methods available for studying the nervous system include the selective destruction or deactivation of parts of the system, with concurrent observations on other parts and on behaviour; the stimulation of highly specific areas, even single neurons, by electrical or chemical means; the monitoring of activity, again highly localized, in terms of electrical and/or chemical changes. The degree of complexity, precision and sophistication involved in much current work is truly astounding and we have learned an enormous amount – especially about events within single neurons, where the transmission of excitation, rapid though it is, usually involves whole sequences of chemical reactions. Yet insofar as all this has thrown light on the processes underlying behaviour, it has been as much to reveal unsuspected complications as to clarify existing problems. More and more detailed knowledge of local chemical processes does not necessarily produce an understanding of the role played by those processes with the cell's integral functioning. At higher levels of organization the co-ordinated activity of interconnected neurons depends not only on the anatomical structure of the networks involved, but on their constantly changing 'functional structure' – i.e. the pattern of interconnection is itself determined by how the system is operating at the time. We thus need to make some sense of what the whole system is doing *before* we can grasp the effective organization of its components.

As an alternative, or preferably as an addition, to 'looking under the bonnet' we can *invent* intervening stages, structures, or processes, designed to account for what we observe on the surface. It is in fact very difficult to think about events 'as such' without at least some implicit picture or theory about what they are or what gives rise to them. Although some psychologists, like Skinner, have maintained that they can manage without such theoretical props, most find that an *explicit* model helps them think more effectively about their observations, and also to make predictions about what behaviour to expect in different circumstances. To the extent that these predictions turn out to be true or false, this increases or undermines confidence in the theory and in further predictions based on it. Inventing theories, testing predictions based on them, and adjusting or replacing the theories if the predictions turn out to be wrong, gives a basic, if perhaps somewhat idealized description of scientific method, in psychology as elsewhere. This chapter will look at what has happened, in the course of such a process, to some of the main assumptions and features of earlier learning theories. In this connection, let us first draw attention to a rather different and intriguing relevance that the use, testing and modification of theories has for models of learning.

We said earlier that it is difficult to think about events without at the same time having some theory or picture of their underlying structure. Most of our actions – turning the steering-wheel of a car, asking someone to pass the salt, boarding a particular train on the way to work – involve expectations and assumptions, usually implicit, about the way things work and about the consequences of what we do. Life would hardly be possible otherwise. Sometimes, of course, those expectations turn out to be wrong, and it is mainly on such occasions that we become aware of having in fact anticipated something. Having put a coin into an automatic coffee-machine, we are likely to be surprised if instead of coffee we get a recording of Handel's *Water Music*. Whatever it is that provides the basis for surprise is presumably there all along, even when things go according to plan; and it seems reasonable to suppose that it forms an integral link in all our interactions with the environment. We are, in effect, using a model of the world, not necessarily verbalized, providing a basis for predictions on which we act, and which our experiences confirm or contradict. System- atic contradiction usually leads to some change in the model. There seems to be a distinct similarity between the 'scientific method' and descriptions of what goes on in learning.

There are parallels also at the more basic level of natural selection. Here too we have invention (genetic change) and testing (behaviour based on the modified genetic structure). A well adapted organism is an *embodiment* of a good and relevant theory about its environment; and in this case it is part of the definition of a 'good theory' that it is reproduced in the genotype of future generations. Equally, a 'bad theory' disappears more or less rapidly, depending on how inaccurate its predictions are, and how crucial.

All this suggests that our model of learning should *itself contain*, perhaps as a central feature, the capacity to develop models or representations of the world – models whose growth and modification would proceed, at different levels of complexity, in a manner analogous to that adopted in a more explicit and self-conscious manner, by scientists. After all, without such a capacity the present enterprise is unlikely to get very far. Ironically this is a view of learning which, with some notable exceptions, was long rejected by learning theorists, and is only now gaining wider acceptance.

How has this transformation come about?

### Stimulus–response psychology

Early theories of learning are best understood as determined attempts to avoid all reference to 'private' mental processes, and to replace them by some mechanism for linking publicly observable stimuli available to the learner with his equally public responses. Such a mechanism would generate behaviour *as a response to stimulation*, and learning would i..volve its more or less gradual modification under the influence of the environment. In particular, mechanistic accounts would have to be found for all those aspects of behaviour which we normally explain in terms of purposes or goals, and in terms of expectations or knowledge *about* the world.

There is a convention that explanatory models should be kept as simple as possible; they also tend to be inspired (and limited) by the kind of technology that is well understood at the time. In the present case one serious limitation is already implicit in the very formulation of the problem: it encourages one to think of the learner's experience in terms of stimuli, of what he does in terms of responses, and of a relatively straightforward association between them. This S–R picture of behaviour was characteristic of most approaches to learning, and it is one whose implications we want to examine in this chapter. We also want to take a closer look at the nature and operation of *reinforcers* in instrumental learning, which will lead us to the problem of purposeful or goal-directed behaviour; and at the *conjunction* of events as the basis for what happens in classical conditioning, which raises the question of how and to what extent properties of the environment come to be represented within the learner. But to begin with let us follow up a question that was raised in Chapter 2: do we really need to assume that different processes are involved in the learning that takes place during classical, and during instrumental conditioning? Can we be sure that the defining relationships, as seen by the experimenter – stimulus–stimulus and response–consequence sequences respectively – are in fact responsible for the observed changes of behaviour?

## One or more learning processes?

In ordinary learning situations these two types of relationship invariably coexist; and in the 'auto-shaping' phenomenon (p. 54) we had an example of a reinforced response (pecking at an illuminated key) that became established, but not because of reinforcement. What looked like a clear case of instrumental conditioning turned out to be, at least to a large extent, classical. There have been a number of attempts, in the interests of simplicity, to demonstrate that learning might *always* be the modification of behaviour by its consequences, or that it might always depend exclusively on the pairing of stimuli. There are, however, a number of experiments that would seem to settle the issue in favour of there being two *distinct processes*, normally occurring together, and responsive to the contingencies represented by classical and instrumental conditioning, respectively. Here are just two examples.

As we mentioned in the last chapter, not only will pigeons start pecking spontaneously at stimuli that regularly precede food, it is difficult to *stop* them from doing so. Williams and Williams (1969) set up a lighted-key→food-presentation sequence, and then introduced the proviso that food would only be delivered when the birds did *not* peck at the key during the brief period that it was lit up. If behaviour was modified exclusively by its consequences, the pigeons should simply have left the key alone. However, not only did they start to peck at it, they maintained this behaviour at a rate that secured them only a small proportion of the potentially available food. It is difficult to account for this result other than as a consequence of the (occasional) light–food sequence eliciting a particular type of innately determined response as a CR. It is an arrangement which would work well enough in normal circumstances – but evidently, if it does turn out that a different kind of behaviour produces better consequences, pigeons have difficulty in rising to the occasion. (See also the examples of 'instinctive drift' in Chapter 3.)

By contrast, consider the following experiment with human subjects (a Russian experiment, reported by Miller, 1969). Electric shock to the fingers produces *vasoconstriction*, i.e. constriction of the surface blood-vessels. If shock is used as a UCS in Pavlovian conditioning, the conditioned response is also vasoconstriction. The anticipatory narrowing of surface blood-vessels in a condition of 'danger' has a variety of consequences that have (or had, long ago) general survival value, so it has become the built-in reaction. But in the experiment it was arranged to withhold shock on condition that vaso*dilation* followed the warning signal – and the subjects were able to learn to 'produce' this effect. Since this is the *reverse* of what happens when the outcome does *not* depend on the subject's reaction, it is difficult to avoid the conclusion that it is precisely this reponse–consequence relationship which is responsible. (We cannot of course conclude from this demonstration that such a reversal of conditioned responses can always be brought about by arranging the consequences appropriately; nor that, when it can be done, it happens as easily as learning a response which is not 'counter-prepared'.)

Experiments of this kind, together with others which attempt to rule out the possibility of one or the other form of learning by physiological means, point very convincingly towards the existence of two processes. One makes it possible for an animal to 'anticipate' the occurrence of a variety of important events by producing a predetermined response – or a range of such responses – usually appropriate to the situation. The other permits the more detailed reorganization and modification of behaviour in line with its consequences. Both processes occur in pigeons as well as in persons, but there are big differences in their relative importance in the two cases. Classical conditioning appears to involve a more basic, and in an evolutionary sense, older form of learning, which can be found in some measure even in very primitive animals. Instrumental conditioning, which allows a more 'finely tuned' adaptation to the environment, increases in importance with increasing cerebral development. For example, in circumstances similar to the earlier pigeon experiment, rats also start off with some prepared responses, but can more easily learn to refrain from making them.

What then can we say about the operation of these processes? Let us start with one of the most persistent issues in learning theory – the attempt to elucidate the nature of reinforcement and of reinforcers.

## Reinforcement and motivation

Clearly not all consequences of action are reinforcing. One can identify reinforcers in a purely pragmatic way as those events that lead to a strengthening of the behaviour that produces them. But this is simply a definition, and it immediately prompts the question: 'What is it about reinforcers, so defined, that gives them this property? And what is it that happens at the time that facilitates the appropriate behaviour on subsequent occasions?'

Food and water are frequently used to reinforce the behaviour of animals. But there is a condition for their effectiveness: the animal has to be in a suitable state; it has to *want* food or water. At the same time, whether or not an animal actually carries out some behaviour sequence that it has learned by means of, say, food reinforcement, usually also depends on its being appropriately 'motivated'. So we could add to our question about the nature of reinforcement, one about motivation: what is it about hunger, for example, that produces 'food-seeking' behaviour, when in the same external circumstances a satiated animal might sleep, or groom?

It may seem at first sight that the answers to both these questions are really quite obvious, and related: to be motivated is simply to want something, and reinforcement consists of getting it. An animal that wants food will try to obtain some, will search for it; and the clue to the effectiveness of food as a reinforcer under these circumstances lies precisely in that it is what was being searched for.

Unfortunately this does not, by itself, get us very far. As an explanation it is simply an appeal to familiarity; being hungry, wanting food, and doing something about it are 'obviously' related in our experience. But suppose that, instead of an animal heading for its feeding-place, we had some *device* travelling to an electric power point – i.e., it moved towards it from wherever it was released, avoiding obstacles (with increasing efficiency), and finally plugged itself in. If now, by way of explanation, we were told 'it wants to get itself recharged', we would probably say 'never mind the metaphor, how does it work?'

To talk about the wants or aims of a suitably constructed machine is not in fact as far-fetched a metaphor as it might seem; equally the 'how does it function' approach can quite legitimately be applied to organisms, human or otherwise. This does not imply a belief in the identity of man or animal and any existing machine, nor should it belittle their differences. It is simply that for certain kinds of understanding it is helpful to think of them *as if* they were machines, to ask what *sort* of machines they would have to be, and what sort of internal functions they would have to perform in order to produce observed behavioural end-products. Applying this approach to motivation and reinforcement, what could we come up with?

Suppose that we take hunger, food search and eating as a prototype. Starting with a satiated animal, hunger comes about as a result of deprivation. Hungry animals do things that lead sooner or later to finding food. Food reduces the effects of deprivation, and, in adequate quantities, returns the animal to its satiated starting-point. This cycle is reminiscent of the internal *homeostatic* mechanisms that maintain a whole variety of physiological and chemical variables within limits required for survival. A departure from equilibrium, such as a rise in temperature, sets up processes like sweating and the dilation of surface blood-vessels which counteract the disturbance. This kind of arrangement is called *negative feedback*, and its basic features are exemplified in devices such as thermostats, governors controlling engine-speeds, or the stabilizing circuits of radio amplifiers.

In many cases the balance cannot be restored by calling upon internal processes alone: behaviour is required. If it gets too hot, we must *do* something to cool down, and food deprivation can in the long run only be rectified by eating. Like homeostatic regulation, some required behaviour might be 'wired in'. But imagine also the following arrangement. Suppose that a disturbance that cannot be rectified homeostatically gives rise, in the first instance, to more or less random behaviour. (More or less, depending on the extent of innate adaptation.) When, in the course of such activity, an event occurs which reduces the degree of disturbance, suppose this has the effect of establishing and strengthening some sort of connection between the immediately preceding behaviour and the circumstances in which it occurred. Such a system would build up precisely those behaviour patterns that repeatedly restored internal equilibria; it would *learn* by extending, in effect, existing regulatory mechanisms to include appropriate behaviour.

### Hull's model of behaviour

A highly influential model of behaviour and learning, incorporating such a feature, was put forward by the American psychologist Clark Hull (1943, 1952). It stimulated a great deal of research and underwent many extensions and alterations, but as an integrated model it has by now disappeared for all practical purposes. Its importance for us lies in that it illustrates in a very compact form some of the main assumptions that dominated the way psychologists thought about learning during a large part of this century.

Hull's central concept was *habit*, symbolized by $_sH_r$. The subscripts s and r stood for *stimulus* and *response*, and the quantitative value of the *habit strength* represented the degree of association between a particular stimulus and a particular response. Learning consisted of the building-up of habit strength, or rather the strength of a whole variety of such associations.

To represent the motivational aspect of behaviour, Hull introduced *Drive* (D), a state of arousal produced by organic need. The actual tendency to respond to a given stimulus was then given by $D \times {_sH_r}$.

Existing S–R linkages would thus become operational to an extent depending on the level of drive. In this way Hull separated the immediate effects of learning from actual behaviour.

This basic framework was rounded off by an assumption about the nature of reinforcement. Hull proposed that reinforcement *was* drive reduction, and thereby completed a system which would (a) generate behaviour and (b) modify itself by incorporating and strengthening 'successful' variations. Strangely enough however, the mechanism proposed for the generation of behaviour – S–R linkages – took little account of what was known about the operation of the underlying homeostatic processes, whose regulatory function the learned behaviour was supposed to extend. The idea of feedback was incorporated into the *modification* of behaviour, into learning, but not into its production.

What we have described is just the nucleus of Hull's system, which contained many additional variables and had been developed to a considerable degree of detail. It was this characteristic that greatly helped to stimulate research, and thereby also led to the eventual demise of the model.* We are here concerned only with certain basic features: the attempt to pin down the nature of reinforcers, and the rather more implicit commitment, symbolized here by $_sH_r$, that we have already referred to – although Hull did not intend the S–R link to correspond directly to an actual structure, the stimulus, the response and the line between them became the fundamental conceptual entities in terms of which a whole generation of psychologists approached all problems of behaviour and of learning.

Difficulties encountered by the reinforcement = drive reduction equation – difficulties which affect the rest of the model – can be summarized in two ways:

(i) There are many kinds of behaviour and examples of reinforcement which simply do not match the pattern of food deprivation, search and consummation that Hull used as a prototype.

(ii) There is, if anything, a better case for relating reinforcement to an *increase* in drive rather than to its reduction.


## Drives without needs

Hull based his ideas of the operation of drive and drive reduction on conditions like hunger, which are brought about by deprivation and constitute a potential threat to the organism – eating restores the situation. There are many kinds of activity and associated rewards which just do not conform to this pattern. Escape from pain, for example, is reinforcing but is hardly a case of making good the effects of deprivation. An earlier formulation proposed by Miller and Dollard (1941) seemed to take care of this case: they suggested that drive was simply excessive stimulation, from whatever source, with reinforcement a move

* Hull would have maintained that this was precisely the mark of a good theory: that it should be sufficiently precise in its predictions to facilitate its own overthrow. But it is also possible, in a detailed theory involving many variables, that time is spent on making a whole variety of peripheral adjustments, thereby unduly prolonging its life despite more fundamental flaws.

towards a more acceptable level. Some kinds of behaviour, however, cannot easily be related to any identifiable state of distress or disturbance – in fact often they have consequences which, if anything, involve an *increase* in stimulation – for example, various forms of 'play' or 'exploration'. Human beings often deliberately set out to engage in such activities, i.e. they can function as goals and as reinforcers. Other animals also, especially primates, will learn and repeat behaviour that leads to 'interesting' situations. In an experiment of R. A. Butler's for example, rhesus monkeys quickly learned to solve discrimination problems where the reinforcer consisted of a brief opportunity to look at some moving toy trains.

There are many other examples from ethology, some of which we discussed in the last chapter, of behaviour sequences, often involving approach to some specific stimulus, object or individual where there is no evidence of an associated *need* – at least not in the form of any kind of metabolic stress. If we want to retain the idea of drive as an essential ingredient in the production of behaviour, we will somehow have to extend it to all the cases where, for whatever reason, animals are 'attracted to' particular stimuli, where behaviour is 'goal directed'. Perhaps a reduction of drive in this enlarged sense will coincide with reinforcement. Certainly this would fit more closely with the common-sense notion that rewards consist of getting something one likes – and a tendency to approach could be taken as a behavioural indicator of liking. Note, however, before we turn to the relevant evidence, that by enlarging the scope of *drive*, we have lost its explanatory value. In the original model it was the result of some off-stage metabolic processes, and could be got at, at least indirectly, through various measures of depletion or deprivation. All we have now is the *fact* of 'behaviour towards goal': both it and the associated drive still need to be accounted for. When we consider in addition that there is something about the idea of 'approaching a goal' which does not seem to be within the scope of simple stimulus–response connections, little that is useful remains of the entire system.

## Drive reduction or drive enhancement?

We referred earlier to activities that both humans and animals engage in, to situations they seek out which involve an *increase* in general stimulation and excitement, and which at the same time act as reinforcers. This phenomenon – the coincidence of reinforcement with all the signs of an enhancement rather than the reduction of drive – is far from isolated. It is, for example, a frequent feature of *secondary* reinforcement, i.e. reinforcement by events that have come to 'signal' the immanence of primary reinforcers, like food. This increase in drive has been given the name *incentive motivation* and has been shown to be a function of the amount and quality of the primary reinforcer that is about to follow (or rather 'expected' to follow on the basis of past experiences\*). But the boost of drive, or appetite, has also been shown to occur in the early stages of primary reinforcement – it is exploited and accentuated by the institution of the *aperitif*. McFarland (1973) has suggested that it is a process which helps animals to make clear-cut decisions, by 'locking' them onto a course of action that is showing results, instead of letting them dither and oscillate between a variety of simultaneous goals. (It does not, however, always work for humans –some people find that the effect of moving towards any decision immediately enhances the attractions of the alternatives.)

Several things seem to be going on here at the same time, and our problem is to decide how they are related:

(i) There is a move towards the attainment of a goal;

---

\* It required some fairly desperate measures to incorporate this phenomenon within a 'drive × habit' framework. It was proposed that the mechanism underlying incentive motivation was a *fractional anticipatory goal response* – $r_G$ – a kind of attenuated rehearsal of the eventual full-blown goal response (like eating). To make the idea more concrete: A rat encounters a familiar landmark on its way to a food source. This elicits partial eating responses, whose intensity reflects the full reaction to the food (as previously found); the internal stimulation produced by this 'fractional eating' in turn raises the general level of activity and the rat will run faster. No such fractional eating has, however, been directly observed.

(ii) There is a boost to the behaviour that has brought/is bringing about this approach;

(iii) There is reinforcement, in the sense that on the next occasion the relevant behaviour will occur more promptly.

Is (iii) the result of (i), which might be thought of as a step towards 'satiation'? Or is it a consequence of (ii) – the (temporary) enhancement and maintainance of behaviour that produces (i)? A small amount of food can contribute towards the satisfaction of hunger even as it stimulates the appetite: which, if either, of these processes is critical for reinforcement to occur? Certainly neither can be wholly identified with drive *reduction* as it was originally thought of.

It is often very difficult to answer this sort of question, which requires the separation of processes that normally work together, and it can involve some quite elaborate procedures. We can, for example, by means of physiological intervention, examine the effects of food or water intake through the mouth, and its arrival in the stomach, in *isolation* from each other. In this way it has been possible to show that the stimuli that maintain eating or drinking behaviour need not be the same as those that produce satiation. In doves (McFarland, 1969) reinforcement depends exclusively on events in the beak and throat, while satiation is controlled by signals from the stomach.

Another kind of evidence is provided by the effectiveness, as reinforcers, of events that 'mimic' the genuine article in some of its immediate, but not of its long-term effects. Many animals will prefer saccharine solution, which has no nutritive value, to dextrose, which has, but is less sweet. There are, however, *some* satiation effects with saccharine, and a more clear-cut case against (partial) satiation as the source of reinforcement is provided when the reinforcing 'substitute' actually *increases* the state of deprivation which underlies the behaviour. Thirsty rats will persist for long periods in licking at tubes producing a stream of cool air, even though this dehydrates them even further (Oatley and Dickinson, 1970).

Relevant data has also been obtained from direct investigations of the brain. In 1953 Olds and Milner accidentally discovered that stimulation, with a weak electric current, of specific locations in a part of the brain called the *hypothalamus* acted like a very powerful reward. They developed a technique of implanting minute electrodes, which could then be connected up in a flexible way, enabling animals to move freely, and to *self-stimulate* by pressing a lever. Under these circumstances rats, cats and monkeys rapidly learned the required operation, maintained it at high rates and sometimes over very long periods. Here there is no question of any pre-existing disturbance to be rectified or goal to be approached, and there is little sign of satiation. Detailed 'maps' have now been produced for a variety of species, covering most of the hypothalamus and associated regions, also taking into account the effects of local lesions, prominent interconnections of various sites with other parts of the brain, and neurochemical differences in the fibres involved (Olds, 1977). Apart from locations which produce 'pure reward', there are some where stimulation is aversive, and animals will learn to turn it off. There are other areas in which stimulation produces rewarding effects and, at the same time, *instigates* specific 'drives': sexual, eating or drinking responses are elicited in *satiated animals*. These responses are not fragmentary but co-ordinated and goal-directed, the period of activity coinciding with the period of stimulation. Given the microscopic detail of the networks being investigated, one cannot be sure that the stimulation is not simultaneously and fortuitously affecting quite *distinct* rewarding and drive-producing locations, but the results do seem to point towards some more intrinsic relationship between the drive state produced and reinforcement. Perhaps this is not as counter-intuitive as it might seem. What is being turned on here, and apparently found to be rewarding, is the *active pursuit of a goal* – the pleasures of 'travelling hopefully' are well known.

One additional and intriguing observation may be relevant here. Although there is some degree of overlap, it is possible to demarcate regions for which a particular kind of behaviour is a very *likely* effect of stimulation, so that one can talk about 'eating points', 'sexual points', etc. If such an eating point, say, is repeatedly stimulated in the absence of food, but in the presence of water, it gradually becomes (and remains) a *drinking* point. The significance of this phenomenon is not yet properly understood, but it does again point towards the direct involvement of *goals* in the organization of behaviour, as distinct from any underlying conditions of need or deprivation – even in the case of behaviour related to eating or drinking, where deprivation is clearly an important factor.

### Premack's theory of reinforcement

Let us also look finally at a theory developed by Premack (1965). It focuses attention on *activities* rather than on stimulation, and is based on the observation that the roles of reinforcer, and of behaviour reinforced, are *reversible*. Thus cage-reared rats will often spontaneously run in an activity wheel (or treadmill); at other times, when they are water-deprived, they will drink. If at such a time we make the provision of water conditional on a few turns of the wheel, then animals will *run to drink*. Perhaps more surprisingly, if during a 'running period' the wheel is locked and only released as soon as a few drops of water have been drunk from a tube, then animals will *drink to run*, with the reinforcing relationship the other way round.

To put this in general terms: suppose that at a given time, activity X is more probable than activity Y (in the sense that left to its own devices, an animal would spend more time doing X than doing Y). If we now make the opportunity for X depend on the prior occurrence of Y, then Y will be reinforced, i.e. it will increase in frequency. If at another time the probabilities are reversed and we make Y depend on X, the reinforcement relationship will be reversed also. Premack has provided a great deal of empirical support for this formulation, in which the clues to reinforcement do not lie in any activity as such, but in its relative priority at a given time, and especially in the fact that its occurrence is depressed below the level 'normal' for the occasion. He has also extended his theory, somewhat less convincingly, to cover *punishment*, which becomes identified with the (forced) performance of an activity *above* this level.

The idea of an 'activity' must here be taken to include 'drinking a particular fluid' or 'approaching a particular place', to deal with the rather different probabilities of drinking, say, water and vinegar respectively – differences which are probably better expressed in terms of stimulation than of behaviour. In the form stated it is also more of a generalization than an explanatory theory. It could be taken to imply that there are regulatory mechanisms which tend to maintain various activities at different (and fluctuating) levels, with the possibility of a kind of deprivation effect. A similar idea has come from ethological observations of 'vacuum activities' – behaviour sequences that occur out of context, and simply *because* there has been no 'legitimate' opportunity for some time – e.g. fragments of hunting behaviour in the absence of prey. Premack's account of reinforcement could be interpreted as involving need reduction of a sort, but the deficit being made up would be a *behavioural* one, and would require some rather radical extensions of the idea of homeostasis.

## Learning and goal-directed behaviour

All this, together with evidence discussed in the last chapter, suggests that any model aiming to cope with a wide range of learning and behaviour would not only have to be much more complex, but also to incorporate some different basic principles. Since the fading away of the Hullean system and its derivatives, theories about learning have confined themselves to relatively narrow areas and specific phenomena; none attempts to be comprehensive. Let us, however, briefly consider some of the main features that a more global theory might contain.

The physiological structure that corresponds most closely to the S–R link is a *reflex* circuit, i.e. an arrangement which permits a stimulus input to trigger, more or less directly, a number of muscle contractions. But this is not the only mechanism available to organisms, including quite primitive ones, for producing behaviour. One kind we have already referred to when talking about the homeostatic regulation of various internal processes, one which uses feedback in various forms, is called a *closed-loop* system and sometimes a *servo-mechanism*. In psychology such systems have been invoked primarily in the discussion of human skilled performance (see Chapter 7), but it has been known for a long time that a whole range of simple approach and avoidance behaviours (of insects, for example) are controlled in this way. Since, apart from being quite basic, it is also a rather more effective arrangement for achieving something that needs to be done, it provides a promising basis, or at least an important component, for any model of behaviour.

## A simple feedback system

The essence of feedback control can be conveyed by describing the operation of a thermostatically regulated heating installation. One part of the system may be thought of as representing a *target* – in this case, a particular temperature that can be set. Another represents the *current state*, again a temperature, obtained from a suitably located *sensing unit*. There is an *effector unit* for producing and possibly also for absorbing heat. These are connected in such a way that when the actual temperature detected is below the target, the heating unit is switched on, and when above, the cooling unit is activated (or, more usually, things are just left to cool down).

The diagram given below shows the structure of such a system. Note that the various boxes need not correspond to distinct physical structures. Thus thermostats usually affect the comparison between 'target' and 'current state' in a way that makes it impossible to identify them separately.

The effect of the output (heating) is reflected in the input (the temperature measured): it is 'fed back'. When the arrangement is such that the output tends to *decrease* the gap between target and current state, we talk about *negative* feedback. Such a system is stable, it constantly 'homes in' on the target. (The reverse arrangement, which accentuates any existing discrepancy, is called *positive* feedback; left to itself, it would move in one or the other direction indefinitely.)

Note that what a negative feedback system adjusts is ultimately

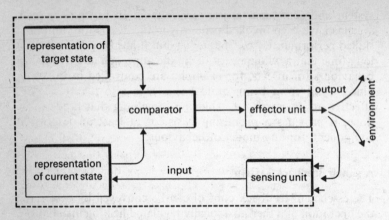

*A feedback system.* The large dotted box demarcates the division between the system and its environment. Arrows should be read as 'operates on' or 'affects'. For rest of explanation, see text

the *input*, or rather, what in the diagram we have called the 'representation of current state' – what the system 'sees'.* What happens to the output is a consequence of this more central objective. For example, most domestic thermostats 'see' the temperature in one particular place (the sitting-room, say); but there are (indefinitely) many consequences of the output (e.g. the temperature in the kitchen) to which they are 'blind' and which therefore do not enter into the process of adjustment. It is necessary to appreciate the fundamental difference between such a closed-loop system and what is implied by an S–R model, which is essentially an assembly of 'open loops'. In the latter case, the stimuli that determine behaviour are defined 'objectively', without reference to the system itself. In a negative feedback system, output is a consequence of a *discrepancy* between the input and an internal standard or target, coupled always so as to reduce the gap: at a very basic

* This point may be of fundamental importance for applying ideas from feedback (control) theory to the behaviour of organisms (see for example Powers, 1978).

level it may be said to have a 'point of view', and a 'purpose' or goal.

Such goals may be simple – a temperature, or a balance between two light intensities to produce an orientation towards a light source; they may also be quite elaborate, involving a particular object or geographical location. That animals *can* find their way towards complex landmarks has been known for some time, but it is only recently that we have come to understand the process sufficiently well to be able to simulate it. (Unfortunately for destructive purposes: there are now missiles that can steer their way towards particular targets by using the appearance of the terrain over which they fly.) Feedback systems in some form thus provide a potential mechanism for any goal-directed activity; what is required is a suitable representation of the target, and an output organized to move the current situation towards it.

### The co-ordination of behaviour

'Output' does not have to mean the execution of some simple response; it could involve the setting up of a subordinate target, or a sequence of targets to be attained in succession and linked by a kind of 'program'. Since even the 'straightforward' positioning of a limb requires the servo-controlled co-ordination of muscle contractions and relaxations (see Chapter 7), an action of any complexity is likely to involve a whole hierarchy of response systems. The developmental biologist Paul Weiss has been one of the main proposers of such a hierarchical structure, from a time (1941) when there was relatively little understanding of the basic control units that might be involved. Although, partly because of Weiss's own work, there is now much more direct evidence, these ideas have been very slow to make an impact on psychological approaches to behaviour and to learning.

What would constitute learning in such a system? When a rat learns to go to 'A' rather than to 'B' for food, it does not have to learn *how* to get to one place or the other. 'A' simply needs to become a 'place-to-be-approached' for the hungry rat, a sub-ordinate goal within the more global one of getting food; but for the achievement of this *sub*goal the rat already has a well-established procedure (in fact, as we shall see, a repertoire of procedures, which can be used as the occasion demands). The learning required involves the incorporation of 'A' as a goal within the chief goal of food – a change at a relatively high level of the hierarchy. Which aspects of behavioural organization can be modified in this way is something that varies from species to species, as we saw in the last chapter. Generally it is at the higher levels that reorganization is possible; a (limited) number of re-sponse patterns may be deployed, and redeployed, for the attainment of superior ends.

## Searching

And what brings this adaptation about? Before looking at the problem of reinforcement within this new context, let us consider a modified form of feedback system which would have much greater flexibility. Suppose that instead of having a particular type of output 'wired in', it can be varied within limits, e.g. it can take the form of approach towards one of several goals. Suppose further that whenever, in the course of such a 'trial' or 'search', a move towards the original target is detected, the search that is currently under way gets a 'boost': it 'locks on', either until the main target is attained, or until once again there is no further progress towards it. Such an arrangement would simply tend to end up with the right behaviour on any given occasion. But if the effect of boosting 'successful' behaviour in this way is also to give it a higher priority on the *next* time round, then we have reinforcement and learning in a form that fits quite a lot of the available evidence. (The suggestion that reinforcement may coincide with the enhancement of current behaviour has been made by a number of writers, e.g. Gray, 1975, who also provides an extensive discussion of the entire issue.)

There is still the difficulty that animals are sometimes reinfor-ced by, and show a continued interest in, stimulation that shows little sign of being satiated – i.e. nothing seems to be 'achieved', no target, even in an extended sense, is being approached. But this normally happens only in unusual or contrived circumstances. Suppose that some form of stimulation is a reliable *indicator* of progress towards an important goal for a particular species, either because the two are coupled in a stable environment or because the animal is so constructed that normally one effect cannot occur without the other. The stimulus could then become reinforcing for the species by natural selection, no provision being made for checking the beneficial effect more directly – remember the rats 'drinking' the dehydrating cool air.

We have used the broad assumptions of instrumental learning theories to illustrate some of the problems created by purposeful behaviour, and arrived at feedback mechanisms as providing a more promising explanatory framework. Let us now use difficulties that have arisen within classical conditioning to show up the need for structures and processes that provide 'models' or 'representations' of the world. These structures will of course also be needed to give an account of purposeful behaviour, of action. In fact, as we shall see, an early *cognitive* theory of learning arose precisely from such considerations.

## Stimulus substitution

Just what is supposed to happen when a CS and a UCS are presented in sequence? The dominant theory, dating from the time of Pavlov, has been that, as a direct consequence of this stimulus–stimulus conjunction, some kind of *stimulus substitution* takes place. Both stimuli produce internal effects. After a time these effects supposedly become linked, the presentation of the CS comes to generate, via this linkage, (some of) the internal effects peculiar to the UCS – and these in turn lead to the conditional response. We have already come across one difficulty with this view – the CR is often rather different from the UCR. But there is another problem, which concerns the nature of the *effective* CS: this can vary, even though the stimulus presented remains the same. When the latter is a *compound* stimulus – one, that is, which can be analysed into a number of components (though in a sense all stimuli could be thought of in this way) – what determines which part or aspect actually becomes involved in learning?

### 'Blocking' and 'overshadowing'

Consider the following experiment by Kamin (1969). He compared two groups of rats: one was conditioned using a compound CS (a noise + a light) followed by shock; the other was first presented with a number of noise–shock pairings, and only then exposed to the same conditioning sequence, involving the noise–light compound, as the first group. Both were finally tested by presenting them with the *light alone*.*

|          | Conditioning sequence | | Result when tested with light |
|          | 1 | 2 | alone |
|----------|-------------|----------------------|------------------|
| Group I  | —           | (noise + light)–shock | conditioning     |
| Group II | noise–shock | (noise + light)–shock | no conditioning  |

Usually when a compound stimulus is used in conditioning, its components, taken separately, each produce a CR. As we can see, this did not happen in the second group, although it received exactly the same number of light–shock pairings as the first. The difference must be attributed to the prior noise–shock experience. Kamin called the effect *blocking*.

Another related phenomenon occurring with compound stimuli had already been observed by Pavlov: a strong or salient stimulus will come to account for most of the conditioning in a compound CS, *overshadowing* the weaker component. The rela-

---

* When, as in this case, the UCS is aversive, conditioning can be measured in terms of the amount of *response suppression* produced by the CS. The technique involves first establishing a base line of activity, such as steady lever pressing on a variable-interval schedule. The CS to be tested is now introduced into this situation. Since aversive stimuli tend to suppress any ongoing activity, the reduction in the rate of response can be used as a measure of the strength of conditioning.

tive failure of *background stimuli* (which inevitably are always present) to show conditioning may be regarded as a partial consequence of overshadowing. But the salience or effectiveness of a stimulus is not simply a function of its intensity – previous experience with the stimulus is another factor, including the experience that its occurrence has *no* particular consequences. Rather than conditioning being a function of individual CS–UCS pairings on their own, it turns out to depend in a complex way on the context – both simultaneous and over time – in which the pairings occur.

### Habituation and the orienting response

Let us look more closely at this experience of 'no consequence', and at the whole idea of a 'neutral' stimulus. No stimulus that an animal is capable of detecting is inherently neutral. When any stimulus occurs in isolation there is typically an attentional or *orienting response* – e.g. head turning towards the source, increased alertness, etc. The phenomenon was noticed by Pavlov, and has been extensively studied by Sokolov (1963). If the stimulus is repeatedly presented without any other consequence, the orienting response (OR) gradually dies away; this is called *habituation*. Any alteration of the stimulus will evoke an OR. But what is more interesting from our present point of view is that the *absence* of a stimulus can also produce a reaction. Suppose that we present an animal with a tone at regular intervals until habituation is complete. If now the tone fails to occur at a point of time where it 'should have done', there will be an OR. The model proposed by Sokolov involved the setting up in the animal of a kind of matching process capable of carrying over into the future an embodiment of expectation; when the stimulus fails to occur, there is a mismatch with the projection of the internal process, and this gives rise to the OR. The important feature of this model is that there are two stages or components – the representation (the state of expectancy) and the consequential response in a given situation. It is a feature that appears to be *required* by the phenomenon (see Gray, 1975, for a detailed discussion) and Sokolov has in fact produced some supporting physiological evidence. A single stage, let alone a simple S–R (or S–S–R) linkage will not do the job.

Consider just one additional example. Suppose that an interval of time is divided up into periods during which a noise is present, and periods when it is not. If now a number of shocks are distributed throughout the interval so that they all coincide with periods of noise, then we get the usual effect of noise–shock conditioning. But if the interval contains a series of *additional* shocks which occur during the noise-*free* periods, then very little conditioning to the noise will occur despite the fact that there is the same number of noise–shock conjunctions in the two cases. In the latter case, the UCSs arrive 'whether the noise is there or not' and it is of course perfectly sensible that under these circumstances no special significance should attach to the noise. But for this kind of relative relationship to be registered requires something rather more complex to take place within the learner than can be represented by simple linkages, or accounted for in terms of conjunctions between specified events.

A mathematical model of conditioning which provides a good fit to most of the available evidence was proposed by Rescorla and Wagner (1972) with subsequent modifications (Rescorla, 1980). In essence, it suggests that there is an upper limit to the degree of association that can take place between any pattern of stimuli and a given UCS. When some stimulus X is paired with a UCS, then according to the model, the increase, on any occasion, in the strength of the X–UCS association depends on the total increase in association that still remains *possible* between the UCS and the whole stimulus complex within which X occurs. Applying this to the Kamin example, if the noise–shock association is already maximal, there is no further conditioning which may take place during the second stage of the experiment, when the light is added to make a compound CS. In consequence, there is no *share* of conditioning which can accrue to the light on its own. This could be put in a more familiar way by saying, for example, that when the noise alone makes the animal expect the shock at the outset, the addition of the light provides no extra information, and consequently does not come to arouse expectations in its own right.

Rescorla and Wagner's model copes very impressively with the effects of both positive and negative relationships between events, as well as with the demonstrated effects of there being *no* relationship. It remains, however, essentially descriptive, and does not propose any particular mechanism. A variety of somewhat more specific suggestions have been made to account for what happens, containing appeals to such *cognitive* concepts as *expectation, attention, information, cue-function,* etc. (See, for example, Bolles, 1979, and MacIntosh, 1975.)

## Cognitive learning theories

There is nothing new about cognitive explanations of learning and behaviour, even within experimental psychology. The name of Edward Tolman (1932, 1959) is especially associated with such an approach. Tolman was impressed by the *flexibility* of goal-directed behaviour, and cited experiments designed to demonstrate that the result of learning is not so much a fixed, new behaviour pattern as a 'model' of some part of the environment, available for use when the need arose. Thus there were 'latent learning' experiments, in which the exploration of a maze without drive and without reinforcement showed substantial benefits when reinforcement was subsequently introduced; others in which rats, having learned to *run* their way out of a maze, could successfully *swim* out if the maze was flooded. These results are not surprising, but difficult to account for in terms of simple stimulus–response, or for that matter, stimulus–stimulus connections. A whole series of 'place-learning' experiments illustrated that animals will learn 'to find their way about', but that the particular manner or method of moving does not form an essential part of that learning. Tolman saw the changes that occurred as primarily cognitive, he talked about the development of 'expectancies', of 'cognitive maps', and the 'readiness' to use a variety of 'means' towards given or learned 'ends'. He failed, however, to indicate what sort of mechanisms could

embody these conditions, in particular the bridging of the gap
between a 'map' and actual behaviour; he was consequently
taunted with leaving his animals 'buried in thought'. His fellow
learning theorists did not have this particular problem – for
them, what an animal learned consisted of nothing but particular
response tendencies. They had other difficulties, however, and
as we saw, cognitive accounts of learning are once again being
put forward. What makes them any more acceptable now than
when they were proposed by Tolman?

Tolman recognized and tried to face up to two fundamental
aspects of behaviour, whose essential characteristics could not
be generated by the types of mechanism familiar at the time: its
goal-directedness, and its use of representations of the world. A
better understanding of servo-mechanisms has at least put us on
a path towards realizing some aspects of the former. And largely
because of developments in the computer field, it is now possible
to devise and envisage systems that may, at least in some limited
sense, be said to 'expect', 'recognize', 'search in memory', generally to form, modify and use representations of some relatively
simple worlds. We may be certain that the way they do these
things is very different from that of any animal; but at least we
can be reassured that a reference to, say, 'expectation' does not
involve an appeal to some unapproachable mystery. Such cognitive terms would now be taken to refer to the systems required
to produce the relevant phenomena, and we have at least some
idea of what such systems might look like. The new wave of
*cognitive psychology* has produced a variety of models inspired
by computer-based techniques, and some of these will be referred
to in the chapters on memory and on language. It is, however,
at present still true to say that this approach is characterized
*primarily* by the underlying confidence that all manner of representations, thought- and decision-processes *can*, in principle,
be modelled – which means that at least the corresponding
phenomena may now be acknowledged and investigated with an
easy conscience.

There is still, however, an important area that remains relatively neglected, and that is the integration of behaviour organization, of the control of *action*, with representation, memory,

*knowledge*. Computer-based cognitive models tend to concentrate on symbol manipulation, and there is a danger that animals, while no longer buried in thought, might be paralysed by information processing. There is a need to join the dynamics of motivation to problem solving, the work on control systems to that on representation. Deutsch (1960) made an early and isolated attempt in that direction, and there has been a recent synthesis by Gallistel (1980), who maintains that a proper concern for *action* has in fact been alive and well all along, in the border country of psychology and biology.

Early learning theories produced an inadequate model of behaviour partly as by-product of their *prior* concern with learning. The mechanisms suggested for behaviour were a direct reflection of the relatively crude methods available for bringing about behavioural change in the laboratory. They failed most conspicuously to account for behaviour in more natural settings – the primary domain of ethologists. The models of action, of performance, that are emerging from that background have in turn been relatively unconcerned about learning, and a learning theory that fully exploits this more sophisticated understanding is probably still some way off. In particular, this understanding has not yet made any significant impact on the methods available for bringing about change – which has been the explicit preoccupation of operant conditioning. These methods, as far as they go, remain valid, even if the implicit theory does not. Perhaps the next development on this front will be a shift of emphasis, from the modification of *behaviour* to that of *goals* and *objectives*.

# 5. Language

The ability to speak has often seemed the most striking difference between the behaviour of humans and that of other animals; it is Man's most conspicuous species-specific behaviour and has enormous consequences for human learning abilities. It could even be argued that the ability to speak renders human learning abilities quite different in principle from those of other species. Whether or not it has quite this effect, the use of language is a highly salient and important aspect of human activity and in this chapter we shall attempt to discuss both how language is acquired and how its use affects other learning.

Our ability to use language, to speak and understand, to read and think in words, is so much a part of us that an effort of the imagination may be necessary to comprehend the sheer extent and complexity of the behaviour we are exhibiting. Many of us, of course, have had the experience of visiting a country whose language we do not speak and of suffering inconveniences on that score. But this is not the same as doing without language. We may be reduced to grunts, gestures and pointing at phrase-books, trying to explain that our valet has been captured by bandits, but there is no question that language underlies our attempt to communicate and our hosts' efforts to understand: it just happens that the languages involved are different.

One thing which might strike us when trying to define human language is the vast range of things that can be said, compared to the restricted range of things that can be conveyed by other methods of communication. It is easy to say to a fellow-traveller, 'This road was very dangerous yesterday when snow restricted visibility and it will be closed next week for repairs', but it is impossible to convey much of this by using, say, traffic lights. This may seem an unfair, not to say ludicrous comparison because traffic lights are *designed* to convey only three simple instructions, but it does begin to illustrate some of the differences between human language and other signalling systems. There are, first of all, a lot more different units – words in the sentence – than are available to a traffic light. English contains some hundreds of thousands of words of which we may habitually use some ten or fifteen thousand. So the sheer number of different identifiable units is already a distinguishing feature of human languages.

Another characteristic of human language is that the words can be combined in an almost infinite number of ways to produce meaningful results. It is quite possible to utter a sentence that has never occurred before which will nevertheless be readily understood by its hearers. Words cannot, of course, be combined at random, there are rules of syntax which restrict the range of meaningful arrangement, but these are general rules about the organization of words and do not prevent the construction of entirely new sentences. A normal adult has at his disposal a very flexible means of informing, persuading, amusing or reprimanding another member of his language group, he can talk about the past, the future, about things which have never happened and, of course, he can talk about the nature of the language he is using. But a young child cannot do any of these things and so we have the problem of accounting for the change. It had perhaps better be said at the outset that, although a great deal of information about the course of language acquisition has been collected, there is little agreement at present about the nature of the underlying process.

Before examining the possible mechanisms involved it might be useful to look at the basic structure of human language. We have already seen that one of its characteristics is the large number of meaningful units. We have a large number of words, not because we can make many more different sounds than members of other species, but because we organize the sounds we can make into a much larger number of significant combinations. This enables us to 'say' a great deal more than other animals but the ability is undoubtedly itself a partial consequence of having a great deal more to say.

## Language structure

The basic sounds of a language, roughly the vowels and consonants plus stresses and pauses, are called phonemes. The number of phonemes, and the actual phonemes used, varies from language to language but is always quite small. It ranges from approximately fifteen to about sixty; English has some forty-five phonemes. This is not very different from the range of sounds used by other species – chimpanzees, for example, use about twenty-five. But in human languages these few sounds provide the basis for many thousands of words and the words, in turn, can be combined to produce an unlimited number of sentences. This characteristic crucially distinguishes human language from the natural communication systems of all other animals.

We have already mentioned the rules for the combinations of words which are part of the structure of any given language. These rules are learned by children at the same time as they are acquiring the vocabulary of their language. One interesting feature of this process is that the rules are transmitted from adults to children usually without either party being able to state them explicitly. Farb (1977) provides an interesting example of the way in which rules are used consistently without an ability to state them and in some cases with only partial awareness that a rule exists at all. The words 'linger', 'singer', 'anger' and 'hanger' are pronounced with different 'ng' sounds by most native English speakers. 'Linger' and 'anger' tend to be pronounced with an additional hard 'g' after the 'ng' sound but the additional hard 'g' is not present in the pronunciation of 'singer' and 'hanger'. The rule which seems to operate is that when a word is derived from a verb by the addition of 'er' the 'g' is not emphasized; when a word is not derived from a verb in this way the 'g' is sounded. While few people know this rule, or even realize that a rule exists, a relatively unfamiliar word derived from a verb such as 'bringer' is invariably pronounced with a soft 'ng' sound while words not so derived such as 'longer' have a hard 'g' sound.

This is of course a rule of pronunciation, but the more basic rules of the appropriate combination of words – the rules of grammar – seem to be absorbed in a similar indirect way. Most people would recognize that 'Telephone boxes seldom pay their income tax on time' is a grammatically correct English sentence despite being nonsense, whereas 'Income seldom boxes their pay time on telephone tax' is not. But this recognition does not depend on being able to articulate the rules to which the first, but not the second, group of words conforms.

Children usually begin speaking just before they are two years old and by the age of four or five, although their speech is still recognizably different from that of adults, they have mastered the basic structure of their native language. They acquire these rules, without any explicit instruction in grammar, from the incomplete sentences and variable syntax of the adults surrounding them. Almost all children learn to speak provided that they are in contact with adults who speak, and the acquisition of the structure of a language by such an early age with little, if any, explicit guidance or instruction must be regarded as an awesome intellectual feat.

Adult speech is not, of course, a complete jumble and there is an element of *teaching* in the fact that adults speak differently to children, particularly young children, from the way in which they speak to other adults. Cross (1977), among others, has shown that they use shorter sentences, that the sentences tend to be well formed and intelligible, usually have concrete reference to the present and rarely to the past. Even four-year-olds modify their speech for two-year-olds and so a child who is just beginning to speak is in effect provided with a special simplified model. On the other hand, when parents express approval – give reinforcement – for what a child has said, it is usually on the grounds of truth or appropriateness rather than the correctness of its grammatical structure (Brown and Hanlon, 1970); explicit instruction in correct grammatical usage is not by any means a prominent feature of language training in the home.

We have implied that there is something special about human

language and certainly humans are the only species (on this planet) to use language so extensively. But other animals do communicate with members of their own species and sometimes with members of other species. A brief consideration of what this involves in different cases may throw some light on what is so distinctive about human language.

## The communications of animals

There would seem to be three types of animal activity that have some claim to be regarded as language behaviour: the mimicry of animals such as parrots and myna birds, the complex in-formation – conveying systems of bees and some other social insects and the achievements of some primates, notably chim-panzees, in learning sign language; the manipulation of symbols; and even some rudimentary human speech.

Parrots and myna birds can imitate the human voice very closely, in some cases to such an extent that it is difficult to distinguish from human speech. Some very important features of language are missing in such mimicry, however. Individual utterances are not *used* to achieve particular, corresponding *ends*; nor are their components rearranged in any systematic way to produce other utterances. We do not regard such birds as being able to speak, as having a language, and we indicate this by using the term 'parrot fashion' to describe mechanical mindless repetition, devoid of understanding.

The communication system of bees, however, is an entirely different matter. Von Frisch (1967) has shown that a particular 'dance' performed by bees on their return to the hive from a successful foraging expedition can indicate the direction and dis-tance of a source of nectar. The main axis of the dance indicates the direction while the speed of performance is inversely related to the distance, or more precisely to the effort needed to get there, since head-winds and changes in altitude are taken into account. More remarkably, when the dance is performed inside the hive and the bee moves in a vertical plane instead of a hori-zontal one, the angle between the vertical and the axis of the dance is the same as the angle between the direction of the sun and that of the nectar source.

The bee's dance has some of the characteristics of language behaviour in that it uses *symbols* (the elements of the dance) to communicate the distance and direction of a source of food. The symbols are used in a flexible way to indicate nectar at different distances and directions and the information provided, and eventually used by the audience, relates to objects which are not present at the time – in no sense is it an immediate response to a stimulus. The language is, however, extremely restricted in its range of topics. There is no way in which it can be adapted to deal with imaginary or *possible* situations, to give orders or ask questions or indeed to communicate anything about present conditions apart from the distance and direction of food. One cannot, therefore, regard the communication of bees, although it is a remarkable biological adaptation, as constituting language in the human sense.

If we are looking for the capacity to develop a more elaborate language we might reasonably examine the other primates, our closest zoological relations, and there has in fact been a great deal of work, notably with chimpanzees, to investigate their potential for speech and for language generally.

What happens when we provide such an animal with an environment resembling that of a child as closely as possible? Environment does not here mean simply a place with a given layout and containing certain objects, but includes people and the way they behave. Obviously the degree of approximation that can be achieved must depend on the animal. The extent to which we can follow normal patterns of *child* rearing when dealing, say, with a young rat is severely limited. But a young chimpanzee can without *too* much difficulty be integrated into a household as though he were a child. For example, W. N. and L. A. Kellog (1933) brought up a nine-month-old female chimpanzee together with their nine-month-old son exactly as though they were brother and sister. Although at the outset the chimpanzee learned a whole variety of physical skills more rapidly than the child, including responses to simple verbal instructions, the child had caught up in most things after a period of nine months, and was beginning to develop language behaviour of a kind that was totally absent in the chimpanzee.

There have been other attempts to teach apes to speak (e.g. by Hayes and Hayes, 1951) with similar results. After three years of training, again in circumstances closely resembling those for bringing up a young child, the chimpanzee was able to use a few isolated words like 'mama' or 'cup' in an appropriate context, but that was about the limit of its linguistic achievements.

The use of language, however, is an abstract ability by no means restricted to the production of speech. It could be that chimpanzees have difficulty in organizing heard and spoken sounds in a manner suitable for speech but possess the potential for language; they are, after all, capable of goal-directed or purposeful behaviour, using the term purpose as a description rather than an explanation.

This possibility has been exploited in more recent research in which chimpanzees and other primates have been taught to use words from visual languages. Salient work in this area has been carried out by Gardner and Gardner (1975) and by Premack (1976). The Gardners taught the American Sign Language, originally devised for deaf children, to their chimpanzee Washoe while Premack has created an artificial language using coloured plastic shapes which his chimpanzee, Sarah, has learned to manipulate in a meaningful way. This work has stimulated a large number of other studies, some using other visual languages and other species such as gorillas. Such experiments are inevitably time-consuming and laborious; Washoe, for example, was raised in a manner similar to that of a human child except that all communications to her, or in her presence, were conducted in sign language. It is also necessary to maintain continuity, as far as possible, in the relationship between trainers and the experimental animal. There can be no doubt, however, that these efforts have paid off, at least in terms of the vocabulary acquired by such animals, most of whom are credited with a large repertoire of words. Koko, for example, a gorilla trained at Stamford University by Patterson (1978) is said to use more than 400 signs of the American Sign Language.

Many research workers in this area claim that their subjects not only use 'words', assigning the appropriate symbols to their referents correctly, but have developed the ability to use language. This is a much larger claim and is based on the animals' alleged ability to use their words creatively in constructing new sentences which, as we have seen, is a critical aspect of human speech. Much has been made of certain rather dramatic observations; Washoe is said to have responded to a duck with the two word response 'water-bird' while Koko called a zebra a 'white-tiger'.

These claims have come under sustained attack from other research workers, notably Terrace and others (1979), who adopt the position that '. . . an ape's language learning is severely restricted. Apes can learn many isolated symbols (as can dogs, horses, and other non-human species), but they show no unequivocal evidence of mastering the conversational, semantic, or syntactic organization of language.'

These criticisms are severe and are based not only on critical analysis of the data produced by other experimenters but on systematic observations of the behaviour of a chimpanzee called Neam Chimpsky (a playful reference to the well-known linguist Noam Chomsky whose views on language behaviour are relevant to the issue) who was raised to speak the American Sign Language by Terrace and his colleagues. Extremely detailed records of the signs used by this chimpanzee were kept, including records of the order of signs in multi-sign utterances, and some of the discourse between him and his trainers was videotaped.

Terrace's assertion that the symbolic behaviour of chimpanzees does not constitute language behaviour in its full sense is based on detailed analyses of chimpanzee utterances, leading him to conclude, among other things, that long emissions of words by the chimpanzee are 'not semantic or syntactic elaborations of his short utterances' in contrast to the initial long utterances of a child. There is, in any case, a startling difference in the rate of growth of MLU (mean length of utterance) with age between chimpanzee and children; even deaf children have shown much more significant rates of growth than chimpanzees. Terrace's central criticism of the view that apes can learn to use language is essentially that all such apparent language behaviour can be explained on a simpler basis (he points out in passing that if judgements about a child's ability to use language were based on its earliest utterances we may have doubts here too: we know that humans can use language because adult forms of language develop, not because small children string two or three words together). The meaningful utterances of chimpanzees and apes have all apparently been produced in situations which maximize opportunities for problem-solving behaviour, and decisions that their performance constitutes language have rested on interpretations made by their trainers.

Such serious criticisms have not been accepted with equanimity by investigators convinced that their chimpanzees or gorillas really use language. A controversy has been generated which lacks some of the restraint one might expect in scientific disputes. The acerbity in itself may indicate that the evidence is inconclusive and at the moment the only verdict on the language behaviour of apes may well be 'not proven'.

We have spent some time discussing the linguistic abilities of animals which, apart from their intrinsic interest, are relevant to theories of language acquisition in humans.

Perhaps because of an ill-fated attempt by Skinner to explain all verbal behaviour in terms of simple operant conditioning, psychologists seem to have eschewed global theories of speech development in favour of more limited and useful studies of how children's speech actually changes over time. There are, however, profound differences in approach to the problem of language acquisition, one of which, originally generated by Noam Chomsky (1976), is concerned with the degree to which the ability to acquire language is inborn in children.

**Nature of language acquisition**

Differences between those, such as Piaget, who believe that language is primarily a learned phenomenon dependent on the development of appropriate intellectual abilities together, of course, with adequate experience of speech from other people, and those who view language as primarily an innate ability, such as Chomsky, appear absolute. Typical statements such as these, from Chomsky (1980); 'investigation of human language has led me to believe that a genetically determined language faculty, one component of the human mind, specifies a certain class of "humanly accessible grammars"' and 'within a given speech-community, children with varying experience acquire comparable grammars *vastly under-determined by the available evidence*' (our italics) seem to leave no doubt that, in his view, the ability to use language is almost wholly determined by innate factors.

Piaget, on the other hand, while equally hostile to those termed 'empiricists' both by him and Chomsky (empiricists are supposed to be those who believe that children inherit very little in the way of preordained intellectual structures except perhaps a susceptibility to repeat reinforced actions) is equally determined in his view that language is subordinate to general intellectual structures which have developed as a result of the child's transactions with the environment.

Chomsky's beliefs seem to be founded on the discovery of rules of grammar which have not been explicitly taught and which are common to all known languages (this criterion of innateness is briefly discussed in Chapter 8; in fact universality is neither a sufficient nor a necessary condition for a quality to be innate). But the fact that children receive very little *direct instruction* in speaking, when one considers the complexity of the linguistic competence of mature speakers, does seem to call for explanation. Chomsky's position is a simple one; no known theory of learning is adequate for this explanatory task, therefore language is innate.

Piaget, and of course learning theorists of other persuasions, tend to take the view that linguistic ability is in principle explainable on the basis of learning even if no current theory can do it and, in any case, to simply call the ability innate is hardly an explanation.

Despite the interest aroused by Chomsky's views, it is possible to doubt whether they are of any practical importance whatever.

After all, even Chomsky recognizes that particular children learn particular languages and it would seem a totally appropriate scientific endeavour to try to find out how they do it. Nonetheless, language learning has been approached by some investigators from the point of view that an important organizing capacity for language is inborn.

## The nature of early language behaviour

This approach, based on the idea that a common 'deep structure' underlies all human languages with their varying 'surface structures', proposes that in order to learn a given language children must be born with a knowledge of the deep structure of all languages, that children in fact have an innate 'language acquisition device'. While no one would doubt that learning a language depends on certain innate characteristics, the idea that it depends on the possession of an inborn language acquisition *device* may seem like saying that learning to balance on a bicycle depends on the possession of an innate understanding of the mechanics of leverage. The idea may have more plausibility than this however. McNeill (1966) posed the problem of building a device that could learn the rules of English sentence construction, using as its input simply a collection of English sentences, in such a manner that it could then generate its own (correct) novel sentences. This is, of course, what a child does. What properties would such a device need? McNeill proposed that in order to be able to organize the input the device must have information about the structural properties of the language, that a sentence has a subject and predicate for example, since such information is not contained in the ordinary English sentence. It is not too clear how such information would help a small child; how useful would it be to know that nouns exist when he would still be unable to identify them in the sentences he heard? Nevertheless attempts have been made to establish the existence of a language acquisition device from observations of children's early speech; an example will illustrate the approach.

Braine (1963) suggested that young children have rules for the construction of two-word sentences which he called 'pivot grammar'. The basic idea is that there are two categories of words, pivot words and open words. Pivot words of one type always occur in the first position in a two-word sentence, if they occur at all, and those of the other type always occur in the second position. Open words can occur in either the first or second position. Examples of the first type of pivot would be 'more' as in 'more milk', 'more toys', while an example of the second type would be 'gone' as in 'milk gone' and 'Daddy gone'. 'Milk', 'toys' and 'Daddy' would be open words.

It had been suggested by McNeill that when using pivot grammar children respect advanced grammatical distinctions in that adjectives all occur as pivot words. If this were substantiated it would constitute indirect evidence of some innate understanding of developed grammatical classes, but it has been shown by Brown (1973) that by no means all children use pivot grammar and that those using it do not restrict their selections of pivot words to adult grammatical classifications. It seems, in general, that there is very little evidence that consistent grammatical classes or relationships exist in children's language from the very beginning, which would be likely if an innate language structure existed.

With reference to animal language it is not clear whether the development of 'true language' by animals would prove that a language acquisition device was unnecessary for speech acquisition or whether it would prove that animals also had a language acquisition device. But the continuing doubt about animal language does lend credence to the idea that learning a language is somehow different from learning other sorts of skills.

Before looking at the possible contribution to language development of such learning processes as imitation or reinforcement, there is another issue which closely parallels the dispute about innate language acquisition mechanisms – the question of the relationship between language and thinking.

**Language and thought**

Historically this problem has sometimes been expressed as a question about the relative priority of language and thought, whether we think because we have acquired the verbal skills to do so or we acquire linguistic forms *in order* to express the thoughts we have. Obviously if we use particular cognitive operations before we express them in the verbal form appropriate to our culture it casts serious doubt on the idea that language structures are inborn.

There is an additional but related question concerned with the relationship between mature thought and speech. In its simplest form it might be expressed as 'Can we think about things for which we have no words?' or in a slightly more elaborate form 'To what extent does the nature of our language determine the way we think about things?'

The idea that language determines the forms of thought has been most clearly expressed in what came to be known as the Sapir–Whorf hypothesis. Sapir expressed this by saying that 'human beings . . . are very much at the mercy of the particular language which has become the medium for their society . . . the "real world" is to a large extent built upon the language habits of the group', and Whorf concluded that 'we dissect nature along lines laid down by our native languages'.

The basic idea of the Sapir–Whorf hypothesis is that the way people think, indeed the only way they *can* think, is determined by the language they speak. In its strongest form this hypothesis suggests that if a language does not have a future tense, say, then speakers of that language will not be able to think about the future or, at best, will be severely impaired in their ability to do so. Proponents of the theory have made much of the fact that languages differ in the detail of their vocabulary as it applies to different parts of the world. Eskimos, for example, have several words to distinguish different kinds of snow for which there are no equivalents in English. It is inferred from this that English-speakers cannot distinguish, and hence think about, these types of snow as well as Eskimos.

It is fairly easy to demonstrate that different languages categorize both natural and social phenomena with different degrees of refinement. If the entire economic structure of a society depends on ownership and breeding of cattle, its language is likely to contain different and more sophisticated terms for describing them than the language of people who only come across packaged pieces of beef in a supermarket. But it is not justifiable to argue from the presence or absence of single words to describe a particular object or event to the ability to detect or think about the object or event in question. If we are forced to deal with snow for some purpose such as skiing, predicting avalanches or making snowballs we can describe it in a more detailed way than we do when simply noting that it is snowing. 'Hard-packed snow', 'soft snow', 'crisp snow' and so on are all readily understandable phrases in English and the absence of a single word to describe each condition does not preclude thinking about it.

It seems likely that the new words which enter a language will relate to objects or situations with which the speakers of the language are involved or preoccupied at the time and which they *need* to talk about; the existence and use of particular words will in turn help to draw the attention of members of the linguistic community to corresponding aspects of the world. In this sense the relationship between thought and language is clearly a reciprocal one.

Languages, however, differ in structure as well as detailed vocabulary. For example, Whorf has shown that the Hopi language, of which he made a particular study, does not have the past, present and future tense structure of English and that time is not quantified in the Hopi culture, which emphasizes sequence rather than duration.

The problem with such arguments is to decide the causal sequence. It is fairly easy to show that different cultures emphasize different aspects of experience and that their language is adapted to expressing those things that seem important in the culture. It is not at all clear, however, that the nature of the language *determines* rather than *reflects* the way in which the members of a society view the world. It has also been pointed out that languages of quite different structure occur in societies of similar social and material culture and languages of similar structure in quite divergent societies.

From the point of view of speech acquisition the question is what relationship exists between a child's developing ability to speak and his increasing ability to think more competently. Thought could be dependent solely on the acquisition of appropriate forms of speech (a developmental variant of the Sapir–Whorf hypothesis); alternatively speech may follow closely the development of cognitive abilities. Other logical possibilities include the total independence of speech and thought (which seems implausible) or some form of reciprocal development which may or may not preserve a degree of independence for the two areas of development.

### Speech and cognitive development

A direct way of studying the relationship between speech development and cognition is to record the language behaviour of children while assessing, as independently as possible, the stage of cognitive development reached. Such studies in general seem to indicate that new cognitive abilities precede the ability to express them in appropriate verbal form. Bloom (1970) showed that children's use of negative statements developed through three stages and the words used to express a new stage when it first appeared were the same as those used for earlier stages on their first appearance. In other words, the use of a new cognitive category did not follow the acquisition of its correct mode of expression but the way of expressing it was learnt after the cognitive ability developed. This view that cognition precedes language is strongly supported by many detailed observations of the development of children's speech.

In order to examine the process of speech development it is necessary to observe particular children in detail while their speech is evolving, noting not only what they say but paying close attention to the circumstances in which they say it. An obvious example would be whether a child shakes its head, expressing negation, while it speaks. Frequently a degree of interpretation is necessary; a child may pull something towards him or push it away, in both cases uttering the word 'take'. In the first case it is reasonable to assume that the child means 'I am taking this' or 'I will take it' while in the second he probably means 'take it away'.

Using careful examinations of context in conjunction with the recording of children's utterances, psychologists and linguists have charted the development of children's speech in some detail in recent years. One study carried out by Roger Brown and his colleagues was based on two-hour samples of speech taken from three children every fortnight over several years.

In these observations the speech of the child together with the situation, including speech by any adult present, such as the child's mother, was carefully recorded. In this way it is possible to relate the development of actual speech with apparent meaning in a systematic way over time.

One striking finding from this study, which has been replicated in others, is that the child's ability to use a concept seems almost universally to precede his ability to express it linguistically. Most of us have heard children say vehemently 'Joe car' while at the same time grabbing and holding tight to the Dinky toy in question. We have little doubt that the child means 'In my considered view this vehicle belongs to me', or perhaps just 'Joe's car'. The point is that the child is expressing possession before he is able to add the possessive 's' which is the grammatically correct way of indicating possession in English.

In the Brown study it was noted that in the earliest stage of language development adults attributed to the child four types of meaning associated with verbs, 'imperative', 'past', 'intention' and 'present temporary duration', all of which the child expressed by using an unmarked form of the verb. An example of 'past' usage would be a situation in which a child said 'toy drop' when a toy had just dropped.

At the next stage children began to use the correct form of the verb to express the meaning they had already been credited with expressing in an ungrammatical but semantically clear (given the situation) form.

This theme, that the ability to express meaning precedes its correct linguistic formation, runs through such observational studies. It is hard to resist the conclusion that the ability to think in a particular way is a necessary (even if not, as we shall see, a sufficient) condition for the development of the correct verbal formulation.

Such a view is strengthened when the development of speech in children acquiring different languages is studied, and particularly by observations of bilingual children. It has been noted that in English the forms of negation acquired by children are usually in the order 'non-existence', 'rejection' and 'denial' while in Japanese the order is 'non-existence', 'denial A', 'rejection' and 'denial B' (there are two forms of denial in Japanese, the second being more complex).

Allowing for the considerable differences in language structure these are remarkably close developments and suggest that the cognitive abilities of the children are developing in the same way and controlling their acquisition of language rather than the language determining their conceptual development. It is also notable that as each new form of negation is acquired it is first expressed in a primitive form. In English, for example, 'no more' serves as the introductory form of a new negation until the correct grammatical usage develops.

Bilingual children have been observed to acquire a particular concept at the same time in both their languages, probably again indicating that the ability to use the concept is a prior necessity for its expression in either language. There are some exceptions to this finding for bilingual children which we shall discuss in a moment, but first one more example of this particular relationship of thought and speech.

This relates to the use of the perfect tense, 'I have seen'. The use of the perfect tense embodies a fairly complex concept and develops relatively late, around four and a half years old. Its meaning may perhaps be explained as making a statement about the past which still has current relevance. Time relationships of this kind are difficult for children and, as we have said, appear fairly late in development but the child has the verbal ability to utter phrases in the perfect tense long before he does so; and when he does use the perfect tense for the first time his utterances are non-standard. In other words the ability actually to say the words 'I have seen' does not mean that he will say them with the adult meaning attributed to them, and when he does mean 'I have seen' he says it in a different way. Cognitive development in this instance seems peculiarly unrelated to purely linguistic skill.

Much of this evidence points towards a form of development requiring the establishment of certain cognitive skills prior to language acquisition. Can we assume, therefore, that language is totally secondary, dependent solely on the existence of the ability to use a particular concept and existing merely as a form of expression of thoughts which are already present?

It seems that this may be an overstatement of the case; there may be a certain degree of independence in language development stemming from the nature of language itself. Some evidence for this derives from the study of bilingual children mentioned earlier where the acquisition of concepts in both languages is *not* parallel. Slobin (1973) quotes evidence on two children learning Hungarian and Serbo-Croatian at the same time. The meanings of some English prepositions such as 'into' and 'onto' are expressed in Hungarian by inflections on the noun, but in Serbo-Croatian they require a preposition as well as inflections. The children both used the inflections correctly in Hungarian before they used the more complex equivalent forms in Serbo-Croatian.

While this may appear to raise only the question of grammatical difficulties peculiar to specific languages (Omar, 1973 has shown, e.g., that Arabic-speaking children only master the very complex forms of the plural by about the age of fourteen while English-speaking children do so by about six) it does suggest that language may have its own inherent problems in acquisition. This possibility is strengthened when one considers certain pathological conditions. Aphasic children may appear to be of normal intelligence yet are unable to speak. Frequently they are able to acquire symbolic abilities, to use signals, yet are unable to construct grammatical sentences. It may be that there is a specific linguistic ability possessed by normal humans which is as necessary as cognitive ability if speech as we usually understand it is to develop.

In other words cognitive development may provide us with something to express (and if it didn't we would not speak) but we may also need a parallel development of the ability to structure language before we can express the meanings we have.

## Speech and behaviour

The use of language is part of the *fabric* of human behaviour – not simply one kind of activity amongst others, but one that plays a special mediating role between the individual and his environment. At a highly complex level we can see this in the use of theoretical language briefly discussed in an earlier chapter. Verbal or symbolic statements can be used to describe the world and hence provide a reference and guide for action. At a more mundane level, a great deal of everyday behaviour is related to some sort of verbal formulation – utilizing instructions or descriptions provided from outside, orally or in writing, or generated by the individual himself as a stage in ongoing activity. Quite apart from making explicit plans and referring to them in the verbally remembered form 'What was I going to do next?', many actions are preceded by verbal decision and situations are identified verbally as an integral part of one's reactions to them. Even in the course of highly practised, 'automatically' performed activities, the experience of difficulty frequently generates a burst of verbal behaviour – internal or sometimes overt – in an attempt to sort things out. It is out of this that further activity develops.

All this is part of our common experience but it is worth enumerating briefly how the availability of language has specific relevance for human *learning* abilities. Information, for instance a book on the techniques of trout-fishing or the instructions for a new kind of can-opener, can exist in written form and hence is available, for transmission into verbal or semantic memory, to anyone who can read. People can change their *behavioural* dispositions relatively permanently, can learn, by reading and storing in some symbolic form information about an activity they have not yet performed. Possible processes of retention of such material will be discussed in the chapter on memory; for the present it is sufficient to note that the possession of language provides an additional dimension of learning for humans.

Learning via the use of language is not merely convenient, it also enables one to acquire information that would otherwise have to be discovered for oneself. The implications of this are enormous, spanning both time and distance in such a way that the existence of many central human activities, science, law and many others, would be inconceivable without it.

Language provides two other specific aids to learning. First it offers an interactive facility between a learner and teacher; the learner can ask questions, understand the answers (if not he can always ask another question), explain his difficulties and so, again, learn to *perform* without the necessity of overt trial and error. In addition the use of language provides a means to control one's own activity in such a way that control over the environment can improve. An example of a very simple kind may illustrate how this self-controlling function of language improves and changes with age. In one series of experiments reported by Luria children of various ages were required to respond to light signals presented to them, by exerting pressure on a device which provided a continuous record of the pressure exerted. If asked to press when a light appeared children between the ages of two and five years tended to continue pressing intermittently even in the absence of the signal. When asked to press for a red light but not to press for a green one no stable co-ordination between signal and response developed. On the other hand, with verbal reinforcement for correct response, discrimination was quickly established, though not *maintained* without it. In contrast to this, children of three and four could, after verbal instruction alone, respond *verbally* to the signals by saying 'Go' in one case, and 'Press' or 'Don't press' in the other, showing a stable correspondence between signal and response. The dynamics of making verbal responses appear at this age to be more highly developed than motor reactions, which incidentally suggests that different neural systems may be involved.

Children were now asked to combine motor and verbal responses – saying 'Go' and pressing at the same time. The effect of this depended on the age of the child. With the youngest it led to a further disruption or to the inhibition of the motor response. Next came a stage where the making of any verbal response – 'Go', 'Press', 'Don't press' – *all* facilitated pressing, this time, however, in a controlled way, pressing occurring once only in conjunction with the verbal response. Thus, in the discrimination experiment, motor discrimination could be achieved by pairing pressure with a verbal response such as 'go', which was made to one signal only. At yet a later age – around four and a half years – the *significance* of the verbal response could be related to action, so that saying 'Press' and 'Don't press' could be combined with the appropriate movement. In all cases, omitting the verbal response led to the previous instability of the motor reactions.

It appears from these and other experiments that from an early age verbal responses begin to have a greater stability than other types of reaction; that verbal responses made by the subject can be used to mediate between signals and manual (or other) reactions, thus bringing these under greater control; and that the nature of the control exercised changes from a situation where speech acts just as an additional, though more effective 'impulse' to movement, to one where the meaning of the words spoken by the subject can be utilized. At about the same time, control can be shifted from *external* to *internal* speech. The experiments make explicit a process that is likely to occur under ordinary circumstances and Luria argues that the development of speech is closely related to the development of deliberate or voluntary action in general. The experiments also suggest the possibility of utilizing the mediating role of a child's own speech to accelerate control over its activity.

## Development of concepts

Many words used to refer to events, situations or objects have more than a single application. Although on a given occasion we may talk about a particular house or about a dog we happen to own, words like house or dog can be used in a wide variety of situations involving houses and dogs of very different shapes and sizes. The words used denote classes or categories of objects or events that are, for certain purposes, treated alike. They give verbal expression to a concept. In fact a concept is defined as a common response (often but not always verbal) made to a category of experiences which have some property in common.

If a child can separate all red objects of varying shapes and sizes from green objects, then we accept that he is using the concept red. To take an extreme example, if a rat can learn to approach all triangular objects, regardless of their size, position and colour, and to avoid objects of other shapes, then we could say that the rat had *some* concept of a triangle. The rat, of course, does not call the objects triangles (the child may not call his objects red) but he is giving evidence that he is responding to the common property of having three sides and disregarding all other variations, and this is sufficient for us to say that the animal is using a concept.

It is obvious that possible concepts differ widely in complexity, ease of concrete reference, range of applicability and so forth, and to describe them all as concepts is not to suggest that the same processes of concept formation operate in all cases; it merely emphasizes the general tendency to organize experiences into classes for convenience. We could not handle a world in which we had to learn a response to all the experiences we could in fact discriminate and we reserve precision of response for those situations in which we are especially interested. We usually use about twenty names for colours, for example, while workers in dye factories may use more, but even they do not attempt to name the thousands of colours we can discriminate. Before we consider differences in the types of concepts we can acquire, however, what can be said in general about the process of concept formation?

An early view of Hull's was that all the objects included within a concept must have identical elements, that the concept response is in fact a response to identical stimuli appearing in different contexts. This has frequently been shown to be wrong and perhaps represents the most extreme attempt to explain thinking in the simplest possible stimulus–response terms. Work carried out by Smoke, for example, showed that concepts can be developed where the only common characteristic is an invariant internal relationship in the items falling within the category. One of his concepts, labelled 'zif', included all cards on which three dots were marked in such a way that the distance between the two farthest apart was equal to twice the distance between the two closest together. It is possible to draw three dots in all sorts of ways which all conform to this requirement, and conversely dots can be located to look quite like members of the concept class without having the correct relationships between their distances.

We have mentioned concepts defining a class of objects with common stimulus elements, or with common internal relationships; but what about concepts like 'edible', 'attractive', 'lethal' or their substantive equivalents? The common feature of the instances which comprise these classes is a particular kind of effect which they have, in this case on people or animals. Subsequently we might discover that they have other properties in common, but in the first instance many things or situations are grouped together on the basis of evoking a common response or reaction from another group – ultimately, of course, from people. Some concepts, like 'poison', depend on our biological make-up, others, like 'hammer' or 'carving knife', are generated by characteristic activities. Definitions of 'marriage-guidance counsellors', 'advertising agency', 'cold war' – indeed all the terms in common usage and the corresponding concepts constitute a reflection of people's interaction with their physical and social environment from the most basic to the most complex. Conversely, this interaction will be influenced by the concepts that we have learned to use. The idea of a chair or seat arises naturally in a species predisposed to sitting; the labelling of an object as a chair invites its being treated appropriately. Learning concepts involves a great deal more than simply applying a name to the members of a class.

Concepts differ also in their degree of immediate reference to physical objects, their concreteness. Generally speaking the more abstract they are the more difficult they are to form. Concepts such as 'gene' or 'gravity' come later in the development of a science than 'cell' or 'weight'.

Relative difficulty in the development of different types of concepts may usefully be thought of in terms of the readiness with which the common associations necessary for the formation of a concept are evoked by the various items. This has been tested directly in experiments in which subjects are presented with a number of single words and are asked to give the most immediate sensory asociate of the word (cat, for example, might evoke the responses 'furry', 'graceful' and 'quick'). The stimulus words are then grouped and presented to other subjects who are asked which concepts are exemplified by the words. The most frequent response then tends to be a concept which has a high probability of association with all the stimulus words individually. Easy concepts are therefore those formed on the basis of the most likely response to the individual object while difficult concepts are dependent on common responses which have a low probability of association with at least some of the individual items.

If we are required to link a hovercraft and Nelson's monument, we would be unlikely to connect them on the basis that neither has wheels; if the items were a hovercraft and a toboggan we would be much more likely to do so. The skill of course is to arrive at unlikely concepts which are also useful.

## Concept formation and concept attainment

A child confronted with a variety of spherical, elastic objects that can be bounced, thrown or rolled, might develop the concept of ball – though it is unlikely that it would spontaneously invent the same (or indeed any) word, or that the category of objects would coincide exactly with that conventionally included under the heading of ball. This would constitute a case of concept invention or formation. It is not, however, the process whereby the great majority of concepts are in fact arrived at. Children are born into a community within which a very large number of concepts already exist and in whose language they are reflected. Thus the child comes across spherical bouncing objects, which are accompanied by the word 'ball', furry animals called 'cats' and so on. The single word applied to a variety of objects draws attention to them as members of a single class, and helps to create in each new member of the community the same concept structure that is already shared by its existing members. The problem confronting the child is not so much one of *forming* concepts, as of *attaining* existing ones, and part of this consists in learning to use the corresponding labels correctly.

Broadly speaking, the ability to respond to features of a learning situation which go beyond its immediate sensory properties increases with the complexity of the animal and reaches its culmination in human beings. *Naming* is particularly effective in drawing attention to common properties, and as a consequence of having a single name applied to a limited number of objects or situations people are able to extend it to other, not yet encountered instances.

Properties defining a concept are not always explicit. When confronted with real objects that are to be categorized, the attributes from which a selection is to be made may remain completely unspecified. What are the properties of a block of wood? Its colour, weight, height, surface texture, shape, density, volume, sharpness of its edges, evidence of dry-rot attack – the list could be extended indefinitely, and it will be apparent that the 'properties' themselves are concepts which may or may not be available to a given individual.

Although it is not necessary to be able to name a given feature of a situation in order to use it as a basis for discrimination, it is a decided advantage. For example Spiker, Gerjouy and Shepard (1956) carried out an experiment with children between the ages of three and five, who were divided into those who could refer in some appropriate way to the middle-sized member of three stimuli (i.e. who could describe it as 'middle-sized' or by the use of some equivalent phrase) and those who could not. The former group was found to be significantly superior at a concept attainment task which involved choosing the middle-sized stimulus from sets of three, the absolute sizes being varied. Being able to *name* a particular object or attribute does of course imply the ability to discriminate the relevant features of the stimulus situation. But in addition to this, having a name available increases the chance that these features will be attended to.

The concepts which a person uses constitute a kind of filter system for the infinite variety and complexity of the information which impinges on him – there is a strong tendency to see and respond to the environment in terms of available concepts. To the extent that language is the predominant factor in the formation of the concepts we use, it is basic to most of human behaviour including those cases where spoken or written language as such is not observable.

Language is, above all, the means by which abstract concepts can be developed. And, conversely, the abstractness of our concepts facilitates our ability to use language.

Premack (1978) has argued that a key distinction between the conceptual abilities of different species can be thought of in terms of the degree of abstractness of which they are capable. He defines abstractness in terms of a transfer situation. If an animal which is trained to turn left when shown two triangles and turn right when shown a triangle and a square subsequently turns left on presentation of two circles and right when shown a circle and a diamond, it has a concept of 'same–different' which is abstract to some degree. If such an animal *always* turns left when two similar items are presented and right when the items are different (provided the difference is sufficient to be discriminated) then its concept of same–different is maximally abstract.

We have discussed earlier in this chapter the varying degrees of abstractness of different concepts – 'density' would usually be regarded as more abstract than 'weight' – but abstractness is also a property that a particular concept held by a given individual can possess to varying degrees.

Simple 'action' concepts such as 'giving' show different degrees of limitation in different species, many restricting giving to very specific types of interactions such as parent to child and sometimes to an adult as part of a mating ritual, whereas giving in the human situation is an action of unrestricted possibilities and is therefore more abstract.

The degree to which concepts have a wide range of reference in different species is paralleled by the degree to which learning in a new situation is absolute or relational. A pigeon, for example, can be trained to respond differently to a pair of identically coloured keys than to a pair of keys of different colours but its success in making this distinction is a function of the difference between the non-identical keys. For humans, chimpanzees and dolphins *success* in such a task will not depend on the degree of difference (provided the objects can be discriminated at all), but the speed with which the decision is made will be inversely related to the degree of difference.

All these species (probably all vertebrates) can respond both to the absolute and to the relational characteristics of the stimulus but the balance is different, relational-responding increasing as one ascends the phylogenetic scale. There is thus an interaction between conceptual development in the realm of abstractness and the degree to which language behaviour can develop, this interaction representing again the interdependence of language use and levels of conceptual thinking.

# 6. Memory

When we temporarily forget a well-known fact, or suddenly remember a long-forgotten childhood incident, questions seem to arise; we are reminded of the existence of memory and of its normally unremarked functioning. One dictionary gives as its definition of memory 'the store of things learned and retained from an organism's activity or experience as evidenced by modification of structure or behaviour or by recall and recognition'.

It is worth looking critically at this definition to see how far it provides a useful concept of memory. First, it defines memory as a '*store*' whereas we shall emphasize the role of memory as an active *process*. It is, on the other hand, very wide, encompassing retained characteristics which are subsequently expressed in behavioural change as well as in tests of recall or recognition. It could be argued that it is a little too wide, the inclusion of 'structure', for example, would imply that the loss of a limb as a result of accident (activity or experience) would constitute part of memory. Even if we understand structural changes only to refer to irreversible developments in the central nervous system it is questionable whether everyone would want to regard these as memory.

We cannot push a dictionary definition too far, perhaps, and it is probably sufficient to accept its width and to look more closely at the nature of the memory process. Contemporary approaches to memory tend to emphasize its role as part of the overall activity of information-processing which includes problem-solving, concept formation and indeed thinking in general. Memory is frequently seen as a three-stage process, the stages being termed 'encoding', 'storage' and 'retrieval'. From one point of view, of course, these are merely logically necessary categories. Unless material is put into a form which can be received or recorded by the storing process (unless it is encoded) it will not get into the store. Unless it is stored it will not be available for retrieval and unless it is retrieved it will not affect subsequent behaviour (be remembered). Nevertheless acceptance of the fact that material must be put into storage and taken out again (the latter process sometimes involving a quite deliberate search) focuses attention on these processes. An example of a memorizing task may help to illustrate them.

If we come across the words 'strawberry' and 'farkleberry', which one are we most likely to remember? Both are real words denoting fruit, but 'strawberry' is probably much more familiar to most people and the one which will be remembered better will probably depend on the conditions under which the word is encountered.

If people are specifically told that they will be asked to recall the word 'strawberry' in one week's time, they will regard this as a trivial task and will in fact almost always be able to respond correctly if subsequently asked 'what was the word you were presented with a week ago?'. If, on the other hand, people are asked to remember 'farkleberry' for a week the reaction will be quite different. First they will almost always ask for a repetition of the word. Then they ask how it is spelled or what it means. If told it is a fruit, they may ask what kind of fruit it is. Depending on how seriously they take the task, or how obliging they are, they will repeat the word to themselves a number of times, check the spelling, ask further questions about it and attempt to fix the word in memory, to learn it. None of this is necessary for 'strawberry'. When asked to recall 'farkleberry' some people will do so correctly but others will fail to achieve a complete reproduction. The responses will range from 'Yes, I do remember you asked me to remember a strange word, but I forget it,' to 'It was a long word, beginning with "f", some kind of fruit, but I can't quite recall it.' *

---

* One of the authors believes this is incorrect. His view of the word farkleberry is 'once heard never forgotten'. If the reader shares this view he may wish to substitute a word of his own, obscure but less striking, and continue with the analysis.

The difference in familiarity of the two words colours the instructions we are effectively giving. In one case we are saying 'learn the word farkleberry and remember it for a week', but in the other case the instructions are quite different. We are not saying 'learn the word strawberry' because most people already know it. We are saying, in effect, 'learn that the word strawberry is the one which we shall ask you to recall in a week'.

It is tempting to say that strawberry does not have to be encoded, merely indicated, but this is probably an oversimplification. Certainly, the process of encoding farkleberry is more obvious; its spelling, meaning and derivation all seem to be relevant to the task of memorizing it and indeed the major aspect of this particular learning task seems to be that of linking the new material to material which is already in store.

Normal adults already have a long-term memory containing many items or concepts about which they already know a great deal, but about which new things can still be learned, such as that the word must be recalled next week. Entirely new concepts can also be entered into long-term memory but the process of encoding new concepts is probably different from that of learning new things about already existing concepts. The use of the phrase 'long-term memory' implies that not all memory is long-term and it is indeed unlikely that a single process of memory underlies all retention, although at the moment we are looking at long-term memory tasks.

## Memory for complex material

A series of experiments which were carried out by Bartlett (1932) have been belatedly influential in studies of encoding and retrieval. His essential method was to present his subjects with a complex and ambiguous stimulus, a folk tale in an unfamiliar idiom or a drawing of an indeterminate animal, allow them to read the story or inspect the drawing and then, after various intervals, reproduce it. The provision of unusual material in a memory task, of course, highlights the need to encode or assimilate the material, as we have seen.

The changes in the material after successive reproductions were striking and certain general processes seemed to operate in the successive reproductions of almost all Bartlett's subjects. The accounts tended to become shorter and simpler and usually more coherent. Unexplained elements of the original story tended to disappear if they were peripheral or be provided with explanation if not. Additions to the story tended to be in line with the subject's own expectations or experience rather than arising from the story directly. The change was not total, of course; striking characteristics of the original served as structure for the reconstruction and sometimes even became exaggerated with time. These changes are not unlike the changes in information content of a rumour as it is passed from person to person, and indeed effects similar to those produced by one person over time can be demonstrated quickly by providing one person with a stimulus and the next with the first's reproduction and so on.

An example of the changes which can occur was provided in a class demonstration carried out by one of the authors. A story told to the first subject concerned a small boy who ran away from home and, in the course of escaping a dangerous situation, made himself very small and hid in the kernel of a nut. The final version of the story, after several subjects had told it in turn, concerned a small boy who ran away from home, joined the army and became a colonel.

Such results illustrate the reconstructive element in recall and are consistent with qualitative changes in memory. Experimentally they are easiest to demonstrate when the original stimulus is ambiguous and complex. This is not surprising because an ambiguous stimulus is one we find difficult to categorize. And it seems that memories are organized, at least to some extent, in terms of pre-existing categories.

Whenever there is a mis-match between existing category systems and the properties of a new stimulus the possibility exists of some effect of this kind. It should be emphasized, however, that Bartlett's results have been taken to imply more than simply that learned material is distorted during learning; the distortion – assimilation to pre-existing structures – continues after removal of the original material.

Bartlett's work was important in drawing attention to the active nature of the encoding process but did not provide anything approaching a testable model of the process of memorizing. More recently attempts have been made to describe specific models which might produce testable predictions. Where these rely heavily on the use of language (as is frequently the case) they have been described as models of semantic networks.

## Semantic network models

The basic assumption in such theories is that there are a large number of locations within memory, each related to a particular concept and containing, or connected to, representations of the concept's properties (the use of the term location need not imply that a concept is stored in one particular physical place in the brain). These locations have been called nodes.

Such models of the semantic network are obviously first assigned properties describing what people are known to be capable of and then given additional properties the implications of which can be tested experimentally. We might start by looking at the sort of questions people can answer about a concept we know they already have. If asked to describe a mouse, people might say, for instance, that it is small, is a mammal, has four legs and a tail and that there are different kinds of mice such as field mice. They will, in general, not say that it swims, has fins and is a fish which would be typical responses to 'salmon'. Clearly the concept 'mouse' is connected to the concept 'mammal' and 'four-legged' whereas 'salmon' is not. But such a statement about the semantic network tells us nothing more than we know. We need to specify the form taken by connections within the network in a manner that will allow us to make predictions in a new situation.

One possibility is that concepts are connected hierarchically within the semantic network in a way which corresponds to their level of inclusiveness. This would imply that 'mouse' is connected to 'mammal' which in turn is connected to 'animal' and that 'salmon' is connected to 'fish' (but not to 'mammal') and 'fish' in turn to 'animal'.

In addition, we could assume that the properties of concepts are stored at the most general level to which they apply, thus 'can swim' is stored with 'fish' not with 'salmon' and 'breathes' is stored with 'animal' not with 'fish' or 'mammal'.

These properties are characteristic of a model developed by Quillian and they yield the prediction that it should take longer to respond to a question such as 'does a canary have skin?' than to one such as 'can a canary sing?'. According to this model 'having skin' is a property stored with 'animal' whereas 'can sing' is stored with 'canary' since not all birds and certainly not all animals can sing. Thus answering the question 'does a canary have skin?' involves the subject moving up two levels in his semantic network and then checking the properties at that level while 'can a canary sing?' requires merely that the properties of the original level concept are examined. It is, of course, assumed in the model that moving from one level to another and then retrieving a property takes longer than simply retrieving a property from the same level.

Such a prediction can be tested by examining the reaction times of subjects as the number of levels to be traversed in answering a question (according to the model) increases. In one study Collins and Quillian (1969) produced results which upheld the prediction by finding a linear increase in reaction time as the number of levels increased. Unfortunately this result has not been universally found. Rips, Shoben and Smith (1973), for example, discovered that subjects took longer to decide whether creatures were mammals than whether they were animals even though mammal is a sub-category of animal and thus, according to this model, stored nearer to the name of the particular animal.

This may reflect the fact that people are less familiar with the concept 'mammal' than they are with 'animal' but given that they know the meaning of both words, a simple hierarchical model would predict that 'animal' responses should take longer than 'mammal' responses. As Baddeley (1976) points out it seems that this model is defective in several respects. There is no provision in the model for the effect of the number of items in a category, thus although it takes people longer to decide that an item does not belong to a large category than to a small one (even when levels are equated for both sizes of category) the model does not account for this. In addition, we have seen that familiarity may have an effect on reaction time and the general factor of frequency of association between an item and the category to which it belongs seems to have a similar speeding-up effect which is not catered for by this model. It has been shown that general properties of large classes (e.g. 'has skin') said to be stored at the higher level of concept, are less likely to be evoked as a defining characteristic when a low-level concept is presented. When this effect of associative likelihood is taken into account, the differential reaction time for questions about properties vanishes although it remains for questions concerned with class inclusion.

Finally, it may be that one of the formal properties of the model is incorrect. It seems likely that not all properties of items in the system are stored at the most general level in the hierarchy to which they apply. The fact that snakes and eagles both move may not be stored with 'animal' but may be stored separately with 'snake' and 'eagle'; as their characteristic movements are very different this does not seem surprising. Clearly this model is incorrect in its first formulation but it does at least generate predictions about behaviour which are not trivial, are not predictable from 'common-sense' and are testable.

The last decade has seen the development of a number of such semantic models of memory, some of considerable complexity and power, but we will just mention one of the predictions generated by one model, called Human Associative Memory or HAM, devised by Anderson and Bower (1973), because of its unexpectedness and elegance.

HAM is a model which represents a sentence in memory by a structure of associations and assumes that the associations linked to a common object would be independent. To test the independence of associations the authors presented the subject with two sentences having a common object such as 'the child hit the landlord' and 'the minister praised the landlord'. Such pairs of sentences were always separated by sixteen other sentences during presentation.

Subjects were subsequently given various cues to the original sentences and asked to recall the object. Such cues might involve just the subject from the original sentence such as 'the child ... the ...', or the verb 'the ... hit the ...', or both the subject and the verb from the original sentence 'the child hit the ...'; as might be expected, providing both the subject and verb leads to higher recall than provision of either alone.

Anderson and Bower, however, provided a fourth type of cue, a partial sentence containing the subject of one of the pairs of sentences together with the verb from the other, e.g. 'the child praised the ...' This produced the highest recall rate of all. As the cue sentence never occurred at all in the original list, it is by no means obvious that this will be the most successful cue for recall unless direct deductions are made from Anderson and Bower's model. They assume that the two original sentences are independently associated with the object 'landlord'; the combined cue sentence has a tendency to elicit *both* the original sentences, hence it will produce the highest probability of recall. This is called the cross-over effect.

While Anderson and Bower's results show this effect the prediction is not borne out under all conditions. Foss and Harwood (1975) have shown that the cross-over effect does not always occur and that when recall probabilities using single items (subject only or verb only from the original sentence) are compared with recall probabilities when providing two items (subject and verb from the original sentence) the latter produces recall probabilities higher than the sum of probabilities associated with single items. This implies that the links in the semantic network representing memory for sentences are *not* independent associations as specified by the H A M model.

## Perceptual memory

So far in this chapter we have explicitly or implicitly emphasized the remembering of material which is either straightforwardly verbal or has a significant semantic content. And in view of the highly developed verbal abilities of human beings, it is appropriate perhaps to focus on this typically species-specific learning ability. But we can remember non-verbal material and in some cases with very great facility. Our inability to forget how to ride a bicycle or to swim even after many years is proverbial, and such accurate memory does not seem adequately explained by the freedom of the acquired skill from 'interference' in the intervening years. We also have an experimentally demonstrable high retentive ability for pictures (if tested by a recognition method) and for particular qualities of sound; voices are frequently recognized on the telephone even after very few words have been spoken.

We can often recognize familiar voices even when we cannot distinguish what is being said, but we cannot usually describe the voice in such a manner that anyone else would immediately recognize it (with the exception of very squeaky or deep voices or very unusual accents and even then we could not give a definitive description, only an indication of one or more peculiarities). Our ability to remember sensory impressions in terms of being able to recognize them, without being able to recall them in the sense of producing a response which completely characterizes the stimulus, suggests that we have perceptual memory systems which may be somewhat distinct from the types of semantic memory we have been considering so far. At the same time it is unlikely that sensory or perceptual memory is totally separate from verbal or semantic memory. We are familiar with the fact that odours, for example, are potent retrieval cues; also the use of imagery when committing material to memory is very common and is in fact the basis of many mnemonic systems.

Despite wide awareness of the fact that odours are very effective in triggering memories, little systematic work has been done on olfactory memory beyond establishing that this form of retention is very resistant to forgetting. Engen and Ross (1973) have shown that while people may distinguish between smells with only about 70 per cent accuracy, the smells can be retained with 70 per cent accuracy for up to at least three months, and accuracy only drops slightly after a year. Such long-term retention may help to explain the effectiveness of smell as a retrieval cue, but the imperviousness to forgetting itself needs explanation. Suggestions have been made that the olfactory sense is linked to the limbic system, which is concerned with emotion, implying that smell may have had an early role in the evolution of the process of learning, but such speculations are too broad to be of much help in explaining retrieval.

The much greater importance of vision is reflected in the range of research carried out in the field of visual memory, about which a great deal is known. One form of visual memory is of very short duration and it is appropriate to discuss this in the general context of memories of varying retention period which was briefly mentioned earlier in this chapter.

## Types of memory

While there has been much controversy about how many kinds of memory we have and what their different properties may be, there now seems to be fairly general agreement that processes with at least three different time-scales are involved. These processes are a sensory store, a short-term memory system and a long-term memory system. It should be emphasized that, while these three retention systems can be distinguished both in terms of the time intervals involved and in terms of the form taken by the stored material, they cannot be regarded as totally independent and – more importantly – they cannot be regarded as exhausting the list of memory functions we might have.

Sensory storage refers to our ability to maintain a one-to-one (but rapidly decaying) image of a sensory experience. For a fraction of a second we can still see a visual stimulus that has vanished, hear a sound that has just stopped or feel an object our fingers have just released. Under ordinary circumstances these images are often not noticed because the next 'real' stimulus is being experienced, but it is fairly easy to demonstrate their existence. The lag in vision, for example, is the basis of our ability to see whole moving pictures on a television screen, which actually presents us with a *succession* of simple stimuli which only become meaningful because a large number of items which are not physically present at the same time are 'seen' all at the same time. Neisser has coined the term *icon* for this very short visual image which has been studied in some detail following the attention drawn to it by the work of Sperling (1960).

Sperling used a technique in which a number of letters were exposed to a subject for a very brief interval of time (usually one-twentieth of a second) and the subject was then asked to report what he had seen under various conditions. In one experiment Sperling presented three rows of four letters each and then signalled either that the subject should report the total display or only one of the rows, the top row being signalled by presentation of a high-pitched tone immediately after the display was withdrawn, the middle row by a medium pitch tone and so on. When the tone is sounded immediately after the display (when the visual image is presumably at its strongest) the subject can report three or four of the four letters on the row, whereas if he is asked to report all the letters in the display he will usually only succeed in reproducing four or five. Since it does not matter which row he is asked to report and he is not told which row until *after* the stimulus has been withdrawn it seems that the whole display persists for a very short interval but the time taken to 'read off' a few letters allows the image to decay. There is just about time to read off one row – any row – and then the image has decayed beyond recall.

In such experiments the items to be reported were chosen by means of their position in the display, and further studies (Turvey and Kravetz, 1970) have shown that items can be specified on the basis of their shape, but only the physical characteristics of the stimulus can be used for the purpose of indicating which to report – people are unable to respond if asked to report numbers from a mixture of numbers and letters. This emphasizes the 'sensory' or physical nature of this form of retention, it maintains a *replica* of the stimulus for a very short time, sufficient presumably for it to be transferred into some other form of storage, but if it is not so transferred it is lost. It is in effect a very rapidly decaying visual memory system.

This brings us to the short-term memory system. If we look

up a telephone number in order to dial it we do not rely on the visual image from the directory lasting long enough for it to be dialled, we say the number over 'in our heads'. We may repeat it more than once (this 'rehearsal' process has been assigned considerable importance in theories of the memory process) but if we are successful in dialling correctly we may well find, after the telephone call, that the number has been forgotten. It has been held long enough for our purpose in the short-term memory system but has not been transferred to long-term memory. We *can* remember telephone numbers over long periods of time, of course, and those we use frequently are remembered, but most people have had the experience of retaining items for just long enough to be used and then forgetting them forever.

But the obvious question arises, why distinguish this kind of forgetting from 'ordinary' forgetting – or this kind of memory from 'ordinary' memory. There are reasons why this seems to be a useful distinction, which relate particularly to the way material is coded or processed in short- as opposed to long-term memory and to the manner in which material is lost from these two systems, is forgotten. Before going on to distinguish between them we might usefully consider the process of forgetting which has generated an enormous body of research while retaining much of its mystery.

We expect to forget things, of course, particularly if long periods of time are involved. We talk about memory 'fading' or being 'a little rusty'. These expressions are simply ways of *referring* to the fact of forgetting – but in the choice of metaphor used there lurks a theory. Over a period of time colours fade and iron rusts, unless special precautions are taken. It is not time itself, but processes happening in time that lead to corrosion and decay – nevertheless, some events require special intervention to bring them about, others will occur unless positive steps are taken to prevent them. One possible process of forgetting is that it comes about simply through disuse; that it is in the nature of whatever forms the basis of memory to erode and vanish unless kept in existence by suitable exercise. As an alternative we may suppose that forgetting takes place because of what happens to an individual during the retention period, i.e.

interference with retention is produced by specific external influences.

Yet another possibility is that systematic changes occur in the processes storing the learned material, in other words internal events which cannot be described simply as decay may alter what is remembered, and of course, some or all of these processes may occur in combination.

Interference, which is discussed in more detail later in this chapter, was regarded as the main cause of forgetting for many years, until studies of short-term memory again raised the possibility that memories may decay spontaneously.

The view that items stored in short-term memory decay was one held by some of the earliest workers in this area. Short-term memory had not attracted wide attention until demonstrated in two experiments carried out in the late fifties by Brown (1958) and Peterson and Peterson (1959). The basic technique used by Peterson and Peterson was to present three consonants to subjects and then ask them to count backwards in threes for periods up to eighteen seconds, by which time the consonants were largely forgotten. It was, perhaps, striking that such a straightforward item could be forgotten so rapidly and the experimental demonstration of this effect caused an upsurge of experimentation and development of theory in the area of short-term memory.

Both Brown and the Petersons regarded their results as demonstrating the effects of decay of the memory trace in the absence of rehearsal and a differential process of forgetting has frequently been emphasized as one of the features which distinguishes between short- and long-term memory. Some theorists have proposed decay of the memory trace as the short-term forgetting process while others have favoured a process of displacement in which new candidates for the short-term store displace old ones, while until fairly recently, forgetting in long-term memory has been regarded as primarily brought about by interference from external events.

But different kinds of forgetting are not the only distinguishing characteristics of the short- and long-term systems. Additional factors are the small size of short-term memory – usually not more than six or seven items can be held in short-term memory compared with the effectively unlimited size of long-term memory – and the fact that material seems to be coded differently in the two systems.

Verbal material in short-term memory seems to be stored on the basis of sound. This may perhaps be seen most clearly if we look at the types of errors made when reproducing material from the various memory systems.

Confusion in the visual storage system seems to occur on the basis of shape; 'O' may be reported instead of 'C', while in the short-term memory system 'E' is more likely to be replaced by 'X' (which begins with the same sound) than by 'F' (which tends to *look* very similar). These errors on the basis of the sounds of stored material in the short-term memory are thought of as reflecting the acoustic nature of the storage system operating in this process; errors in the long-term memory system are much more often of a semantic kind, words of similar *meaning* (not shape or sound) tend to be confused.

It should be emphasized that *tasks* designed to examine the operation of long- or short-term memory may not always operate solely on the basis of the underlying *mechanism* they are designed to test. An obvious example occurs when we test short-term memory using words as items to be memorized. The particular words may be dealt with in an immediate recall task largely on the basis of an underlying short-term memory process, but the subject's awareness that they are words, rather than meaningless sounds, depends on their being stored in his long-term memory.

We have already indicated that different types of errors seem characteristic of the different memory systems, but since in experiments we must always test a whole human being and not one of his isolated memory systems, it is reasonable to ask if there is any further evidence which would lead us to distinguish between these systems.

A fairly striking confirmation of the existence of separate memory processes derives from a study of certain clinical evidence. Some forms of brain damage produce characteristic defects in memory and it seems likely that some brain-damaged patients can be regarded as having a defective long-term memory with unimpaired short-term memory, while others have a defective short-term memory while retaining an apparently intact long-term memory.

An example of the first type is provided by patients suffering from Korsakov's syndrome, which is an amnesic condition observed in some extreme alcoholics. Such patients may show severely impaired long-term learning abilities for all material since the onset of the condition; during a conversation lasting twenty minutes they may relate the same incident twice without recognizing, on the second occasion, that they have just told that particular story. Others may not know what day or year it is or may not be able to name the hospital they are in or who is currently prime minister. At the same time, such patients may have a normal memory span for material presented for immediate recall. This seems to indicate a deficient long-term memory without damage to the short-term memory and is strong indirect evidence for different underlying memory systems. Patients with a defective short-term memory with apparently undamaged long-term memory have been described by Warrington and Shallice (1969).

One such patient had suffered brain damage when injured in a motor-cycle accident, and while slightly aphasic in that he had difficulty in selecting a word from time to time, had no general amnesia, was able to talk normally and showed no long-term learning loss. His memory span was very short however, being about three items for spoken material, suggesting that his short-term memory had been affected by his injury.

Such evidence is suggestive, of course, rather than conclusive. It is extremely difficult to interpret behaviour resulting from accidental brain damage of unknown extent and it has also been suggested that some of the difficulties exhibited by patients with long-term memory defects may be due to problems of retrieval rather than storage.

Summarizing, however, we seem to have a sensory storage system which retains a literal copy of a stimulus for a fraction of a second, a short-term memory system which retains an acoustically coded representation of the stimulus for a few seconds and a long-term memory system operating on a semantic basis on which we largely depend for most of our retention. It is long-term memory which is in many ways most relevant to learning and it has historically generated most research. Much of this was based on general notions of the association of ideas, and studies of forgetting within this tradition have concentrated on interference between the learned material and other experiences which the learner has had before or after learning the 'target' material.

## Interference as a cause of forgetting in long-term memory

Many questions about memory, such as 'can memory be improved', 'what is the best way to memorize' or 'should I study just before the examination or two weeks before it', can be re-phrased as, 'why do we forget' or 'why do we forget some items and not others?'. We could of course counter the question by asking 'why, for that matter should we remember?' And this reopens the whole problem of learning in its full generality. At the moment, however, we are concerned with those cases where there has already been evidence of learning. A man is introduced to someone and later addresses him by name. A student has just translated a prose passage from French to English. A rat finds its way through a maze without errors. Why should any of them fail on a future occasion?

One reason could, of course, be that the occasion is in fact different. Words seen in one context are often easier to translate than when seen in another. We frequently fail to recall people's names and who they are if we see them under unfamiliar circumstances. If we look for factors influencing retention, we must examine the occasion when retention is being assessed, and also that of the original learning as well as the intervening period.

We have mentioned several possible causes of forgetting earlier in the chapter. One conceivable cause of retention loss, particularly in short-term memory, may be decay; alternatively, material may be 'displaced' by new input, since one characteristic of short-term memory is its limited capacity. Neither of these seems a likely candidate for long-term forgetting, and the other main process suggested, interference with retention by specific external events in the interval between learning and recall, was regarded for many years as the primary cause of forgetting in long-term memory.

This has been an attractive idea to many theorists and, while it is not as clear a process as it may first appear, it does seem to have some explanatory power. If interference were a major factor in forgetting we should expect that if, shortly after learning something, an individual is somehow shielded from all experience and then retested, retention would be near perfect. Two experimenters, Minami and Dallenbach (1946) trained two groups of cockroaches to acquire a particular form of avoidance response. The experimental group were placed in a 'non-behaving' state by being subjected to contact over a large part of the body surface, which produces immobility in cockroaches. The control group were forced to engage in activity during this time and both groups were then tested for retention of the avoidance response; the immobilized group performed significantly better on this test than the activity group, showing that loss of retention was at least partly attributable to behaviour during the period between learning and test.

Essentially similar experiments have been carried out with human subjects, though the method for bringing about non-behaviour is rather different. Here the experimental group sleeps after the initial learning, usually of verbal material, while the control group go about their normal activities. Again, there is less impairment of retention in the sleeping as compared to the active group.

Experimental investigations of interference factors in forgetting have tended to follow this basic pattern. Two or more groups of subjects learn the same task to a specified criterion. They then engage in various types of activity and then relearn, or are simply tested on, the original material. Any systematic differences in performance at retest can be ascribed to differences between the effects of the interpolated activities. Such effects are usually referred to as *retroactive inhibition or inter-*

*ference* if they involve impairment of the original performance.

Interest has mainly been focused on introducing a second *learning* task between the initial learning and retest. And, as might be expected, the effect of such a second learning task depends on its similarity to the first. Suppose, for example, that subjects originally learn to assign names to ten unfamiliar objects, i.e. they learn to make specific responses to a set of stimuli that are provided. Of the infinite number of possible second tasks we might consider four sub-categories: (a) where both stimuli and responses are identical to those in the first task, (b) where the stimuli are the same, but the required responses are different, (c) where the stimuli are different, but the responses are the same and (d) where both stimuli and responses are different.

Type (a) is a situation where the subject is simply continuing to practise the original task and this obviously helps rather than hinders; whereas (b) would be expected to produce interference, confusion is usually the result when on separate occasions people are called upon to behave in different ways under similar circumstances. The special form of type (b) in which the stimuli and responses of the first task are arranged in different pairs in the interpolated task produces the greatest effect of all. Type (c) does not usually produce interference and can produce some facilitation while (d) produces various degrees of interference depending on the degree of similarity between initial and interpolated stimuli and responses.

There are considerable difficulties in trying to define 'similarity' and attempts to obtain general rules relating degree of similarity between first and second task to extent of interference have not been very successful. It will suffice for our present purpose to salvage the general result that if the responses required in the first and second task are different, then interference increases as the stimuli in the two tasks become increasingly similar. This might suggest the following model of what takes place. The first learning session produces a set of stimulus–response tendencies. During the second learning period a conflicting set is built up and during retest there is some sort of competition between responses, leading to impairment in the production of the first set. There is some evidence for a process of this kind. During retest people often make responses appropriate to the interpolated task which are now errors. However, this is not the whole story. Where the tasks are to some extent incompatible, the responses compete at the time of relearning, but there is also competition of responses at the time of learning the interpolated task and in order that the interpolated task may be learned the responses of the original task must in some way be suppressed. This has the result that at retest the original responses are less likely to be emitted than they would have been without the interpolated learning, quite apart from the competition factor which interferes with them. They have in effect been weakened.

Some evidence supporting this interpretation has been found, for example in a study by Barnes and Underwood (1959). In this experiment an attempt was made to eliminate the effect of response-competition at recall by asking the subjects to give both original and interpolated task responses when recalling the first task. They were also allowed to take as long as they liked in making their response. All subjects learned the original task to the same criterion (being able to recite it once through perfectly) and were then given various degrees of interpolated learning. As the amount of interpolated learning increased the subjects were naturally more able to recall the interpolated responses but less able to recall the original responses. As it is assumed that response-competition at the recall stage is eliminated by this technique, the effect is considered to be caused by the unlearning of the original task at the interpolated stage.

Unlearning has been an attractive idea within the general context of interference theory where the comparison with extinction in conditioning has often been made. But although the idea accounts for the fact that the tendency to omit – or forget – a correct response and the tendency to replace it by some specifically learned alternative do not quite go together, it runs into other difficulties. It is found that the more intensely the first task is learned, the less retention is affected by the second. This is to be expected. But if we increase the amount of effort given to learning the second interpolated task there comes a point where there is no increase in interference; there can even be relative improvement in the retest performance of the first task. On the model we have just considered, we should expect interference with the first task to increase steadily with the amount of practice given to the second.

A straightforward stimulus–response model does not do justice to the behaviour we are considering. Reports from experimental subjects indicate some of its inadequacies. Frequently, before the emission of the overt response, different possible responses are considered, until eventually one is accepted. Increased learning of the second set of S–R pairs leads to fewer false responses during retest, since they are increasingly recognized as belonging to the second set, and are in consequence not 'passed'. This process of checking seems to be at least partly independent of the process which produces possible responses for scrutiny – responses known to be wrong can sometimes 'suggest themselves' – with irritating persistence.

While interference as a general process affecting the recall of the stimulus–response associations of a prior task in the laboratory setting can be adequately demonstrated there are, as we have seen, difficulties in precisely describing the mechanisms. Postman (1976) remarks, 'One cannot help but wonder why after so many years of patient experimental effort interference theory today finds itself entangled in so many empirical inconsistencies and theoretical complications.'

A general answer to this question which might suggest itself is that the associative 'meta-theory' underlying interference theories might be inadequate. Alternative approaches to the mechanism of remembering have been developed in recent years, some of which have been stimulated by the difference in performance shown by people given recall and recognition tests in memory experiments.

### Recall and recognition

There are several methods of measuring the amount retained by a subject. The most obvious one is the ability to reproduce, to recall. A measure of how well an actor can remember his lines is the accuracy with which he can speak them. But this is not the only measure. Even though failing to produce the words, he might still recognize them when presented in conjunction with others. This aspect of retention is most clearly evident in the retention of pictures, where we quickly learn to recognize but where any sort of reproduction is quite a different matter. While recognition is often possible without recall, recall usually implies recognition and is, therefore, a more comprehensive test of memory.

There is also a third possible indicator. Returning to a part he has not played for some time, an actor might fail to recall any of it. But if we compare the amount of work he has to put into 'refreshing his memory' with the effort that went into the original learning, we would find that in general it was much less. Again, 'something' has been retained. All these – recall, recognition, and the saving in the amount of relearning necessary – are aspects of retention (of learning); and they form the basis of more systematic measuring procedures in the laboratory.

Suppose the material to be learned consists of a list of words, and they are presented to the subject one after the other. After the first complete presentation the list is presented again but the subject can start trying to anticipate each word before it appears. The presentation is continued until some criterion has been achieved, such as two consecutive perfect sets of anticipations. In order to measure retention after an interval of time, we may now use the same procedure – which is essentially a method based on recall – and score the number of errors.

It is also possible to use a 'free-recall' procedure in which the subject is asked to reproduce as many words from the list as he can, regardless of order. A recognition method would involve presenting the words in the original list mixed up with some others and asking the subject to pick out the words from the list he had learned. As has already been pointed out, recall is usually the more stringent measure since what is recalled will almost always be recognized. It is possible, by using new items in the recognition list which are very similar to the old items, and hence very confusing, to depress the recognition score below the recall score, but this has to be specially contrived – recognition almost always leads to higher scores than recall. Why should this be so?

One answer to this question which various theorists have found attractive is that different processes are involved in recognition and recall and, specifically, that the recognition process involves fewer stages.

## Two-stage theories of remembering

Kintsch (1970) has suggested that recall involves two stages, retrieval and decision, while recognition only involves a decision process. In recalling an item the person has to search for it and then decide whether it corresponds to an item he has previously encountered. Such a formulation, of course, begs many questions. When the recognition items are words the person may well have seen them all before and the decision is not simply 'are they familiar?' but 'were they encountered at the appropriate time?', i.e. 'when I was learning the particular list of words in question'. This, however, is the essence of two-stage theories; recall requires an additional search or retrieval process while recognition only involves a decision about the appropriateness of the item.

In addition to the almost universal finding that recognition scores are higher than free recall scores several variables produce differential effects on recall scores while having negligible effects on recognition scores. Brown (1976) points out that if material to be learned consists of words chosen from a limited number of categories, as opposed to being entirely unrelated, recall scores are increased while recognition scores are not. Similarly high familiarity words are better recalled than words of low familiarity but are not better recognized. Finally, if subjects are presented with material and instructed to learn it, instead of being presented with the items in the course of carrying out some other task, their recall score will be much higher but recognition scores are hardly affected. Such evidence supports the idea that recall involves two stages while recognition does not, but it does not specify in any detail how the processes of retrieval and decision actually work.

**Retrieval**

Retrieval of items stored in memory has been compared to the use of a catalogue when finding items in a library. The use of this metaphor highlights one important aspect of retrieval at least, that it depends on encoding. Unless a book in a library is correctly listed in the catalogue it will not be found (except by chance), and so it might as well not be there. Similarly retrieval of an item from memory depends on the manner in which it was encoded when first encountered. Examples of encoding discussed earlier in this chapter indicate at least two aspects of the encoding processes available to people – first that multiple encoding is possible and second that some choice exists concerning the encoding system to be used with a given item.

One way of looking at encoding is to regard it as a procedure whereby a list of the attributes of an item to be encoded is entered into memory. A hedgehog might be encoded by listing 'small', 'spiky', 'insectivorous' and so on, and it would share some, but not all, of these attributes with a porcupine. Mistakes in recognition tests of memory suggest that something of this sort may go on, as errors frequently share many attributes with the items for which they are mistaken. An ingenious experiment carried out by Brown and McNeill (1966) on the 'tip of the tongue phenomenon' also supports this view. They presented subjects with dictionary definitions of infrequently used words and asked the subjects to name the word. When subjects could not recall the correct word, but felt it was on the tip of their tongue, they could often correctly report its first letter, give words that sounded the same or report how many syllables it had. This suggests that the word had been originally encoded in various ways and that the meaning of the word was linked, at least partially independently, to the various encoded attributes.

Considerable research has been devoted to the actual encoding processes available to people and the importance of the context in which an item is encountered, including the task required of the subject, has become evident. One widely used approach to differences in encoding has been termed the 'depth of processing' given to an item, when first presented, as determined by the task required of the subject (Craik and Lockart, 1972). Most work in this area has distinguished three 'depths' to which a word might be processed. When presented, the subject may be asked 'is this word in capital letters?', and a correct answer would only require 'structural' encoding, a fairly shallow form of processing. The question could be, however, 'does this word rhyme with another (specified) word?', which needs 'phenomic' encoding which is presumed to be rather deeper. If the question were intended to elicit 'semantic' encoding it would take the form 'does the word fit into the following (given) sentence?'. This is presumed to be the deepest processing. Evidence has been found that recall scores vary with the form of encoding required by the task.

In the examples given the presumed depth of processing can be inferred from the nature of the task but in wider applications of this theoretical approach it has proved difficult to provide an independent measure of 'depth', and this approach has proved less useful than originally hoped (Baddeley, 1978; Nelson, 1977). Perhaps the most striking effects produced by specific encoding procedures, and those most amenable to voluntary control, are those produced by the use of imagery or by other methods of rendering the items more 'meaningful'.

### Active encoding

Paivio (1969) has shown that the degree to which a word conjures up a visual image is a much better predictor of the likelihood of its being recalled than measures such as its familiarity or the number of its associations. Subsequently many experimental studies in which subjects were instructed to form images in relation to the material to be learned have shown that this procedure is an important aid to memorizing. It is not certain, however, that the process of forming a visual image is, in itself, the crucial factor. Studies in which subjects were instructed to form sentences using the items to be learned have also been successful in producing higher recall scores. There is even some evidence that material which is originally hard to visualize can be recalled if the subject is subsequently given a cue requiring him to reinterpret the material. Auble and Franks (1978) have shown that if subjects are presented with an incomprehensible sentence plus, five seconds later, a cue enabling them to elucidate the sentence, better recall will be produced than if an easily comprehensible sentence without cue is presented. This suggests that the activity carried out by the subject, regardless of its mode, is the operative factor in providing ease of recall.

Much of what has been said about encoding and retrieval relates essentially to isolated items or events which have to be memorized but much of our experience, on the other hand, is concerned with carrying out large numbers of related acts extending in time and space. An actress of our acquaintance tells the following story. At a certain point during a play she had a sudden total block, she was completely unable to remember her next line. Without thinking about it she proceeded to the next piece of 'business' – taking a cigarette out of a box on the table in front of her and lighting it – whereupon she was immediately able to recall the next lines. Two things are indicated by this; first, the memory for the necessary physical act was cued by the last words spoken prior to the act, which did not itself need to be remembered 'consciously', and, second, the operation of the correct physical act cued the retrieval of the next piece of verbal material from memory. It suggests strongly that there exists an overriding 'plan' which incorporates memorized items of different kinds and which can proceed, at least some of the time, in the absence of awareness.

It is a characteristic of human behaviour that it is ordered in a sequence of acts of many different types; we are sometimes aware of the 'plan' we are currently executing, sometimes not. When the activity seems to consist of a well-ordered and successful sequence, especially when it has been learned, we tend to describe it as a skilled activity. The study of skill forms the topic of the next chapter but the example could serve to remind us that theory in the area of human behaviour is in an elementary state of development and also that the division of topics into 'memory', 'skill', 'training' and so forth is somewhat arbitrary.

# 7. Skill

There are several related uses of the word skill, and we need to make some distinctions among them at the beginning of this discussion. We may talk about skill in the sense of driving a car, typing or fencing, i.e. we may refer to particular, more or less complex activities which require a period of deliberate training and practice to be performed adequately, and which often have some recognized useful function. The emphasis here is on the activity, on the achievement, frequently on the manipulation of some specialized piece of equipment – though we also talk about social skills, mathematical skills, etc. On the other hand someone may be described as having skill in, or being skilled at performing a particular task, in the sense of being proficient or good at it – the emphasis being on the level of performance of which he is capable, rather than on the characteristics of the task. In this sense it is possible to talk about having or lacking skill in the use of a sewing machine, but also in the use of a knife and fork – which would not normally be singled out as a skill in the former sense. The stress is on the activity in the one case and on the person in the other; and we single out those activities as 'skills' in which it is possible for an individual to distinguish himself in some way, showing competence which is not normally achieved without some special effort.

In this chapter our concern will be with the individual, with competence, and with proficiency. This may manifest itself in the exercise of recognized skills like driving, in the playing of games like tennis, or marbles, also in more widespread accomplishments such as riding a bicycle, tying shoe laces or just walking. We want to examine the conditions under which skill develops, the factors making for more or less rapid achievement of a given criterion, and we want to do this in a way which is only incidentally concerned with the particular type of activity involved.

## The characteristics of skilled performance

What are the signs by which we recognize proficiency, what is it that distinguishes the performance of the expert from that of the beginner? To the extent to which there is some sort of product involved, there will be faster output of higher quality, and this is the kind of criterion of good performance with which most assessment is concerned. But since output and quality are specific to a given activity, it does not help us in the present inquiry. We are looking for a description of *how* a task is done, in terms that might provide an insight into the general features – if there are any – of the change from early to expert behaviour. It will simplify matters if we confine ourselves for the moment to the consideration of *motor skills*, i.e. activities in which physical movement is the predominant, or at least the most obvious, element.

Skilled performance, when compared to its inexpert counterpart, is characterized by an appearance of ease, smoothness of movement, confidence and the comparative absence of hesitation; it frequently gives the impression of being unhurried, even while the actual pace of activity may be quite high. The skilled man 'seems to have all the time in the world' compared, say, to the learner driver whose progress is more like a sequence of emergencies. In skilled performance there are no surprises, in the sense that surprise involves a lack of readiness for the situation that has arisen – indeed increasing skill involves a widening of the range of possible disturbances that can be coped with without disrupting the performance.

This is perhaps the most striking feature of a high level of proficiency – it involves being ready at the appropriate time for a whole variety of events that *may* occur, including the direct consequences of the activity itself. The novice driver is caught unprepared not only by slightly unusual behaviour of traffic or pedestrians, but also by the movements or situations that he has himself brought about – as when, having completed one manoeuvre such as gear change, he is required to begin another, such as turning. The consequences of his actions are also more varied and uneven, and in this respect his task is doubly difficult. He is unprepared for what happens, and the range of what may happen is greater. The expert, by contrast, somehow always manages to be ready, there are no hesitations. If one watches an adult tying his tie, one can notice how at each stage, as the ends are manipulated, the hands rapidly move into position for the next stage. A good tennis player moves into place much earlier than a beginner, reacting to and anticipating situations which are created in part by himself and in part by his opponent.

### The sensory components of skill

We are dealing here with the unfolding of a sequence of move-ments which bear the character of co-ordination and integration in *time* – indeed the element of exact timing is highly evident. But what are the components of the sequence, what is it that is being co-ordinated and organized? We tend to think of skill in terms of movement, of what is *done*. A task analysis, such as an industrial 'Time and Motion' study, usually breaks down an operation into a sequence of component movements. Attention is focused on *output*; what is often ignored, partly because it is taken for granted and partly because it is difficult or impossible to observe directly, is the *input*.

The tennis player takes account of his opponent's moves, the car driver obviously watches the road. These phrases, however, conceal the complexity of what is involved. There are many things about the movements of a tennis player, or about road conditions, on which attention may be concentrated. This is not simply a question of directing the eye towards some things rather than to others, but of selecting the features that we 'take in'. While looking at the same object, we may, for example, attend now to its colour, now to its shape, now to its surface texture – or to particular aspects or combinations of these. The 'information' that arrives at the eye can be dealt with in different ways, and the development of new ways of perceiving, of 'processing' the available information, forms an integral part of what is more appropriately called a *sensory*-motor skill. When the clues to required action lie in some aspects of the environment the learning process must involve the development of a selective sensitivity towards them.

It should not be thought that selective attention is confined to seeing. In hearing, we are constantly listening to, or for, certain aspects of the total sound pattern that impinges on the ear – at a party, for example, we are usually able to pick out the voice of the person with whom we are in conversation (or sometimes, by preference, what is being said in another conversation near by).

Attention may also be divided between different kinds of sensory message, including those arising from within the body, e.g. toothache or hunger pangs. Confronted with a mass of available information, we learn to ignore much that is irrelevant to the task being executed at the time. To the extent to which an instructor is aware of this aspect of a developing skill, he may be able to find more effective means of directing the attention of the learner.

It is important to realize that proficiency does not necessarily involve the explicit recognition of contributing factors, and it is partly for this reason that someone who has acquired a skill is not always particularly good at helping to produce it in others. Even highly skilled people are often only vaguely aware of what they do, and are usually quite unconscious of the part played by various sensory modes in regulating their activity. This is especially true of information arising from the activity itself. A very effective way of demonstrating the contribution made by particular incoming signals towards the performance of a task is to eliminate or to distort them. Thus we can illustrate the role that hearing one's own voice plays in speaking, by feeding a noise into the ears of the speaker with the use of earphones. The raising or lowering of the noise-level directly affects the loudness of speech, often without awareness; it is as though the volume control of the noise-generating apparatus is directly coupled to the speaker himself. We know that we tend to raise our voices in noisy conditions, but this is not so much a deliberate act for the benefit of other people, as an automatic one in response to not hearing our own voice sufficiently clearly.

Although it is the sound received through the ears which is normally the main factor in controlling the level of output, there are other sources of information available which may be used. Sound is also transmitted by bone conduction, and in addition sensations in the mouth, throat and chest bear some relation to the loudness of the voice. It is possible to learn to rely on these rather than on airborne sound, for controlling the quality of output. It is in fact a common feature of developing skill that some control of activity is transferred from senses that provide a link with the external world to internal or *proprioceptive* senses not requiring conscious attention. Thus while current activity is monitored and regulated in this way, information from outside can be taken in in advance of the time that it is needed.

## Making *appropriate* movements

It is of course not enough to attend to particular cues; one must also produce movements that are appropriate, given one's objective and current position. In a highly practised skill this usually happens quite unconsciously, and is somehow 'obvious': if I want to switch on the light, once I have located the switch my hand just moves in the right direction. That this involves a problem becomes more explicit if we think about the construction of a robot capable of this sort of achievement. It would need a motor system of some kind to carry out movements; sensing devices to register the location of the target, and also of the current position of the relevant limbs; but it would also need a system for translating information about relative locations into the right instructions to the motor system for bringing the moving arm into contact with the target. To achieve this in anything approximating to a skilled way would in fact need something rather more subtle than this, but these elements are minimum requirements. (The early S–R models of behaviour fall short even of these, in that there is no real provision for referring 'stimuli' to the current position – or more generally, to the current state – of the organism itself.)

Another way of demonstrating this translation aspect of action is to change the 'meaning' of incoming information for the execution of some well practised task. If we try to trace a pattern on paper while looking at both pattern and moving hand in a mirror, there is a considerable disruption of performance, at times almost amounting to paralysis. A well-established and 'automatic' relationship between visual image and movement has been changed, and a conscious translation has to intervene. However, with continued practice a new skill develops, incorporating the modified relationship, until once again it becomes relatively spontaneous and unthinking. Now the *removal* of the mirror temporarily produces difficulty in tracing. More dramatic but essentially similar results are obtained if spectacles which turn everything upside-down are worn for extended periods of time. Not only do people eventually learn to move about efficiently and without hesitation, but subjects report that towards the later stages of the experience there are periods when the world is actually *seen* the right way up. Again there is temporary disorientation and difficulty in movement when the spectacles are removed. Such results, together with observations of the gradual development of hand–eye co-ordination of young children, indicate that the automatic movement of a limb towards a selected point involves a learned relationship – though possibly a 'prepared' one.

When we are using a machine or instrument to achieve some desired goal, it is more apparent that the relationship between what we *do* and the intended *result* is something that has to be learned. Given the visual image of car bonnet, road and kerb, there is to start with nothing self-evident about the movements required to keep the car on a straight course, or to take it round a corner. This relationship involves not only the direction and extent of movement, but also its timing – we have to learn the 'response characteristics' of the system being operated. After prolonged and continuous practice with a particular type of machine – again cars provide the most familiar example – it becomes increasingly like a part of one's own body. The *body-*

*image* extends beyond the skin to wings and bumpers, and reversing into a tight parking space one can almost *feel* the slight crunch against the car behind *at the point where it actually takes place.* At the same time we acquire a confident and implicit knowledge of how to achieve certain effects – like accelerating or slowing down within a given time or distance – which approximates to the way we know these things in relation to our own limbs. Brake-failure or a 'sticking' accelerator is a very disturbing experience, even when it occurs in circumstances where there is no immediate danger. It is as though relevant aspects of the machine came to be represented within us as an integral part of our perceptual and motor systems: the disorientation, when there is malfunction in this extended system, may provide the merest hint at the experience of people who, through neural damage, lose normal control over parts of their own bodies.

### Display–control relationships

Although the detailed consequences of turning a steering wheel have to be learned, this turns out to be a good deal easier than it would be if, by the use of different gearing, a clockwise rotation of the wheel sent the car to the *left*, rather than the more normal arrangement. It seems there are 'natural' relationships between movements and their consequences, even when, as in 'instrument flying', they involve the use of artificial displays – and such relationships are more easily acquired than others. To the extent that it is possible for a designer to arrange these relationships at will, he can make the operation of his equipment simpler to learn, and also reduce the risk of mistakes being made under stress. As part of *Ergonomics* or *Human Factors Engineering*, a recognition of the importance of such *display–control relationships* helps to improve the coupling or *interface* between people and machines. In more recent years with the introduction of computers into an increasingly wide range of situations that often involve people without special training, the design of this interface has had to allow for problems of 'communication' in a much more extended sense; interacting with a computer is in some ways like a *social* skill.

## The time element in skill

We have already referred to the smooth unhurried quality of skilled performance, to the way in which the competent driver, for example, is all set to carry out each manoeuvre at the moment that it is needed – in contrast to the more fragmented, panic-prone behaviour of the beginner. This difference reflects a variety of changes in the way in which perception and action are organized, and hinges on the fact that the translation of information into appropriate response takes time – quite apart, that is, from the time required for the execution of the movements involved. Driving affords many examples of this time needed to react – such as when cars follow each other too closely at speed and the leader puts on his brakes. But even in such a simple task as depressing a key in response to a signal, a finite period of the order of one tenth of a second elapses between signal and *onset* of movement. This is called *reaction time*, – a *simple* reaction time in the example just given, where only one signal and one response are involved. When any one of several signals may occur, calling for one of several corresponding responses, the time required is called a *choice* reaction time and is generally longer – though the relationship between number of choices and time taken to respond is not a simple linear one and also depends on stimulus – response compatibility. We will return to this relationship when we discuss models of skilled behaviour towards the end of the chapter.

## Doing several things at once

A brief consideration of an activity like driving clearly shows that we are able to carry out several movements at the same time, even when these movements have to relate in a prescribed way to the environment – think of all the things that go on if we change gear while turning. Since we cannot look in two directions at the same time, this raises a problem about how the necessary information about extent and direction of such simultaneous movements is in fact obtained and transmitted. But there is also another kind of limitation on dealing with overlapping or closely spaced information.

Suppose that two signals requiring different responses follow each other in close succession. If the interval between them is shorter than the reaction time needed for the first, then there is an additional delay before the second response is initiated. This delay does not arise from any difficulty at the sensory end – the two signals might be clearly visible without change of fixation, or indeed they might involve different sensory modalities; and the responses could be the pressing of two keys with the right and left index fingers respectively, so that there is no conflict between movements. It is rather as though the task of *deciding what to do* about the second signal cannot begin until the first signal has been dealt with; as though there is a single location or 'channel' through which incoming information must pass in the course of translation into response, so that the second decision has to queue until the channel is clear. Apparently we are unable to cope with more than one 'item' of information at the time. How then do we ever manage to perform tasks which require continuous and often complex adjustment to a changing environment?

A simple card-sorting task can illustrate the problem and part of its solution – the reader can easily try it for himself. Two different methods are used to sort a pack of cards into red and black. In method one, the cards are held face down, so that each card is seen only after its predecessor is already in position. In the other method, they are held face upwards, but the same turning movement in sorting the cards is used (i.e. they are placed on the table face up in the first case, and face down in the second). Although the movement is identical in both cases, the speed of sorting is far higher in the second case than in the first.

The reason for this difference in speed is that in the first method the time taken for deciding where a particular card is to

be placed is necessarily additional to the time needed for movement – the required information simply does not become available until the previous placing has been completed and the new
card turned. In the second method, while one card is being
placed, the colour of the next one is visible, and so we have an
opportunity of 'preparing' the next movement while the present
one is being carried out. We are able to do this because a simple
placing movement, once initiated, requires no further visual
supervision – it seems to be taken care of by an internal 'program' whose execution does not prevent the sorter from setting
up the next.

### The development of stimulus and response 'units'

The general ability to carry out approximate positioning movements without having to attend to them is something we acquire
in childhood, and it takes little time to master the requirements
of any particular task. We can see the learning process in some
detail if we consider the more precise and complex demands of a
skill like touch-typing. At first, each letter is typed individually,
as a separate act. A skilled typist on the other hand will type
whole words and even phrases as a unit – i.e. the pattern which
comprises the whole sequence of movements making up the word
or phrase appears to be ready at the outset, and simply 'runs
itself off'. With the arrival of this stage, one can copy-type *behind*
the material that is being read, building up one 'program' while
executing the last one. Since the execution of movements takes
longer than their preparation, the increasing size of internally
programmed response units makes for a more leisurely translation process, and removes the element of 'flap' which is so
characteristic of an unskilled attempt at speed.

Corresponding to the development of larger units of action
there are larger units of perceptual organization. In the case of
copy-typing these are already established at the outset, in the
sense that words and phrases can be read and stored as a whole.
The growth of these perceptual units can be observed in children
learning to read, who progress – depending on the method used

– from taking in sequences of individual letters, through short letter combinations to the recognition of whole words and phrases. Learning to play a musical instrument usually provides an illustration of both processes in association – the gradual perceptual structuring of the score as it is taken in, together with the growth of integrated motor units or 'plans' for playing that seem to be ready in advance of execution.

In summary, we have emphasized the following features as characteristic of increasing skill: development of selective attention to changes in the environment, including changes produced by the current activity itself; development of appropriate relationships between received signal and response; development of perceptual units of increasing size, translated into internal motor programs, which may be carried out with little or no external supervision – thus making it possible to *overlap* preparation and execution, and arrive at the state of constant readiness which is one of the main characteristics of skilled performance.

It should be realized that some of the 'features' referred to, such as the development of perceptual units or motor programs, are theoretical analogies for, rather than descriptions of, what can be observed. But the analysis of skilled behaviour does seem to require such analogies, which adds further support to a cognitive-cum-control-theory framework for the description of behaviour generally. We will consider the question of explanatory models in a little more detail when we have examined some of the factors that contribute towards the acquisition of skill.

## Helping the learner

The help that an instructor can provide falls into a number of distinct categories. He can describe and explain what has to be done; he can give demonstrations; in some cases he can physically *guide* the learner's movements; and he can comment in a variety of ways during and on the learner's own performance.

## Verbal instructions

The ability to follow verbal instructions is obviously an enormous advantage in any learning situation. We must remember, however, that the information 'conveyed' by words depends on the significance that the recipient is able to attach to them. In one sense the instructions 'raise your right arm' and 'raise your right ear' are equally well understood by everyone; but for most people there is, as part of the received meaning of the first phrase, an awareness of what is involved in *doing* it, which is missing from the second. In the same way, an implicit knowledge of 'how-to-go-about-it' is evoked by 'take the first turning on the left and the second on the right'; but, irrespective of verbal formulation and detail, there are limits to what can be got across in this way to someone learning to synchronize clutch, accelerator and handbrake in making a hill start. There are aspects of this or any other operation which words can only transmit to someone who can already do it.\* What instructions usually can do is identify objectives, as well as things to be manipulated, their locations, component actions and the order in which they should be performed – in short, to provide a kind of framework or approximation for behaviour. In the early stages of skill acquisition learners themselves often use words in recalling what has to be done. Beyond this, however, improvement must come from other sources.

## Demonstration

A demonstration shows what a correct performance looks like. We have developed a general ability to match seen movement with our own actions, and so a demonstration can often provide,

---

\* Often the desired effect can be achieved by a kind of subterfuge – instructing the learner to carry out an action different from the one to be learned, but one which incorporates the desired movement or produces it as a by-product. Thus a tennis coach might tell a learner practising his service to pretend to *throw* his racket at the ball; indeed (using an old one) actually doing so can be a help. The phrase 'throw at' usually triggers off the right response – which someone who can throw already possesses – better than other kinds of description could.

in an integral form, information about the quality, timing and general organization of movements beyond the point where words fail. Here too, however, the observer's own competence limits what he can derive from watching the performance of others – as any visit to the circus or ballet will amply confirm.

## Knowledge of results

Let us look at the role of comments made during and about the learner's activity. We will ignore here any advice that they might contain about future performance, and concentrate on their effect simply insofar as they spell adequacy or inadequacy of what has gone before. There is a clear parallel here to the function of reinforcement, although we are still dealing with *information* rather than a more direct human counterpart of rat-cake pellets. But it is information confirming or negating *approach to a current goal*, and as such would fall within the more liberalized view of reinforcement arrived at in Chapter 4. Such information is usually referred to, in this context, as 'Knowledge of Results', or K R.

There are of course many activities in which the evidence of (relative) success or failure is directly available to the learner, who also has criteria for evaluating it. If you try to trace a pattern while looking in a mirror, you may not, at the outset, know what to do, but you get clear and immediate knowledge of the *results* that you have just produced. This information comes with every movement that is made; it pinpoints its motor source exactly. But there are many cases where an evaluation becomes possible only at the end of a whole sequence of movements. It is helpful for a child to know what a well-tied tie or shoe-lace looks like, but it is not sufficient; a successful outcome might be reinforcing, but as in the case of an over-rapid shaping procedure, it is unlikely to occur. There is a need for information along the way, which can be used to confirm successful progress so far, and this could be provided by a competent instructor.

The idea of competence in shoe-lace-tying instruction may

sound somewhat pretentious, but we can use this humble example to make some more general points about helping people to acquire skills.

*Criteria for judging performance*

The first is that people who are good at tying their laces make little or no use of visual information – doing it properly just *feels* right. But visual cues (i.e., in the more general case, externally available cues) are the only ones we have when we are assessing *someone else's* performance. There may, therefore, have to be some special effort to discover indicators of successful progress that are other than those used by the skilled performer himself.

Such indicators can form the basis of the instructor's evaluation. But they could equally well serve the learner directly, with the advantage that they are then constantly and immediately available. One could say that one of the most important functions of a teacher or trainer is to provide, where possible, criteria which the learner himself can use to judge the quality of his performance. It may take the form of drawing the learner's attention to some cues that are readily available in the situation – for example, changes of engine noise in the context of changing through the gears – or it may on occasion consist of some extra signal which is easy to use – provided perhaps by a special instrument, e.g. a revolution-counter. But a word of warning. The signals that provide knowledge of results in the course of an activity usually come to form an integral part of it – they not only reinforce what has gone before, but can also guide what is going on now. Looking at your fingers while typing or playing the piano can tell you whether or not you *have* moved them to the right place. It can also tell you where to move them, and you may consequently remain dependent on information being provided in this particular form. The ability to move your fingers to a sequence of locations without looking at them requires what is in effect an internal 'map', reference to which can guide the movements to be carried out, and it seems that the development of such a map is greatly facilitated by an *active attempt* to move without visual guidance. A number of studies (e.g. Annett, 1970) have shown that the use of additional or augmented feedback, if it is intended simply as an auxiliary and temporary device, can actually impede the attainment of proficiency without it, by encouraging what amounts to an alternative way of performing the task in question.

Providing K R at various stages of a task also raises the question of breaking it up into components, to be mastered individually. In learning to play a piece of piano music many people will begin by trying out and practising one hand at a time, or will concentrate on difficult passages in isolation from the rest. The advantage of such fragmentation is that information about the performance is more easily evaluated, and appreciable success can be attained earlier. But there are also drawbacks. As we have repeatedly stressed, skilled performance is characterized by its integration and co-ordination – there is a danger that a component activity, carried out on its own, may set up an internal organization that is different from that which is required for it to be a part of a larger or more complex whole. The linking up of components, simultaneously or in sequence, is always more than simply an addition, and requires practice in its own right. It is impossible to legislate in advance about the optimum size of the initial learning unit, which is likely to depend not only on the nature of the task but also on the individual learner.

### Learning from success and from error

Knowledge of Results can provide confirmation of success, but it can also signal failure or error. Do we learn as much from our mistakes as from our successes? This question recalls the comparison between positive reinforcement and punishment as factors in learning, but the parallel would be at least partly misleading. The issue concerning punishment was whether it was effective in *stopping* something from happening. The question now is how much, if at all, we can progress towards getting something *right* through the discovery that we have just done it *wrong*. Here it will be useful to distinguish between the motivational effects of K R, tending generally to boost or discourage current behaviour, and the informational. As far as the latter is concerned, even if it simply takes the form of a 'right' or 'wrong', the amount of usable information made available can vary greatly depending on the situation. If, for example, there are just two possible responses or courses of action, to learn that the choice made was wrong tells us as much as the discovery that it was right; but at other times, to find out that there has been an error tells us very little, unless the error signal also provides a clue to the nature of the mistake and to what is needed to correct it. Instructors need to bear in mind that it is not very helpful for a learner simply to discover that some complex performance was inadequate.

After allowance has been made for differences in the information *available* in K R after successful and relatively unsuccessful performance, there remains the question of the effect of that information on subsequent performance. To be adaptive, these effects need of course to be different. A successful performance should be confirmed, become more strongly established.

An adaptive reaction to error would be the generation of a new (and preferably more appropriate) response. How *new* response patterns (new hypotheses) are generated is an important and relatively neglected issue. For the moment we may simply note that the maintenance or strengthening of an existing response pattern seems to be easier than its modification – a kind of inertia effect. It is therefore desirable to establish correct patterns as early as possible – much of the effort in mastering a skill can go into getting rid of inappropriate habits.

An experiment by von Wright (1957) provides a good illustration of this point. It involved the learning of a sequence of choices in a kind of moving maze. A strip of paper was mounted on rollers and concealed from the subject by a screen. The paper moved past a slot in the screen, making visible a short section of the strip at any one time. On the paper were drawn a connected sequence of diamond-shapes as illustrated in the figure below. Subjects had to move a stylus so as to avoid 'blind alleys', indicated by a line across the path. In the initial version A of the task, this line always appeared on the second half of each diamond, so that it became visible only *after* the corresponding choice had already been made. On the very first trial, subjects usually made their choices on some systematic basis, such as always going to the same side; but starting with the second trial, they attempted to make correct decisions at each choice, on the basis of the previous run. Although K R was provided immediately after each choice, and although this was a case where it had an equivalent informational content after correct and after incorrect choices, errors made during early trials proved very persistent.

Von Wright also prepared two other versions of the maze. The second, B, contained exactly the same sequence of choices as the first, but there the blockage occurred in the first half of the diamond, so that it was visible *before* each choice was made. Version C simply omitted all incorrect sections of path.

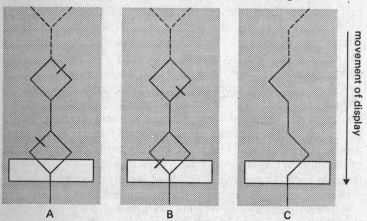

Three versions of the same choice point in von Wright's 'moving maze'

He then examined the performance of two further groups of subjects. One started with four trials of version B, then transferred to A and continued to a criterion of two consecutive errorless runs. The other similarly started with C before transferring to A. Here are the mean number of trials per subject to achieve criterion:

Group 1 (version A throughout) – 23·25;
Group 2 (4 trials with B then A) – 10·45;
Group 3 (4 trials with C then A) – 18·80.

Groups 2 and 3 learned significantly more quickly than Group 1, although the amount of information available was the same for all of them. The advantage must have derived from the first four trials in which Groups 2 and 3 were able to utilize this information uncontaminated by discrepant responses.*

To complete the picture, we really need information on the performance of subjects who receive different proportions of their training on B and on A. B is in effect an *externally guided* version of a task that must eventually be carried out without guidance. Suppose that *all* training were guided: after how many such trials – if ever – could we expect perfect *unguided* performance? The indications are that in order to arrive at such an achievement, the subject must make unguided decisions during some stage of the training, and this does not necessarily happen while guidance remains available. If we think of skills more generally, one problem of training can be seen as finding a balance between effort directed at getting early responses approximately correct with the use of appropriate external aids, and practice situations which require the learner to dispense with such aids.


### The transfer of training

With the exception of accomplishments like moving one's ears, or the more exotic yoga exercises, most skills are made up of components which are shared with, or similar to, those of others. Many sports overlap in the muscle groups they use, and all of them benefit from efficient heart action – consequently, distance running can contribute towards a better performance at football,

* The superiority of Group 2 over Group 3 probably results from a greater *transfer* (see the next section) of what is learned during the first four trials, to the trials with version A. Version B resembles version A in actually *presenting* the choice points, even though it then tells you what to do. Version C, by omitting the incorrect paths, *looks* like a different situation, even though it is logically identical.

boxing or rowing. Craft skills like carpentry involve, among other things, the ability to handle a variety of tools which may then be brought to bear on a range of tasks from making a bookshelf to reproduction furniture. Some components are so basic – like the ability to match a seen location with the appropriate hand movement – that they enter into virtually everything we do. To some extent, therefore, when we are learning a 'new' skill, we are building on and utilizing a variety of sub-skills that have been developed previously, either on their own or in other contexts. There is still, of course, an important element of organization that is specific to the skill in question – whether it takes the form of timed and closely integrated motor patterns, or of more cognitive structures, co-ordinating several distinct operations as in a craft. Nevertheless, it is possible to benefit to some extent from prior training and experience – in effect, from a *transfer* of training.

The idea of components or of similarity, however, requires further analysis. If we consider again the example of mirror drawing, we might think of the operations of tracing the outline of a particular pattern with and without mirror as being highly similar; and yet practice under one condition interferes with performance in the other, i.e. we get negative transfer. Tracing a pattern of very different appearance, on the other hand, might seem to be dissimilar a task; yet there is considerable benefit from practising one pattern with the use of a mirror to being able to trace another under the same conditions. Significantly, there is also positive transfer from mirror drawing with one hand to using the other.

The important aspect of similarity which this example illustrates is that found in the *relationship* between stimulus input and motor output. This relationship is different in the mirror and no-mirror conditions, but remains the same within them; we can in fact expect to find positive transfer between tasks in which the stimulus–response relationships are the same; negative transfer or interference between tasks in which the same stimuli require different and incompatible responses; and little or no transfer between situations involving radically different stimulus inputs.

The activities involved in any formal learning or training procedure are inevitably restricted, yet it is hoped that they should facilitate a far wider range of achievements than those that were actually practised. Certainly this is true of the general education we receive. The idea is that acquisition of a number of basic physical and intellectual skills will provide a good basis for a wide range of activities involved in later everyday life or for further more specialized learning. Naturally, the question arises to what extent such a basis is actually provided and whether there are any particular features of learning content and presentation that promote widespread transfer to new situations.

## Facilitating transfer

We no longer believe in the all embracing virtues of particular disciplines, like classics, simply to 'train the mind', enabling its owner to cope with virtually any demand that might subsequently be made on him – though it does appear, after all, that an ability to read and write one's native language and to carry out the basic arithmetic operations make useful ingredients in most forms of life.

Views and decisions about what is an appropriate content for education, the relative emphasis on the arts or sciences, on cognitive or physical skills, are influenced by many different considerations, to some of which we will return in the chapter on education. It is, not only a question of finding the best basis for a given set of requirements in later life, but also of what those requirements will, or should, be. In the present context, we would like to emphasize just one very general feature of training which can facilitate transfer.

Consider as an example 'oddity problems'. These involve being presented with three objects, two of which are alike in some way, while the third is different – you have to pick out the one that is different. Chimpanzees can learn to solve this kind of problem, not simply in the sense of dealing with a given triad – but having been presented with a limited number of such problems, they can quickly solve others in which the actual objects used are not the same as those in previous trials. This achievement requires an appropriate capacity in the learner – rats, for example, cannot manage it. But it also requires a sequence of learning trials in which the nature of the oddity is appropriately varied. Protracted practice with a single instance is not enough.

The ability to abstract common features from a limited series of instances is most highly developed in human beings and has been discussed in the chapter on language. Exposure to an inevitably limited number of correctly structured sentences results in the abstraction of implicit 'rules' which can be used for the construction of an indefinite series of new sentences. Even when the abstraction or principle is directly presented, e.g. in the exposition of a mathematical technique or theorem, something additional and important is added by its application in a variety of instances, which facilitates flexibility in subsequent use. This is not something confined to purely cognitive learning. Having achieved proficiency in driving one car, the difference in size, instrument layout and general response characteristics of another can be very disturbing. After one has driven three or four, subsequent ones are mastered much more quickly. It is as though exposure to different instances leads to the elimination of dependence on inessential features, leaving a kind of common denominator. The general point being made is that, individual differences in capacity-to-benefit apart, effective transfer of training to a variety of tasks or situations is best encouraged by an explicit emphasis on a variety of applications *as part of training*.

## Knowledge of results and motivation

Evidence was presented in Chapter 4 that reinforcement often coincided with an increase, a boosting, of current activity. Whether or not there is an intrinsic relationship between these events, there is certainly evidence of similar motivational effects associated with KR. For example, simply providing additional information to people doing a repetitive task (e.g. information about quality, or time taken) can lead to an improvement of quality or speed respectively (though in industry there are usually complicating factors that prevent it from working out quite like that. There are also more general effects. Evidence of success usually increases interest in an activity 'as a whole', and by the same token, evidence of failure or simply absence of information, can lead to its abandonment. To think of behaviour as being organized into larger units, as having some kind of hierarchical structure, fits in well with this observation, but it also raises some unanswered questions. Suppose that a child is playing the piano and gets some encouraging comments: does this reinforce, or otherwise affect, the playing of a particular sequence of notes? the piece of music as a whole? playing Chopin? or the piano? And if failure leads to variation of behaviour, will this take the form of playing differently, or of playing something else altogether, like football?

Learning theories that regard behaviour as consisting simply of an assembly of responses cannot answer this kind of question because they cannot really ask it. But for the time being, and for practical purposes, one can give some rough quantitative advice: if we want to 'shape' the behaviour of an animal (discussed in Chapter 2) then at each stage of the procedure we must set the criteria for success at a level where they can be fairly readily achieved – otherwise there will be little reinforcement, the animal will sooner or later start doing something else, or, if it can, just go away. It is a phenomenon not unknown in human learning situations.

## The retention of skill

It appears that certain kinds of skill, like swimming or riding a bicycle, are never really lost, even after very long periods during which they are not used. There is of course a difference between competence and performance – a difference which stimulus–response theories never adequately dealt with. But even within a cognitive framework, the survival of competence without any practice over many years is intriguing as a form of very stable long-term memory.

Retention is not equally good in all skills. A distinction can be made between *discrete* skills like typing, where specific stimuli are translated into specific movements, and *continuous* ones, of which cycling is a good example – with the former being more readily forgotten than the latter. Motor memory has been much less investigated than verbal memory, and so the reason for this difference is not really understood. The explanation could be along the following lines. If the perceptual and motor components of a skill are largely specific to a particular situation – as they probably are when balancing on a bicycle – this will protect them against interference from new learning during the period not spent in the saddle. And if at the same time, these components are highly integrated among themselves, as they will be in a continuous skill, this will make for a stable, mutually supportive 'structure' in motor memory – whatever form that may eventually be shown to take.

## Theories of skill – execution and learning

We must briefly return to some theoretical issues as they have arisen in the study of skill. What becomes particularly salient here is the contrast between the picture of behaviour that emerges from a detailed examination of skilled performance, and that presented by theories about learning. Looking primarily at discrete acts, like pressing a lever, taking a right turn, etc., and concentrating on the occasions for their occurrence, rather than on *how* they were executed, led to a conception of behaviour as cobbled together from single responses. The idea of a response chain might just about fit the novice pianist, producing one note at a time from an examination of the score, but it is quite inadequate for dealing with a phrase executed at speed, whether from a score or from memory. Such achievements seem to call for the analogy of a program – i.e. a set of instructions which exist, or are set up in advance of their execution, and which contain the necessary features of movement, timing etc. without depending on the occurrence of stimulation, whether of external or of internal origin. The other prominent feature of skilled behaviour is that much of it involves aiming at, adjusting to and tracking, some kind of target, often quite explicitly, as when we try to follow a moving object, in actual pursuit or simply with the eyes. To account for this kind of achievement calls for feedback or closed-loop systems, whose basic properties we described in Chapter 4.

Stimulus–Response–Reinforcement models have sometimes been described as being of the closed-loop type – and in a sense they are, in that the successful consequences of behaviour react back upon the system producing it. On the *next* occasion behaviour will lead more directly to the goal; but the model does not allow for any ongoing corrections, as part of behaviour-in-progress: we are dealing with a relatively *long* loop. (Natural selection completes an even longer closed loop, and provided the environment does not change too rapidly a species will 'track' these changes within an evolutionary time scale, even if there is little capacity for adaptive change within the lifetime of the individual.)

Analyses of skilled performance point to underlying systems of greater complexity – utilizing, for example, not just the straight feedback of distance from a target, but also the rate at which the distance changes, and the acceleration; or various forms of *feed-forward*, in which a kind of 'copy' of the (anticipated) consequences of an initiated movement is made available for comparison with the real consequences, as they unfold. But, as with similar performance models derived from biological work on animal behaviour, we have a much better understanding of how such systems operate than of how they become modified and adapted.

## Closed loops and open loops

Some years ago Adams (1971) put forward an influential 'closed-loop theory of motor learning'. One characteristic of this theory is its emphasis on the element of verbal/cognitive control in the early stages of learning (where frequently one tells oneself verbally what should be done next, or how to do it). But the central proposal is that learning a skill involves the creation of an internal representation or 'image' of movement, built up from the *proprioceptive* sensations that the movements themselves produce – Adams calls it a 'perceptual trace'. With increasing skill performance is progressively guided by comparisons between this 'trace' and the proprioceptive signals generated by current movement. Having learned what a letter 'A' *looks* like, we can use a visual image of the letter as a guide in drawing it. Analogously, the execution of a well practised manoeuvre in gymnastics, say, would be controlled by reference to a 'motor image'. This constant reference to an internalized image is also put forward as an explanation of the continued improvement that usually results from practice, even in the absence of (external) knowledge of results.

The distinctive feature of Adams's theory is not that the learning process itself involves a closed loop – which it does, as must any system producing adaptive changes – but that, in contrast to stimulus–response–reinforcement models, the *execution* of behaviour also depends on feedback. Motor learning consists, in effect, of establishing a feedback loop closer to the 'centre' from which instructions for movement are issued. After this, movement is or can be controlled by means of a constant comparison between the target, in the form of the perceptual trace or motor image, and what has been 'achieved' – as represented by signals coming back from muscles and joints. Once we have become competent at writing, we can manage reasonably well without visual guidance – in terms of Adams's theory this would be done by 'referring' to the motor image. Notice particularly that the incorporation of feedback into execution produces a greater coherence between *doing* and learning. The same visual feedback that guides performance also helps to establish the motor image – though there is some evidence to suggest that in order for it to have the latter effect, it must be used, at least part of the time, 'after the event' – not to provide a current target, but as a confirmation of a target already attained – as knowledge of results, in other words.

## Motor programs

To propose, at this stage, an *open* loop for the generation of (some) behaviour might seem like a backward step. This is after all what we had in the S–R model. There has been quite a lot of recent evidence,* however, to support such a view, in the more sophisticated form of a *motor-program* – an organized package of instructions, issued in a predetermined sequence.

One kind of evidence comes from a consideration of very fast sequences of movements – the pianist's arpeggio, rapid speech – where there seems to be no time for signals to go back and forwards between the 'centre', and the muscles and joints involved in execution. Various studies have also shown that if the flow of information from the periphery is somehow prevented – one of the methods used involves an inflatable cuff around the wrist – reasonably accurate movements can still be produced, even in the absence of vision.

Another appeals to the finding that active, intentional movements can be *re*produced more accurately than passive, guided ones ('the preselection effect'). The argument is that the information coming back from the muscles and joints should be the same in both cases, so that the superior memory for the intentional movement must be a function of *issuing the instructions*.

That movements remain *susceptible* to feedback, even when it is apparently not being used, is not under dispute. One of the interesting features of a skilled performance is that it can proceed quite smoothly and 'automatically' at one moment, yet as soon as something unusual happens – something unfamiliar in the way things look, sound or feel – control immediately becomes more conscious, and activity continues with more careful and explicit attention to what is going on. Not only does this suggest a change in the 'level' of control to one more characteristic of an earlier stage of competence; it also indicates that in some way

* The idea started with the physiological psychologist Lashley (1917), after a clinical study of a patient with a spinal war injury. This had severed the sensory nerves leading back from the limbs, eliminating this source of feedback. Nevertheless, the patient was able to make accurate positioning movements, which persuaded Lashley that control must be altogether central.

the incoming information is being *monitored* all along, with the regulation of movement continuing in a particular way as long as this information conforms to an expected pattern. What is at issue between 'centralists' and 'peripheralists', between protagonists of the open and of the closed loop, is the extent to which this information continues to be required as an *active part* of movement regulation, as distinct from *enabling* another form of control to proceed.

### Schemas

An example of a theory that incorporates both motor programs and feedback control is a 'schema' theory due to Schmidt (1975). Its point of departure is in the 'coming together' of four kinds of signal or information when someone carries out a motor task. They are: (1) the representation of the goal; (2) the movement instructions that are issued; (3) the proprioceptive information coming back from those movements and (4) knowledge of results, i.e. external information about the achievement of the goal. Schmidt proposes that two, partly independent, 'schemas' are built up as a result of this confluence of information. (1) and (2), together with (4), build up a 'recall schema' which will be able, increasingly, to generate appropriate motor programs. (1) and (3), together with (4) build up a 'recognition schema', and in fact the two schemas build up in interaction with each other.

The other important feature of the theory is reflected in the use of the term 'schema'. The object is to provide a model that does not have to specify movement instructions, or criteria of success, in complete detail, and thereby to overcome what have been called the *storage* and *novelty* problems. In essence these problems arise from the *enormous* variety in the movements that are actually performed in any skill. To specify these in advance down to the last detail would require more storage capacity than is available. It is also difficult to see how *new* movements (or much more generally, new actions of any kind) could ever come to be performed, if such detailed specifications were necessary.

Schmidt's theory is itself somewhat schematic in describing how this might be done, but there are some promising clues in the very nature of negative feedback systems, and in hierarchical organization. If a system can select responses according to whether or not they produce approach to a target, then interaction with a variable environment will generate an unlimited number of response sequences. If the organization of the system is also hierarchical, then the higher levels can give their 'instructions' by setting goals that do not have to specify in detail how they are to be attained, and these details can be provided *progressively* by lower levels in the course of execution. The challenging problem is to understand how, in the course of practice and experience, the pattern of such generalized instructions comes to be established: it is again the process of abstraction from a limited number of instances, that we have already referred to.

These are outlines of just two kinds of theory in what has recently become a very active field. For many years, psychologists interested in learning tended to keep away from the detailed study of motor control for the same reason, one may suppose, that made them avoid the 'free-range' behaviour of animals: these are uncomfortable topics if you adhere to a model based exclusively on association. Now that the spell has been broken, the task is to realize the full implications of much more sophisticated ideas about *performance* for the process of adaptive change. And here the fundamental property which these models share (including those that incorporate motor programs) may provide a key to progress in our understanding of learning processes in general. Like learning, performance itself is seen as essentially adaptive and goal directed, though on a shorter time scale; the processes that take care of meeting *immediate* targets merge into those that produce more long-term changes. We may think of learning as the effect of a range of feedback loops that lie between, and are continuous with, at one end, those loops that produce detailed adjustments to the current situation, and at the other the 'ultimate' loop of natural selection. Insights obtained in one part of this continuum may well prove useful in the others.

# 8. Human Development

In Chapter 3 we discussed the inverse relationship between the adaptability of a species and the degree to which it is already competent to operate in its environment at birth. If a species is capable of adaptive development during the lifetime of its individuals the newborn members of the species must be relatively uncommitted at birth. The young must also be protected during the period when they are not competent to survive in the environment; the long infancy of humans is presumably a reflection of the very large difference in the skills available to mature people and newborn children. This chapter is concerned with the processes which bring about such a change.

As mentioned previously, development is controlled to some extent by the genetic constitution of the individual. Provided the person survives, developmental changes controlled genetically – usually called the process of maturation – will proceed in a more or less inevitable way. This is not to say that the physical environment has absolutely no effect on processes which are genetically controlled; height, for example, is affected *both* by genetic constitution and by nutrition, but within very wide environmental limits the deciding factor is the gene structure.

Another way in which genetic endowment controls development is a process called epigenesis, in which the expression of the genes occurs *provided* certain forms of psychological experience occur. It is as if the genetic instructions 'permit' certain forms of development but only under particular conditions. An example of this would be the development of binocular vision. Certain receptor units in the central nervous system are genetically designed for binocular vision but will only become operative if binocular experience is available during specific periods in early life; if it is not available at these times this capacity will not develop. Both these forms of genetic control produce effects which are normally irreversible within the lifetime of the individual.

Finally there is the effect of experience on development. Babies can learn from a very early age and subsequent learning skills will undoubtedly be dependent on what has been learned earlier. However, the effects of learning *per se* are not usually regarded as irreversible in quite the same way as are the effects of genes on development.

We have spoken rather cavalierly of three processes underlying development as if these processes could be precisely described and their effects precisely delineated. This is obviously not the case; a significant part of research on human development is devoted to carrying out this task and, indeed, to discovering what abilities may be already present at birth, because we often seem to credit babies with much less ability than they actually possess.

Research on development has concentrated on a number of issues. First there are widely differing views about the *extent* to which experience after birth controls development. This dispute, sometimes referred to as the nature–nurture controversy, has at times generated great heat, especially when it has been concerned with individual differences. It is possible to ask to what extent the observed differences in human adults in degree of aggressiveness, intellectual ability, visual acuity, masculinity or whatever characteristic one may choose are determined by genetic factors or by the effects of experience during life.

It is also possible to ask, for example, to what extent we *all* have to learn to see, as opposed to having innate visual abilities, or to what extent we must all learn about language. It has sometimes been assumed that the latter types of ability, which (with very few exceptions) we all seem to exhibit in much the same way, are innate, whereas those in which obvious variations occur, such as intelligence or personality, are not. But, as Cellérier (1980) has pointed out, sickle cell anaemia is not found in all members of the species but, where it is found, it is innate, whereas our susceptibility to gravity, though universal, is not (except, presumably, in that having mass is innate).

Despite this, much emphasis has been placed on the contribution of environmental factors to individual differences while the origin of more general abilities has usually (though not always) been approached in a more objective manner. This may be related both to the *clarity* with which differences in intellectual ability and personality between people can be detected and to the *value* attached to certain manifestations of these characteristics – high intelligence for instance.

While many psychologists and most geneticists would agree that about 80 per cent of the observed variance in I.Q. scores found in people in western society is attributable to inherited factors, such an assertion is frequently attacked as racist or fascist propaganda. Whereas, since most people develop the ability to see, and any residual differences in the manner in which visual perception is organized in different racial or social groups is detectable only by somewhat esoteric methods, interest in the maturational versus experiential factors in the development of vision has tended to be confined to specialists in that area.

A commitment to the environmentalist explanation of individual differences has often been linked to progressive political views on the grounds that innate differences might seem to justify hierarchy and privilege. But Chomsky (1975) has argued that this position could equally be consistent with a political system in which people were moulded into forms which best served 'their' interests by those, of course, who define what those interests should be. We will consider the question of 'manipulation' in the final chapter; for the moment it is worth noting that the sources of all characteristics are of both practical and theoretical interest. An understanding of the development of vision in small children, for example, in addition to being interesting is often of great importance in cases of potential or actual defective vision.

A second area of research interest has been concerned with the *timing* of certain experiences, much of it stimulated by the findings in studies of animal development described in Chapter 3. Examples would include a sensitive period of between ten and fifty days after hatching during which white-crowned sparrows *must* be exposed to the mature calls of their species if they are to learn how to make them. The most striking of these 'critical periods' for learning is, of course, shown in the process of imprinting and it has been tempting to apply the concept to human development. The suggestion has been made that the smiling response in the human infant may be equivalent to the following response in newly-hatched precocial birds. Linked to this is the question of how easily the effects of such early experiences can be reversed, especially to what extent unfortunate early experiences can be subsequently corrected. There have, in addition, been studies aimed at elucidating the conditions under which early experience can have a controlling effect on development. To some extent these have been brought to a focus by the work of Piaget (discussed below) and have concentrated on whether the variables normally associated with learning, practice, reinforcement and the like, or conditions deriving from Piaget's theory, such as conflict between existing intellectual structures and new behavioural requirements, are the significant factors in behavioural change.

In summary, research on development has been much concerned with the extent, timing and quality of experience, particularly early experience, as it affects psychological development. Some consideration of the work of Piaget will provide a useful starting point since his approach has formed a frame of reference within which much research in this area has been carried out.

## The work of Piaget

The most obvious characteristic of Piaget's work is his postulation of successive periods or phases of development through which every child passes. There are three main phases, each of which is divided into several stages, but the boundaries between these and indeed between the main periods themselves are not seen as sharp dividing lines but as times when the intellectual abilities are undergoing considerable change. In naming these main phases we run into the first difficulty in relating Piaget's work to more general work in this field – his terminology. The first phase is called the period of *sensorimotor schemata* lasting from birth to about two years. The second is the period of *concrete operations* from two to about eleven years and the last is the period of *formal operations*, from eleven onwards. These names relate to the major types of intellectual activity engaged in during the periods.

During the period of sensorimotor intelligence the emphasis is on immediate perceptual and physical response to aspects of the environment – concept formation is in an extremely concrete, largely pre-verbal phase. The first few weeks of this period are occupied by the modification and development of co-ordinations between the reflexes present at birth. The infant gradually begins to follow moving objects with his eyes, to attempt to grasp objects and so on. Between four and eight months a rudimentary purposiveness develops, the child repeats actions which have had interesting results and begins to anticipate. More sustained goal-directed behaviour follows and, after the development of experimentation and exploration, the sensorimotor period ends with the beginning of symbolic behaviour.

The name of the second period, *concrete operations*, emphasizes the fact that during this period the child operates on the environment intellectually – classifies, notes similarities and differences, adds, subtracts, and so on – but still at a concrete level without being capable of much abstraction from the present environment. This period is divided by Piaget into two important *sub-periods* lasting from about two to seven and from seven to eleven years. At eleven the child has a fully organized ability to think logically about concrete objects, but not to deal with abstract concepts. This latter ability develops in the period of *formal operations*. Concrete thinking develops in the sub-period from seven to eleven, while in the phase prior to this the child is still learning to handle symbolic representation and his thought is inadequate in several respects, even for the handling of concrete objects. Thinking at this stage is still *egocentric*, for example the child cannot describe a scene from a position other than the one from which he looks at it; it is also irreversible in the sense that the child cannot detach from the sequence of actual events in the environment and is able usually to handle only one property of the situation at a time. For example, a child will say that two containers of liquid of identical shape contain equal quantities, but when the liquid from one is poured into a narrower vessel will say that there is now more because the level is higher. This changes at about seven when the 'principle of invariance' develops and concrete thinking begins to deal adequately with the environment. The period of formal operations terminates when the child has developed adult forms of thought, including the ability to manipulate abstract concepts, set up hypothetical propositions and so on.

The particular classifications used by Piaget are not necessarily those that would occur to everyone but his observations and the resulting development of theory have provided a starting point for much of the research on intellectual development.

Piaget goes on to suggest various processes which underlie this development. He distinguishes between the unvarying *function* of intellectual behaviour, adaptation to the environment, and the changing and developing intellectual *structures* which subserve this function.

Adaptation – adjusting to and dealing with the environment – is seen as the basic role, indeed almost the definition, of intelligence. Two *sub-processes* carry out the basic function of adaptation, assimilation and accommodation. Assimilation is the process by which a new stimulus or experience is absorbed and responded to on the basis of already existing cognitive structures, whereas accommodation is the change or development of existing cognitive structures to meet new situations.

While these processes are formally opposed they are not necessarily alternatives and may be better thought of as complementary. A situation can only be dealt with approximately by means of available responses, that is, by means of assimilation; but any situation will be different to some extent from all previous experiences and will require some adjustment in current modes of response, that is, it will bring about accommodatory changes. Thus development at a given time will require both assimilation and accommodation but the relation between them alters with age. In the early sensorimotor period, assimilation is probably a 'routine' procedure while situations requiring accommodation may simply present themselves as obstacles. As intelligence develops, the processes are brought into a more articulated relationship whereby the child will seek accommodatory changes – will search for novelty.

This particular method of coping with the environment while continually developing more complex intellectual structures for the purpose brings about, in Piaget's view, a fairly constant order of development from child to child. This is essentially an interactionist view of intellectual development. Within certain limits all children start with the same modes of adaptation to the environment; the characteristics of the physical environment are similarly fairly constant, and so the stages of development are much the same for all children. Ability develops in a fairly constant direction with given abilities inevitably preceding others. An example of the building of more general and more flexible behavioural characteristics on more restricted abilities is provided by Piaget's observations of the development of grasping a visible object. For a child to learn to grasp an object in the field of view seems to require mastery of a prior skill. This is the ability to grasp a visible object when the child's hand and the object are simultaneously in view. When the child is in this stage, a movement of its hand or of the object, taking either out of sight, will at once stop attempts to reach for and grasp the object. But once the operations of holding an object in sight and simultaneously reaching for it have been thoroughly 'linked' the child is ready to develop the more general ability of grasping any visible object within reach, regardless of the initial position of its hands.

This entire system emphasizes much more the order of development of behavioural characteristics and the intellectual structures presumably underlying them than the detailed conditions necessary for the acquisition of a new response. The whole theoretical system emphasizes the dependence of intelligence on previous simpler, more concrete and less generalized structures – on the existence of previous intellectual structures, that is, and not on the previous acquisition of specific responses. Nevertheless the conditions for the emergence of behavioural change can be derived from this approach. Essentially the attainment of more appropriate behaviour depends on the existence of two or more primitive 'concepts' none of which are fully adequate for the situation. When this state of conflict develops it can only be resolved by the emergence of a more elaborate conceptual system which will incorporate the conflicting aspects of the situation as these are mediated by the simpler, existing concepts.

This approach sees intellectual development as a series of conceptual evolutions rather than as a gradual development. There is evidence supporting this view in at least some areas of development.

An important aspect of Piaget's thinking is the idea that individual cognitive development from birth to maturity closely parallels the historical development of scientific knowledge. This fits in with his view that the world is, as it were, *constructed* by each individual on the basis of his interactions with it. Individual experience obviously has an important role in Piaget's thinking, although, as we have seen, he is not in agreement with the essentially associationist approach of most learning theories.

At the same time the interest in processes of learning during this century has been accompanied by an emphasis on the role of experience in development and a relative disparagement of innate factors. Some innate control of development has always been recognized, of course, and the general idea that hereditary factors and environment 'interact' in development has commanded wide agreement.

This is obviously an unsatisfactory position; while true in the trivial sense it is precisely the nature of the interaction that is in question. And the general implication that the environment is the dominant partner in the interaction has in recent years been challenged by various theorists, notably by Chomsky in the domain of language. We have discussed the position of Chomsky in the chapter on language but the means by which the environment produces its effects – the nature of learning – is, as we have seen, a matter of dispute.

It is, incidently, a common assumption both among learning theorists and 'constructionist' theorists of the Piaget school that only one or two processes of learning (those specified by the theorist in question) underlie all adaptive changes in behaviour. This has always been improbable, and as Foss (1965) has pointed out it seems more likely that there are several modes of adaptation just as there are in other aspects of biological functioning.

While recognizing that no one process is likely to mediate all adaptive development there is an obvious need to discover which process best describes conditions for behavioural change in particular circumstances. In early development the two approaches which have most often been used to provide explanations for learning are Piaget's conflict approach and some form of reinforcement theory. Bower (1974) has attempted to evaluate these approaches in the area of object perception in young infants.

Up to about the age of five months babies are prone to two types of inappropriate behaviour when looking at objects. If a moving object is presented the baby can follow it with his eyes, but if the object stops the baby will tend to continue moving his eyes in the direction the object would have taken, paying no apparent attention to the object itself which is now stationary and in full view. This is termed the movement error. On the other hand if a stationary object is first presented in one place and then moved to another the baby will tend to look for it in the place he first saw it, disregarding the object itself which is visible but in another location. This is termed the place error.

These errors could be interpreted as representing two different concepts of the nature of an object, one that an object is 'defined' by regular and continuing movement and the other that an object is regarded as occupying one particular point in space. At about five months the baby changes this way of looking at things, 'realizing' that objects can exist in more than one locality, that their movement is subject to change, and that it is the same kind of thing (a permanent object) that has all these properties. The question Bower investigated was whether behaviour indicative of this more advanced concept arises primarily through reinforcement of the relevant behaviour or because the more primitive concepts are brought into direct conflict, thus forcing the baby to develop the new superordinate concept incorporating the previous two.

The criterion behaviour chosen to indicate that the baby had arrived at the new concept was his continued tracking of a moving object in the appropriate direction, when it disappeared from view from time to time. The apparatus, designed by Mundy-Castle (1970), consists of an object moving regularly along a circular track in the vertical plane and passing in each revolution through two short tunnels, during which it vanishes from sight. If the baby continues to 'follow' the object with his eyes while it is out of sight he is assumed to have mastered the idea that a permanent object is moving continuously along a circular track and passing behind a barrier.

Bower attempted to produce this criterion behaviour using two different 'training' techniques. One group of babies was introduced to the circular movement without tunnels and was thus able to follow the object over the whole circuit. If we assume that being allowed to follow the object with the eyes is interesting, and thus reinforcing, then the tendency to track circular motions should have been learned. The other group was shown an object moving back and forth along a straight track, stopping at each end before returning in the opposite direction.

This presentation provides no training in following an object moving in a circle but, since the object stopped at the end of the track, it did provide a conflict between the two notional concepts of object-as-a-fixed-place and object-as-continuous-movement. If this conflict is resolved, a more inclusive concept of an object which can both move and remain stationary, and is thus not 'tied' to a place or a regular visible trajectory, should develop.

When these babies were tested with the Mundy-Castle apparatus the second group, which had not been trained to follow circular movement, tracked the object through the tunnels much more frequently than the first group. This can be interpreted as evidence in favour of the Piagetian conflict view of cognitive development, or at least as evidence against a crude reinforcement view of learning in this situation. In addition to experimental tests of this kind it has been shown (Bower, 1979) that place and movement errors in babies decline concurrently, which suggests that their disappearances are functionally linked.

It seems likely that an understanding of how, at certain stages of development, a baby integrates simple and limited concepts into broader, more widely predictive cognitive structures, will lead to more adequate interpretations of behavioural development. In order to further this understanding it is obviously necessary to establish what accomplishments are present at various ages. Much attention has been paid to the sensory abilities of small babies, particularly to their vision, and the outline of early visual development is becoming clearer.

## The development of perceptual ability

People have long been interested in what newborn babies see, and there has never been any lack of speculation, or even assertion, about their visual experience. Difficulties in establishing the relevant facts, have, however, until comparatively recently foiled any attempt to develop an understanding of visual development. A baby's lack of commitment to disinterested visual research is matched by his inability to respond to the investigator's questions.

The problem seemed fairly intractable because, by the time young children have developed organized behaviour enabling them to give conventional responses in experimental situations, their vision is already well developed. It thus seemed difficult to ascertain both the degree of visual ability present in very early life and the course of development that occurred before they had acquired abilities roughly within the normal range. Infants cannot describe what they see and cannot even point in answer to questions. More recently, however, there has been a rapid development in techniques for extracting 'answers' from small infants to questions about the visual world as it appears to them.

Pioneering work was carried out by Fantz (1966), who argued that if infants show a preference for one visual pattern over another, by looking at it significantly more, then they must be able to discriminate between them. It is fairly easy to record the time spent by an infant in looking at two (or more) stimuli and so to determine whether the child can differentiate between them. Failure to spend longer looking at one than the other does not prove that he cannot discriminate between them; he may merely like them equally well or, indeed, be indifferent to both, but if he does prefer one over the other he *must* be able to tell the difference. A further development of this method has come to be known as the violation of expectancy technique. Essentially the idea is that an infant becomes bored with the same display, attends to it less and can only be rendered attentive again by a new stimulus. By this means it is possible to explore what constitutes a new stimulus for the infant. Changes in the rate at which babies suck, which are assumed to indicate surprise, have also been used to indicate what types of perceptual rules hold for babies as opposed to older children and adults. Observation of the visual 'tracking' of objects by infants has been used, as we have seen, as a means of determining their ability to recognize permanent objects.

Using his visual preference technique Fantz established that quite young infants (his subjects were aged between one and fifteen months) preferred complex to simple stimuli and could distinguish both pattern and form. He also showed that young infants have a preference for three-dimensional as compared with two-dimensional shapes.

One controversial result reported by Fantz in 1966 was that babies showed an early, and probably innate, preference for human faces as opposed to other stimuli of equivalent complexity. He used three displays in this investigation: a drawing of a human face, a stimulus which had the same elements (mouth, eyes and so on) placed *randomly* within the drawing, and a third display which simply had a black section of equal area to the sum of the elements in the other two drawings. These were presented in pairs to the subject and Fantz reported that even the youngest infants showed a preference for the realistic drawing of a face. These results have not always been replicated by subsequent investigators and the failures have been interpreted as indicating not only the absence of an innate preference for faces, but also a lack of competence to discriminate detailed visual forms. It has been suggested by Harris (1979), however, that this may be an incorrect inference. We have already seen that a weakness of the visual preference technique is that it can only show discriminating ability where a preference has occurred and that the absence of a preference need not indicate a lack of competence. It is possible that many of the stimulus situations presented to infants by investigators have not been sufficiently interesting to generate a preference. It has been shown by Goren, Sarty and Wu (1975) that infants only a few minutes old will track a face-like stimulus provided it is *moving*. When the features are mixed up they are much less likely to track it. It has also been shown that before it is a month old a baby can distinguish between its mother's face and that of a stranger (Maurer and Salapatek, 1976). It is therefore necessary to test perceptual abilities using stimuli which are meaningful, or at least interesting, in the baby's own terms. Using photographs of faces, Fagan (1976) has shown that children of five months can differentiate between the same face in different orientations (e.g. full-face or profile) and between different faces in the same orientation.

Such results indicate considerable sophistication in the perception of shape at an early age and perhaps indicate a special interest in faces. But a particular perceptual ability in regard to faces may also pose a problem for small babies. Field (1979), among others, has shown that at three months old babies may prefer to look at a doll's face rather than at their mother's. Field arranged for four types of stimuli to be presented to the children; a stationary doll's face, a moving doll's face, their mother's face not animated and their mother's animated face. Infants spent most time looking at the stationary doll's face and least time at their mother's animated face, with intermediate times for the other two stimuli. At the same time their heart-rate levels were most elevated when looking at their mother's animated face. Field interprets these findings in terms of arousal or information processing. The idea is that the mother's face is more arousing or demands more information processing (because it provides more information) than the other stimuli, and the babies' need to moderate their state of arousal results in their looking away from their mother's face more than they look away from a stationary doll's face. This would be consistent with other findings such as those of Karmel (1969) who found that babies' preference for complexity in visual stimuli increases with age.

There are indications that some abilities necessary for the correct perception of space have developed by a very early age. Muir and Field (1979) showed, for example, that infants between two and seven days old turn their heads in the correct direction when presented with a sound from a source at right angles to their line of sight. Although there is evidence of quite developed learning abilities at this age – Siqueland and Lipsitt (1966) found that babies could learn that a head movement in a particular direction, after a particular tone, was followed by a sweet taste – it seems reasonable to conclude that there are inborn mechanisms regulating eye-movements in space.

It seems that the *existence* of some important abilities necessary for the accurate perception of the world depend very little, if at all, on what happens after birth. But this is far from saying that experience has no part to play. Abilities for which innate mechanisms are available often improve and become co-ordinated with appropriate experience and great damage can be caused to all visual capacities if this is not available.

Experimental studies using other species, such as cats and rhesus monkeys, have shown the serious effects produced by lack of early binocular experience. If animals are reared so that one of the eyes is always covered, sometimes the left, sometimes the right, the ability to use the eyes together, as in the binocular detection of depth, does not develop. Observations of humans born with crossed eyes are consistent with this, although there is evidence that if the disparity is corrected in the early months of life no permanent damage may result.

More serious deprivation, such as being born with cataracts, can have more fundamental effects. This is a condition in which the lens of the eye is lacking in transparency, so that light is diffused before reaching the retina and no patterns are seen. A baby with this defect would not be able to see 'things' at all – merely shifting intensities of light. This condition can be corrected but if it is not treated before about the age of six months, permanent damage to vision may result. It seems that certain functional systems in the brain are 'set aside' for visual activity but if they are not 'claimed' very quickly they go by default to other activities and are not redeemable.

Children remain vulnerable in this way for up to about the age of three, any extended period of stimulus deprivation being likely to result in 'forgetting' how to see. This aspect of the role of experience is perhaps best described, not as learning but as providing the opportunity for genetic determination to express itself.

Development, however, is not always in the direction of increasing effectiveness and may even, at times, lead to a loss of previous abilities. Wishart, Bower and Dunkeld (1978) showed that the ability to reach out in the dark for a toy which makes a noise, an ability which becomes quite accurate around five months old, disappears thereafter. While this could be related to the increasing reliance on visual feedback to control movements with age, Bower (1979) points out that even blind babies, as well as normal babies given training in reaching out in the dark, lose this ability at about the same time, and this effect therefore seems to be the result of maturation rather than experience. There is thus an interrelationship between inherited characteristics and experience in the development of sensory ability, although the relationship is complex and far from fully understood.

## The development of social behaviour

We take for granted the fact that children will copy both significant and trivial characteristics of adult behaviour; they will walk with their hands behind their backs because their father does and they will also acquire the language and concept system of the people with whom they are brought up. Imitation is important not only for humans: as we have seen some species of birds do not develop the same song as other birds if they are raised in isolation.

There may well be inherited differences in the type of behaviour which can be imitated and in the accuracy with which it can be reproduced. This seems a necessary assumption in order to explain why some species of birds, such as parrots and myna birds, can imitate noises of many different types including human speech, while others, even with the same opportunity, never do.

Evidence has recently been produced that babies as young as

two or three weeks old can copy an adult putting out his tongue (Meltzoff and Moore, 1977) so it seems likely that imitation can be regarded as an innate characteristic of humans also. This skill is quite a complex one for very small babies; they must not only detect the particular facial contortion (putting out the tongue) but also translate this into instructions to their own motor system.

We say that imitation occurs when the learner reproduces behaviour which he has seen (or heard) *because he has seen it*. If a flock of birds fly away when disturbed by a loud noise, we do not consider that the last birds to fly away are imitating the first to take off (although in some cases they may be). All the birds have been exposed to the same stimulus – the noise – and this would result in their flying off even if they were alone. Similarly we consider that children have imitated when they have not been exposed to an appropriate stimulus for the behaviour except the sight of the model's actions. The presumption of imitation is strengthened if the learner has not shown the behaviour before and if it occurs within a relatively short time of the behaviour of which it is a copy.

We can regard imitation as an available, and probably important, capacity which will be operational to a greater or lesser extent in the child's development of specific abilities. But to the extent that imitation is a mechanism active in development it puts a premium on the particular experiences of each individual child. The emphasis becomes, not that of the unfolding of an invariant order of development in response to encounters with the physical world, but of the development of behaviour in inter-action with the people in the environment who can serve as appropriate models.

But emphasis on the immediately overt behaviour of the copier may obscure the full extent of the role that imitation has to play in human development. Bandura (1977) has made a distinction between vicarious acquisition, or observational *learning*, and imitative *performance*. The importance of this distinction is illustrated in a study in which three groups of children watched a model carrying out a novel action. The first group saw the model punished for his action, for the second group the model was ignored, while for the third group the model was rewarded. The imitative behaviour of children in all three groups was noted and, as might be expected, the group who had a rewarded model imitated most, the group with an ignored model was intermediate and the group with a punished model showed least imitations. However, when, without further training, all the children were promised rewards if they would demonstrate what they had learned, they all showed equivalent levels of imitation.

Such results indicate that the acquisition of behaviour as a result of observation of others' behaviour may be much more pervasive than immediate indications of copying would lead one to expect. Bandura has stressed the cognitive elements in observational learning and he and his associates have studied the properties of the modelling situation.

It seems necessary, first of all, for the model's behaviour to be distinctive or salient enough to attract the child's attention. This is an obvious, even a logically necessary point, but it highlights an aspect of development not always fully taken into account. The degree of subtlety with which a child can interpret cues in the environment, not simply cues for modelling but any cue indicating the appropriate behaviour, increases as he grows older, and failure to detect an appropriate cue may often underlie failures to behave appropriately which occur early in life. It may often be the case, for example, not that a child lacks intellectual abilities for dealing with a situation, but that he fails to recognize cues indicating which activity would be suitable at a given time.

Given that a child is paying attention to a particular piece of behaviour, if his observation is to result in learning he must have some means of storing or retaining what has been observed. This again is an obvious point; it gains added emphasis, however, once the distinction between observational learning and immediate performance of the learned act has been made. If the child is to benefit in the long term, so that the imitation can be used at a later, more appropriate time, the observed behaviour must be described and coded in a form that allows it to be retained. We would also expect that improvements in the proficiency with which language can be used will increase both the efficiency of observational learning and the complexity of the behaviour that can be acquired in this way.

In addition to properties inherent in the child – the degree of attention of which he is capable and the extent to which he can remember what he has seen – there are situational variables which greatly influence the success of observational learning. The characteristics of the model, the nature of his relationship to the child, the observed behaviour and its consequences all play a part in determining what the child will learn in any situation.

From these various aspects of the situation, two factors in particular have received extensive study: the nature of the model as seen by the child and the consequences of the model's actions, especially whether reinforcement takes place or not. Much attention has also been paid to whether or not the model is 'nurturant' – that is friendly and presumably compassionate – and how this affects the degree of his influence on the child. Such interest stems from theories of identification in children which hold that strong emotional relationships between parents and children influence the adoption by children of parental values and attitudes.

Models who are warm and apparently trustworthy tend, not surprisingly, to be emulated more than those who lack these characteristics, but it is by no means essential for a model to be friendly or to have a special relationship with a child. The essential property of the model seems to be his ability to arouse a child's interest and, perhaps above all, to engage in actions which point the way to goals the child wishes to achieve.

Finally, as we have seen, the consequences of the model's behaviour has an effect on the degree to which he will be imitated immediately but does not seem to be instrumental in controlling the degree of observational learning that takes place. Similarly, while reinforcement of the child for imitating the model will increase *immediate* emission of responses it is not necessary for observational learning to occur. The essential variable seems to be the apparent relevance of the behaviour for the child, now or in the future.

We have paid particular attention to the role of imitation in children because, while it is widely taken advantage of both by parents and teachers, it is frequently not used systematically enough and its intimate relationship to cognitive development is seldom fully exploited. Within the framework of social learning theory few assumptions are made about the inevitable order of development of human abilities, or about the relationship of particular types of learning to particular periods of a child's life. Nevertheless, as the studies of imprinting show, some species of animals do have sensitive periods during which certain forms of learning are particularly easy. And it seems that if learning of particular kinds does not take place during this sensitive or critical period it will not be possible subsequently. It is natural to consider whether, and if so to what extent, this applies to humans.

### Critical periods for learning

Because of the striking nature of such phenomena as imprinting, the temptation to apply the concept of critical period to human behaviour has been very strong. It fits rather well with the findings that maternal and other forms of deprivation in early childhood seem to have severe and sometimes far-reaching effects. It is a short step from the realization that early learning in children may be important to a belief that it is irreversible.

Bowlby (1971, 1975) has been a major proponent of the view that early 'attachment' behaviour of the human infant to (usually) its mother is a major determinant of its subsequent social behaviour. Attachment behaviours are those that result in nearness or contact between mother and child; crying is an obvious example in early infancy. Bowlby argues that the child rapidly comes to distinguish between his mother and other adults, and also to develop a fear of strangers which will tend to restrict his attachment behaviour to one individual. The need for attachment is seen as a behavioural process existing in its own right and successful attachment to a single mother figure, and maintenance of that attachment, is seen as essential for the normal development of the personality.

Bowlby has argued that absence of opportunity to develop

attachment to a single person, especially if this continues during the first three years of life, produces an 'affectionless' personality which is unable to form deep relationships. There does seem to be some evidence that total lack of opportunity to form relationships with anyone during the first years of life can have far-reaching deleterious effects, particularly on the nature of subsequent relationships. It does not seem necessary, however, that the individual to whom attachment is formed be an adult; in one study of a group of refugee children carried out by Freud and Dann, the attachment of the children for each other seemed sufficient to allow 'normal' personality growth.

The emphasis on the importance of early attachment behaviour has probably had a beneficial effect, in that the importance of child care in early life has been increasingly recognized in recent years.

Children may, however, be more resilient than such a view would lead us to believe. Clarke and Clarke (1976) have recently challenged the view that early learning has such intransigently rigid effects, pointing out that '. . . a child's future is far from wholly shaped in the "formative years" of early childhood. Rather, human development is a slow process of genetic and environment interactions with sensitivities (rather than critical periods) for different processes at different times'.

Again, this cannot be regarded as a final word. As we have seen certain forms of perceptual deprivation in infancy do seem to have essentially permanent effects and it also seems necessary for some form of language behaviour to develop before a certain age if speech is to develop fully. Babies only four days old respond more to human speech than to other sounds, and when babbling develops they make the consonant sounds of all languages. They learn to produce regularly only those they hear, of course, and subsequently find it very difficult to produce sounds they could easily produce as very small children.

Babies can develop the ability to swim when only a few days old and may find it much harder to learn to swim thereafter. There may, in fact, be critical periods for optimum development in many areas.

It will be clear by now that we do not have a fully developed model of human development. That interaction with the environment both for the full expression of genetic potential and for learned abilities to develop, is necessary, is clear enough. It is also evident that the timing and ordering of certain kinds of experiences is important, although doubts remain in many spheres just what the timing and order should be.

The study of psychological development is in many ways one of the most productive and interesting areas in psychology, as well as one of the most important. In view of this importance it is fortunate that many of its problems seem increasingly susceptible to experimental study.

# 9. Mental Illness and Behaviour Therapy

The term *mental illness* suggests both a parallel and a contrast with ordinary *physical* illnesses like mumps or measles. In one case we think of something being wrong with the body – as a result, say, of invasion by a harmful virus – in the other, of something wrong with the mind, something that needs to be put right and may require specialist intervention. One case is characterized by physical symptoms like spots or swellings and often a raised temperature, the other by varieties of abnormal behaviour, sometimes accompanied by strange thoughts and stressful emotions. When the illness is cured, spontaneously or by means of some appropriate therapy, the symptoms disappear and the patient is well, and normal, once again. Part of the implied similarity consists in assuming for both cases an underlying pathology or malfunction as the essence of the illness, with various symptoms as by-products; the contrast lies in the explicit distinction that is made between the physical, the organic, on the one hand, and the mental, emotional and behavioural on the other.

Clearly the distinction cannot be too sharply drawn. Many changes of physical state – such as high fever or alcohol in the blood – are accompanied by changes of experience and behaviour. Some forms of insanity have been shown to be the consequence of infection, as in the advanced stages of syphilis. At the same time, experiences and emotional states can give rise to clear-cut physiological conditions such as gastric ulcers, or excemas – often termed *psychosomatic* disorders. There is now a steady trend towards thinking of illness (and of health) in a more fundamentally integrated, *psychobiological* way – as complex conditions with many different facets or aspects, some best described in medical, some in psychological terms, with distinctions a matter of relative emphasis. This also applies increasingly to therapy: it becomes a pragmatic question of how, in any given case, the whole 'system' is most effectively restored to normal functioning.

## Are mental abnormalities illnesses?

While on the one hand, the boundaries between 'the physical' and 'the mental' are being eroded, doubts have been expressed on the other hand about similarities based on the common use of 'illness'. Some psychologists (e.g. Szasz, 1972) have challenged the basic assumption, contained in the idea of an 'illness', that there is something wrong with *the individuals* who are mentally abnormal. They point out, amongst other things, that standards of normal or abnormal behaviour are often determined by purely social conventions. Using the label 'illness' turns the unusual or deviant individual into a 'patient' who 'needs' treatment; thus, for example, the supression of political dissidents might be carried out under the mantle of 'therapy'. It is suggested that the concepts of illness and therapy are unsuitable, not only in such cases of deliberate and cynical abuse, but right across the board, whenever we are dealing with abnormalities of behaviour.

It is true that by talking about 'illness' we evade the need for *justifying* psychological intervention – or any other kind of intervention for that matter. We should like to postpone any more general discussion of this issue until the final chapter. For the moment, our method for trying to sidestep such ethical questions will be to consider only those cases where an individual's behaviour is damaging to himself; and where in addition he feels the need for – and actively seeks out – help. We shall assume that there is indeed 'something wrong with him' that should, if possible, be rectified. But what *kind* of individual problem are we talking about, and what form should help take when we are dealing with behavioural and emotional disturbances? There are other implications of the 'medical model' which can be questioned.

## Illness and symptoms

The characteristic rash of measles is one of the *symptoms* of the illness – i.e. it is regarded as a by-product of an underlying and more fundamental pathological condition. Although part of the treatment might involve trying to reduce any discomfort arising from the rash, it is assumed that any attempt at a real cure must address the underlying 'cause' rather than simply one of its results. One of the ideas implicit in the medical model for behavioural or emotional abnormalities is that these also are symptoms of some more basic disturbance, so that any treatment which singles them out directly for attention is at best palliative. This would be the line taken by *psychodynamic* approaches, such as psychoanalysis. An alternative view does not accept the illness–symptom distinction, regarding the manifestations as *constituting* the problem. This is the approach taken by *behaviour therapy*, and in a somewhat wider context, by *behaviour modification* – an approach whose inspirations have come from theories of learning.

The orthodox position might be put as follows. Abnormal behaviour is an outcome of learning processes just as much as its normal counterpart. It is simply that special circumstances have produced an undesirable result and now keep it in being. We are dealing, not with an illness, but a severe case of bad habits. What is needed is a detailed analysis of the responses, behavioural and emotional, that make up the problem, as well as of the circumstances in which they occur. We can then bring about all the required changes by an application of techniques derived from learning theory.

Recent years have seen substantial changes in this approach to therapy, both reflecting and contributing towards changes in theory. The emphasis on the environment as generating and modifying behaviour has become less exclusive; there are attempts to allow for some cognitive and emotional *organization* of behaviour, whether normal or abnormal, and a recognition of the possible role of relatively innate predispositions. Nevertheless, learning in one form or another continues to be the process chosen for bringing about deliberate, therapeutic change. What support is there for this point of view?

## The independence of causes and cures

If a state of affairs has been brought about by a given process, then it seems likely that the same kind of process will also be effective in changing it. It does not, however, mean that it is necessarily the only or the best process – and it may not even be available. While we may regard learned abnormalities as best removed by processes of learning, it is not necessary to know how a response was first acquired in order to change or remove it. We can also not rule out the possibility that certain harmful effects brought about by learning might in some circumstances be improved by chemical or physiological intervention. Until we have a much more comprehensive model of behaviour, knowledge or speculation about how a given condition was produced can provide only a very limited guide to therapy: effectiveness must be the overriding criterion.

In the rest of this chapter we will look at some of the ways in which learning can produce maladaptive effects, describe and assess the effectiveness of therapeutic procedures based on learning, and briefly compare this *behavioural* approach to some forms of psychotherapy.

## Learning maladaptive behaviour

If we think of learning as an essentially *adaptive* process, it may seem strange that it should ever produce behaviour that works out to the disadvantage of the learner. Yet this is what can happen. Before looking at some examples, let us briefly examine whether it really does involve a contradiction.

Chapter 3 was devoted to considering learning within the wider context of evolutionary adaptation. It was suggested that the capacity to learn must itself be regarded as an evolutionary development, one that enables organisms to cope with changes in their environment that are too rapid to be 'tracked' by the processes of natural selection. But even learning produces changes that have some degree of permanence, and, depending on content and circumstances, some instances of learning can produce longer lasting effects than others. 'Imprinting' provides a special example, and it copes well with the way in which the pattern of experience of many animals usually unfolds. But if the pattern should for some reason be radically different – e.g. isolation, or exposure to an 'unsuitable' model during a critical developmental period, then the early learning may prove a later handicap. More generally, the fact that a characteristic or capacity confers an overall (reproductive) advantage on a species does not mean that it must therefore produce beneficial consequences for all individuals under all circumstances – especially if subsequent conditions are atypical of the conditions prevailing at the time the characteristic was selected.

## Fear, phobias and avoidance learning

Being afraid of dangerous situations is a perfectly normal and adaptive phenomenon: it tends to make animals and people keep away, or take other precautions, and so avoid injury. Fear can become maladaptive if it is unusually intense; if it leads to the avoidance of situations that are not really dangerous – that may in fact be useful and important – for the individual; or if it occurs without having an *object*, as a diffuse and often acute anxiety. Intense, unreasonable fears of specific objects or circumstances are called *phobias*. Fear or anxiety without object is a common feature of many forms of mental disturbance, so that the acquisition and the extinction of fear is of considerable interest in trying to understand and deal with such conditions.

In Chapter 2 we briefly discussed the classical conditioning account of acquired fear, as well as its supposed role in the relatively long-lasting effects of *avoidance learning*. The experimental illustration of the process involves coupling a 'neutral' stimulus or situation with a painful experience; this produces a conditioned fear response to the stimulus. If a selected action, like moving away, results in escaping the pain, it quickly becomes established; if acting in time avoids the pain altogether then such an avoidance response is often very stable. One proposed explanation of this stability was that the avoidance response reduces the conditioned fear, and thus continues to be reinforced. But the conditioned fear should extinguish – and indeed when an avoidance response is well established, there is usually little sign of any fear to be reduced. A more cognitive account was suggested: the structure of the situation can prevent the learner from discovering that the original relationship between stimulus and pain no longer holds. Clearly this can be maladaptive: the restaurant that served the contaminated food may be under new and more hygenic management.

Avoiding restaurants, even without good cause, hardly ranks as pathological. But there are many people whose aversion for certain situations, animals or objects is so intense that it cripples their lives. Agoraphobia, for example, which is the fear of open spaces, and which results, in extreme cases, in the sufferer being unable to leave the house, is a fairly common phobia which restricts behaviour in a severe and very obvious way. Could such phobias be the result of avoidance learning?

There is no shortage of evidence, both from experimental studies on animals and from human clinical reports, that painful or traumatic experiences *can* give rise to long-lasting aversions. That does not mean, however, that all instances of such aversions must have been brought about in this way. Most people who are afraid of spiders, snakes or rats, even those whose fear is 'excessive', have never had a painful experience involving these animals. There are of course other ways in which people can acquire fear – by direct instruction that something is dangerous, and, more powerfully, by *example*, by witnessing the fearful reactions of others. This is certainly a learning process, albeit of a more complex kind than that envisaged in the avoidance-learning model. But why should these particular instructions or examples arise in the first place, even in parts of the world where spiders are harmless, and dangerous snakes rare or altogether absent?

The chances of being seriously injured or killed by a car are much greater, at least in this country, than coming to harm as the result of meeting a spider. Yet there are relatively few cases of car phobia. Many people have been subjected to very real and repeated danger, such as in combat conditions or during air-raids, but the instances of long-lasting subsequent anxiety are surprisingly few. By contrast, the objects of common phobias are on the whole not dangerous (in many parts of the world); nevertheless, some people are intensely frightened by them, and a great many more find them disquieting or distasteful. It looks as though there may be an inherited predisposition to be afraid or uneasy in certain situations – close confinement, darkness, the presence of certain types of animal – so that it takes relatively little encouragement for some degree of fear to become estab- lished. It has been suggested, in fact, that what happens in the case of most people is the gradual extinction or habituation of innate fear responses to these situations or objects, given that the environment does not reinforce them.

All this does still not explain why *some* people develop very intense fears, when others do not. There is seldom systematic evidence of either direct or vicarious 'genuinely frightening' ex- periences to provide the starting point of phobic case histories. This does not rule out learning as a contributory factor. On a cognitive view, the effect of an experience depends at least in part on the subject's *interpretation* of what is going on. For ex- ample, once you believe that people are threatening or conspiring against you, it becomes much easier to 'find' confirming in- stances; you may also begin to behave in ways that provoke the genuine article. This makes the progress of learning a highly idiosyncratic business, and it can lead by easy stages to a view of the world that is both distorted and stable: a personal and much more complex version of the avoidance-learning phenomenon.

Such personal idiosyncratic learning will of course also depend on a host of early individual differences – which may include differences in susceptibility to frightening and to rewarding stimuli – interacting with the environment. If at some stage this leads into a maladaptive blind alley it is rarely possible to identify with confidence a particular characteristic or sequence of events as the main 'cause' of the deviation. Does this imply a corres- ponding obstacle to therapy?

In general it does not. As we have indicated, responses can be maintained by reinforcements different in timing and quality from those under which they were acquired and behaviour can be changed by changing its *present* contingencies.

## Techniques of behaviour therapy

Several techniques for producing therapeutic behavioural change have been devised, to some extent reflecting the range of problems presented by patients but also based in part on different emphases given to aspects of learning theory. People who seek help because of behavioural problems may not, of course, fall neatly into a category for which a given technique is indicated, and in describing methods of behaviour therapy and their applications we do not intend to imply that an ideal procedure exists for each patient. Much depends on the therapist's judgement, his skill in diagnosis and his ability to adapt the existing techniques to the particular (and sometimes complex) needs of each patient.

Nevertheless, distinct procedures exist and a given behavioural disorder may indicate one technique rather than another. It is tempting to start with phobias, for which several techniques exist, not because phobic problems are the most widely treated conditions but because they are at least superficially easy to define and they represent, in an extreme form, a condition which is shared by many people in a minor way.

Many people suffering from phobias to a disabling degree appear to show no other obvious abnormal characteristics and the removal of such irrational fears often significantly increases the person's ability to live a normal life. One technique for dealing with abnormal fear has been developed by Wolpe (1958). This technique, called *reciprocal inhibition*, aims to replace anxiety in the phobic situation with a new learned response which will be incompatible with the development of fear.

## Reciprocal inhibition

One difficulty found when attempting to help people learn a new response to an anxiety-producing stimulus is to induce them to approach it. The abnormal behaviour is essentially a set of avoidance responses which has been developed over time to protect the person from the anxiety developing in the critical situation, and which effectively prevent him from approaching it.

The process developed by Wolpe involves systematic 'desensitizations' to anxiety-producing situations, starting with relatively innocuous stimuli and gradually moving up to more fearful situations. The essential first step is to discover the situations in which anxiety arises and their order of seriousness. For example, a person suffering from social phobia may be most afraid of addressing a large public meeting and least afraid (while still somewhat anxious) of talking to one stranger. Then these situations are ranked in order of seriousness and the therapist's aim is to desensitize them, starting with the least serious, by prevailing upon the patient to respond, in the presence of the stimulus, in a manner which is incompatible with anxiety. A suitable response for this purpose would be to relax when the stimulus is present, the patient being trained in methods of relaxation before beginning the treatment proper. The patient may thus be asked to talk to a stranger at the same time as he deliberately practises a method of relaxing which inhibits some of the physical concomitants of anxiety. When this has been repeated several times, the anxiety-producing properties of the stimulus decreasing all the time, the patient is exposed to the next (more serious) item on the list of fear-producing situations. Using such a gradual desensitization procedure, people suffering from claustrophobia have been brought to the point where they can remain in a small, dark locked room without anxiety.

Relaxation is not the only anxiety-inhibitor used, although various therapists have found it effective; assertive and other types of responses incompatible with anxiety may be used. Nor is it always necessary to use real stimuli to provoke anxiety; imagined situations can be used if it is difficult or inconvenient to use real-life situations. The details of the procedure obviously depend largely on the pattern of symptoms presented by the patient.

A slight variant of this procedure was used by Öst (1978) to treat phobias involving thunderstorms. It is, of course, impossible to provide thunder and lightning as required for treatment sessions and it was decided to simulate these as realistically as possible. Öst used a tape-recording of a thunderstorm together with a slide projector showing pictures of thunder clouds, the devices being linked in such a manner that when the thunder sounded distant the clouds were seen to be far away and when the thunder was loud, the clouds loomed close. For the lightning a neon lamp similarly connected was used.

One of his patients was a 64-year–old woman who had been afraid of thunderstorms since early childhood and seemed to have acquired this fear from her parents who took excessive precautions when a thunderstorm was forecast. She was unable to remain alone outdoors when there was a prospect of thunder, she listened compulsively to weather reports in the season for thunderstorms and, during an actual storm, experienced severe anxiety, headaches, heart palpitations and an urge to urinate.

The procedure used to desensitize thunder was for her to experience the simulated storm while listening at the same time to a recording of her favourite music. She was instructed to switch on the simulation as soon as she felt calm and then gradually increase the volume until it became uncomfortable, at which point she was told to lower the volume or terminate the simulation. The music was played continuously during this time. When she felt calmer she restarted the display.

When she was able to tolerate the full volume of thunder the music volume was reduced slightly. She had thirteen treatment sessions at the end of which she could tolerate the entire simulated storm without music and with no discomfort. At a follow-up session four months later the patient had experienced several real thunderstorms without her former fears; she reported that 'for the first time for as long as she could remember, the summer had been enjoyable'.

This treatment has been used with considerable success in a wide variety of phobic disorders. Excessive fears of lice, examinations (it should be emphasized that a phobic disorder is characterized by *severe* fear, slight fear of lice and examinations might be regarded as reasonable), toads, injections and tunnels have all been reduced by this treatment. Reduction of fear has often been accompanied by generalized improvement in adjustment and usually no substitute symptoms occur. The overall improvement might be explained as a reaction to the removal of an embarrassing symptom or, as is sometimes argued, the therapeutic procedure itself might be more pervasive in its effects, less restricted to the behavioural manifestation than is usually accepted.

The theoretical justification for the use of reciprocal inhibition has been, as the name of the technique indicates, that one set of responses, including the onset of anxiety and related avoidance behaviour, is replaced by another. The importance of relaxation and graded exposure to the fear-inducing stimuli has been emphasized, the idea being that the inhibition of anxiety in the presence of a mildly frightening stimulus will generalize to the next item in the hierarchy, which in turn is desensitized, and so on until the patient can tolerate previously severe anxiety-producing situations. While the technique is usually successful, the reasons for its success have been questioned. It has been claimed that the importance of the therapist's role has been underestimated, the idea being that the support and encouragement provided by the therapist himself is of more significance than the *technique* of behaviour therapy he is using. While it is clearly necessary that the initial diagnosis is made by experienced behaviour therapists, and expertise is required for the design of treatment programmes, it seems unlikely that the personal attributes of the behaviour therapist contribute much to the success of treatment. Baker, Cohen and Saunders (1973) treated patients suffering from acrophobia (fear of heights) using either a desensitization technique administered by a therapist or one controlled by the patient. The latter consisted of the patient listening to tape-recorded relaxation training together with recordings of fear-arousing events. Both groups of patients improved significantly compared with control patients who had not yet received treatment and the self-administration group showed greater improvement at a follow-up check eight months later than the group treated by the therapist. This does show that the technique itself is effective and perhaps indicates that training patients to administer their own treatment may have greater long-term benefit. It does seem intuitively likely that providing people with the means to modify their own behaviour would help to reduce a sense of dependency on outside causal factors and inculcate greater self-reliance.

Other criticisms of the idea that desensitization works by providing an alternative response have a more solid basis, however. Studies in which the process of reciprocal inhibition is systematically 'dismantled' seem to indicate that the crucial aspect of the process is non-reinforced exposure to the anxiety-producing stimulus. A number of experimental investigations have shown that neither graded exposure to the aversive stimulus nor training in relaxation (the provision of an alternative response) is necessary for phobic behaviour to be extinguished. It may well be, of course, that both these aspects of the full reciprocal inhibition technique are of tactical advantage in easing the introduction of the phobic stimulus to the patient, so that the essential component, the confrontation of the feared object without disastrous consequences, can take place.

Opinion is gaining ground, however, that the essential aspect of treatment for at least some phobic disorders is extensive exposure to the actual situation feared. Emmelkamp, Kuipers and Eggeraat (1978) have shown that walking in busy streets for up to an hour and a half at a time, shopping in supermarkets and using buses and restaurants (all situations producing anxiety in their patients) were much more effective in reducing phobic responses than equivalent time discussing the irrationality of beliefs and attempting to create positive self-instructions.

The investigators used a 'cross-over' design in their study in which half the patients started with exposure to the real situation and half with the discussion sessions and then both groups switched to the other procedure. This permits evaluations of the effectiveness of each technique to be made without reference to the particular characteristics of the individuals concerned.

This particular study is of interest in that it was designed to make a direct comparison between a method of treatment involving non-reinforced exposure to the real situation with one involving discussions intended to produce 'cognitive restructuring'. The latter would presumably result in the patient thinking differently about the phobic situation and, effectively, realizing that it is not in fact dangerous, whereupon fear of it would cease. As we have seen, in this experiment the process designed to produce cognitive restructuring was not as effective as direct exposure to the phobic situation. But, paradoxically, a number of subjects in this study reported spontaneously that their 'thoughts' had undergone a much greater change during prolonged exposure to the feared situation than during discussion intended to produce cognitive restructuring.

It may be that this method of treatment, which is in effect simply placing people in a situation which produces fear, and has been described here as 'non-reinforced exposure to the phobic stimulus', in the learning theory manner, may produce its effects by 'cognitive restructuring'; essentially people may simply come to realize fully that the situation is not dangerous and they thus become unafraid. Such an interpretation obviously casts doubt on 'unreconstructed' learning theory explanations of the success of this procedure but, as we have already seen, wider, and especially more cognitively orientated explanations are currently being extensively used.

This direct approach to the treatment of phobias, usually termed 'flooding' or 'implosive therapy', is quite widely used. The explicit aim is to produce a high level of anxiety while preventing 'escape' and is often continued for quite prolonged periods. Stern and Marks (1973) have shown that one two-hour session is more effective than four half-hour sessions in the treatment of agoraphobics and also showed incidently that real exposure is more effective than imagining the feared situation, as one might expect. While still not used as extensively as systematic desensitization, the procedure does seem effective especially with very severe phobias. Equivalent methods have also been used occasionally to treat compulsive behaviour, especially where this is related to anxiety produced by specific objects.

Meyer (1966) treated two patients exhibiting ritualistic compulsive washing by urging them to handle 'contaminating' objects while preventing them from carrying out compulsive actions such as hand-washing. This was also interpreted by

Meyer as a situation in which the patients' expectations were modified rather than as a simple extinction process.

Extinction has been invoked in behaviour therapy, however, in a technique known as negative practice, in which the patient repeatedly emits an undesired response during the practice sessions. This is a direct application of the experimental observation that learned responses continually evoked in the absence of reinforcement decay and ultimately disappear. When this process is used in behaviour therapy the ability to perform the response voluntarily typically declines and the expectation is that the involuntary and undesired emission of the response – the symptom – will similarly decline.

### Negative practice

This procedure is most suitable for those cases of abnormal behaviour where the most prominent characteristic is a clearly specific overt response. One of the clearest examples of the successful use of the method is provided in early reports by Yates (1960) and Jones (1960) in which the patient was afflicted by four severe tics.

Each of these was treated as a separate response, negative practice being carried out in all four of them. No other treatment was given during this period. Several different detailed procedures were used during the course of treatment (mainly to find the most effective forms of practice) but it may be sufficient to indicate the method eventually adopted for the stomach-contraction tic, which was the most troublesome.

The patient practised the tic as frequently as possible during a period of one hour then rested for a week. During the next week the tic was practised for a short time each day. Then another practice period was held and so on. Seven such one-hour sessions were held and the number of responses made by the patient, the number of voluntary tics emitted during each hour, declined from 259 in the first hour to 12 in the seventh. An eighth session was discontinued after seventeen minutes, during which no responses were observed.

These results cannot, of course, be attributed to fatigue because of the considerable intervals between practice periods, and they represent the almost complete extinction of the voluntary response. Similar results were obtained with the other three tics. While this demonstrates that negative practice can have considerable effect on the ability of a patient to make a given response at will, the important question is whether or not the involuntary emission of the response declines similarly, whether in fact the symptom is reduced.

Although total behaviour throughout treatment was not quantifiable with the same accuracy as behaviour during treatment sessions all available evidence indicates that the patient's condition was much improved. The tics declined markedly during treatment, the patient's emotional condition improved and there was no evidence of the development of alternative symptoms.

At a psychiatric examination some time after completion of treatment the patient was classed as much improved compared with her condition prior to treatment and, by all counts, this form of therapy seems to have produced significant amelioration of the condition. Yates and Jones based this treatment on Hullian learning theory (extinction was seen as the growth of conditioned inhibition) and many detailed predictions from this theory were confirmed by systematic variation of conditions during the therapeutic process.

This procedure has been used in other cases where the major presenting problem was a gross distortion of normal behaviour. Agras and Marshall (1965) used negative practice to treat two patients suffering from spasmodic torticollis, sometimes called 'wry neck', in which the patient holds his head at an extreme angle and has difficulty in moving it. Again the treatment involved the patient in duplicating the tic as many times as possible in each treatment period and also practising at home. This also proved a relatively successful procedure. So far we have discussed the removal of symptoms, either inappropriate fears, inconvenient avoidance behaviour or embarrassing tics. But much research in learning has been concerned with the power of positive reinforcement to increase the behavioural repertoire of the subject and this approach also has its place in therapeutic behaviour modification.

The role of positive reinforcement has been discussed extensively in earlier chapters in an attempt to develop a model for the process of behavioural acquisition but in therapeutic behaviour change a more pragmatic approach is used, developed mainly from the work of Premack. He demonstrated that any highly probable response will reinforce a less probable response, or, to put this into more acceptable English, a person will do something he doesn't want to do on condition that he is allowed to do something he does want to do. Thus rats will run in a treadmill in order to be allowed to drink when they are thirsty but they will also drink in order to be allowed to run in a treadmill if they are confined but not thirsty.

Once the therapist has determined what it is the patient would like to do he can (if the patient has given permission for his environment to be controlled temporarily by the therapist) arrange that the opportunity to carry out the pleasurable behaviour is contingent on carrying out prior actions which the patient is reluctant to perform.

Thus claustrophobia might be treated by making one hour's television viewing conditional on walking 100 yards in the open air. Such treatment obviously requires control over the patient's life and usually involves hospitalization.

Positive reinforcement has not only been used for the treatment of individual examples of neurotic behaviour where the patient has insight into his condition and is able to co-operate with the therapist. It has also been used quite widely to treat groups of patients suffering from the effects of prolonged hospitalization and the system has been described as setting up a 'token economy'.

When people have been in psychiatric hospitals for many years they develop a condition known as institutionalization which is characterized by apathy, inability or unwillingness to make decisions and in general an inability to cope with life outside an institutional setting and even including, it is sometimes claimed, a special stance and gait.

Patients who were originally admitted to hospital on the grounds of extreme psychotic behaviour but who have ultimately been stabilized by the use of anti-psychotic drugs (or have spontaneously improved) are often unsuited for life outside the hospital because of this secondary 'disease' of institutionalization.

The problem of rehabilitating such long-term patients then becomes that of retraining them to act, to behave independently and to take over decision-making for themselves. Token economies are reinforcement contingency situations set up for a group of patients in hospital whereby all 'privileges', such as access to recreational facilities, cigarettes, permission to go outside the hospital and any other pleasurable opportunities normally open to them, are withdrawn and made accessible only on payment of tokens. These tokens are obtainable by carrying out certain specified actions such as getting up in the morning, washing, cleaning the ward or any other activity appropriate to the patient's level of functioning.

These methods have proved successful in dramatically changing the range of behaviour carried out by long-term patients and, when combined with sensitive and well-designed support programmes, in maintaining them outside the hospital.

The psychotic conditions, notably schizophrenia, are typically much more intractable than the phobic and other 'neurotic' problems we have been discussing and token economies are not indicated until patients are considered to be suffering primarily from the *effects* of hospitalization. At this point they are useful but in order to produce permanent rehabilitation they must be combined with adequate after-care.

Positive reinforcement, or its absence, has been allocated a major role in the development of certain depressive or 'helpless' states by Seligman (1975) who suggests that depressive illness (and perhaps the secondary state of institutionalization we have been discussing) can result from experiences of ineffectiveness, can, in other words, be learned.

### Learning and effectiveness

Most of us expect that our actions will have some effective result. We may not always succeed totally in any current endeavour, but we do not anticipate that our attempts to influence events will meet with complete failure, and we certainly do not expect that all our efforts will be nugatory, pointless and devoid of results.

When this does happen, when nothing we do seems to have any effect, and particularly when this occurs repeatedly, we may learn to feel helpless. Seligman identified this 'learned helplessness' as a significant factor in the development of depressive illness, the 'giving up' characteristic of depression being seen as almost a rational consequence of an apparent failure to influence the world.

The idea of learned helplessness developed as a result of studies of avoidance learning in animals and may be regarded as one of the stronger justifications for studying behaviour over a wide range of species. We have, in this book, pointed out both the specific differences in learning readiness from species to species and also some of the broad similarities in overall learning processes among species; learned helplessness seems to be one of these.

A typical experiment of this type exposed one group of dogs to a series of electric shocks which were inescapable. No action on the part of the dog could cause the shock to stop until the experimenter switched it off. Subsequently an avoidance-learning situation was set up in which dogs could learn to avoid an electric shock by jumping over a barrier on presentation of a signal. 'Untreated' dogs, those not given the prior unavoidable shocks, learned this skill readily, but about two-thirds of those given previous unavoidable shocks could not learn to escape or avoid the shock in the new situation. An interesting aspect of such experiments is that the unavoidable shock experience is not equivalent to training in passiveness. If *any* response, even that of doing absolutely nothing, controls the extent of shock, then the animals can learn to make a new, active avoidance response when appropriate. It is only when the events in the external world, in this case the duration of shock, are not contingent on *any* behaviour carried out by the animal that learned helplessness develops.

Even more dramatic effects have been demonstrated by producing a state of helplessness in rats. If wild rats are placed in water they will swim for sixty hours before drowning, whereas, if they are held in the hand until they become immobile before being placed in the water they will swim for only half an hour (Richter, 1957).

It has now been shown in a number of animal studies that a previous experience of being unable to effect events causes a learning disability in a subsequent situation where learning *is* possible, and two obvious questions arise: first, does this apply to humans, and, second, is the process reversible? Short-term experimental studies do indicate that humans are susceptible to this type of learning. Tasks such as proof-reading and problem solving, when carried out under noisy conditions, are carried out better when people believe they can switch off the loud noise, *even when they do not do so*, than when they believe the noise is outside their control. Personality tendencies to attribute the results of actions to external versus internal factors are also relevant, those people who characteristically believe their actions influence events being less affected by prior failure in new learning situations.

These, of course, are experimental results in which the consequences are not necessarily of great importance to the people concerned. To relate such processes to the onset of serious depressive illnesses is much more difficult and one is necessarily reduced to clinical reports. Seligman cites many instances in which the apparent sudden loss of control leads to depression and even death. Prisoners of war promised and then denied repatriation, aged persons forced rather than choosing to go into old peoples' homes, appear to suffer from their failure to control events. It is still not certain that learned helplessness is a major cause of depressive illness, but the evidence that failure to exercise control can transfer to new situations and that it may well affect depression in humans is becoming very convincing.

Can such processes be reversed? Again for conclusive evidence one must turn to animal studies. There are methods of 'immunizing' animals against the development of helplessness or curing it if it has developed. If dogs are allowed to escape shock, before being exposed to unavoidable shock, they can subsequently learn to escape when the situation again becomes within their control. And dogs which have not had this prior immunization, but have been rendered helpless by uncontrollable shock, can be 'cured' in the new learning situation by being forced to cross to the other side of the box about twenty-five to thirty times. Demonstration that these are solutions, as it were, can overcome the inability to act.

It would clearly be inappropriate to extrapolate this model too far, on the assumption that it provides the sole answer to depressive illness. Indeed it has been criticized (e.g. Rippere, 1977) on the grounds that it places too little emphasis on cognitive aspects of human functioning and particularly that it fails to stress sufficiently the self-help techniques which many depressives already use. What does seem clear, however, is that animals in serious situations, and humans in short-term experimental situations, can learn that their behaviour can have no apparent effect on the environment and that this learning can transfer to new situations. Equally, such learning can be reversed. The relevance of such results for human depressive illness cannot be ignored even if its significance were for only a proportion of cases.

Many kinds of abnormal behaviour involve the patient in a conflict situation; he is both attracted and repelled by the same activity or set of circumstances. In cases of phobia, anxiety has the upper hand, and the patient avoids certain actions or situations, to his own long-term disadvantage. Alcoholism, drug addiction and various forms of sexual disorder usually involve conflict in which the *approach* tendency is dominant, i.e. characteristic activity produces reinforcement whose effect out-weighs – at critical times – the misery and distress which resulting physical conditions or social disapproval usually produce. Society often tries to deal with conflicts of this kind by intensifying its disapproval – as where the activity is classified as criminal, thereby increasing the severity of punishment. This is rarely successful even in inhibiting the undesirable behaviour, and certainly does nothing to resolve the conflict. The learning models considered earlier give some clues to their failure.

The effectiveness of reinforcers, both positive and negative, depends critically on their timing. In conflict situations timing can override other considerations of magnitude, and a small reward, close at hand, may loom larger than a distant though more serious punishment. If we try at all to inhibit behaviour by an increase in anxiety, this can more effectively be done by careful timing than by simply increasing the intensity of aversive stimulation. The consequences of 'going on a bender' – even if they follow more quickly and more certainly than those of heavy smoking – are still too delayed to produce avoidance on the next time round. We could expect greater success if disaster could be arranged to follow drinking more closely.

The drug apomorphine produces nausea and has been used in behaviour-therapy approaches to alcoholism. The drug is injected and shortly before nausea develops the patient is induced to drink alcohol. If alcohol closely precedes nausea on a number of occasions, it comes to produce it as a conditioned stimulus, and some limited success has been achieved by this procedure in developing an avoidance of alcohol. It is, however, crude, not just literally but also methodologically, as an example of avoidance conditioning. This general approach to behavioural change, using unpleasant stimuli as an essential part of the treatment, is known generally as 'aversion therapy' and has been used in various forms to treat intractable behavioural orientations which a patient wishes to change.

### Aversion therapy

In its attempts to deal with unsuitable 'approach' behaviour aversion therapy, like other forms of behaviour therapy, may be more appropriate when the condition being treated is a highly specific one. Marks and Gelder (1967) have used the technique with some success in the treatment of transvestites and fetishists (patients who gain sexual satisfaction from wearing clothes of the opposite sex or where sexual orientation is towards personal articles belonging to the opposite sex).

They used electric shock, at first presented when the patient imagined himself performing the abnormal sexual behaviour and subsequently when actually performing it. During the course of this treatment sexual arousal was measured by using the penile plethysmograph which indicates the diameter of the penis and patients' attitudes were measured by the somewhat more pedestrian semantic differential technique.

They concentrated on the deviant behaviour in a highly specific manner, by reducing the response to one female garment, for example, before proceeding to the next.

The period during which treatment was given lasted two weeks and at the conclusion of that period abnormal behaviour had completely ceased. While two patients showed a partial regression within a year this still represents a remarkable degree of success compared with other methods of treatment particularly as four of these patients had suffered from their abnormal condition for over twenty years.

In a subsequent report, Marks, Gelder and Bancroft (1970) showed that among a sample of twenty-four patients examined two years after treatment those previously suffering from transvestism, fetishism and sadomasochism were all much improved compared with their condition prior to treatment, the emission of abnormal responses ranging from significantly less than before therapy to none at all.

Obviously the treatment of abnormal sexual behaviour raises ethical and social questions in addition to questions of effective procedure. It is clear that the desires of the patient should be paramount in almost all such cases and this applies particularly to the 'treatment' of homosexuality. Many homosexuals do not regard themselves as abnormal (and presumably therefore seldom seek treatment) but some do want to change their sexual orientation and in such cases it seems appropriate that treatment is available.

Feldman and MacCulloch (1971) have devised a number of techniques integrating aversion therapy for homosexuality closely and in detail with complex behavioural patterns. In one form of treatment used by them an attempt was made to combat the interest-arousing character of photographs of men for male homosexuals. Patients first individually ranked a set of male photographs in order of attractiveness. The least attractive was then projected on a screen, the patient being able to switch it off at will. It was explained that he should leave the picture as long as he found it sexually attractive. If he did not switch it off within eight seconds, however, he received an electric shock of sufficient strength to make him switch off immediately. Patients were also asked to accompany switching off by saying 'No'.

Once complete avoidance for a particular picture had been established, a schedule of intermittent reinforcement was introduced, aimed at increasing resistance to extinction. For example, in some cases the patient's attempt to switch off failed, the picture remained and he received a brief shock. In others the picture remained for a variable period, but eventually disappeared within the eight seconds, achieving avoidance. When the patient reported indifference or dislike of the slide, and switched it off almost at once on each presentation, the next slide was introduced and the procedure repeated.

Feldman and MacCulloch also utilized patients' relief when male slides left the screen in an attempt to make women more acceptable. Photographs of women were occasionally introduced as the male slide was switched off, thus being associated with anxiety reduction. Patients were also allowed to ask for the return of a female slide, this being a kind of guarantee against the appearance of the shock-producing male. However, such requests paid off only intermittently and in a random manner, so as to increase resistance to extinction.

Results were strongly encouraging, even without allowing for the brevity of the treatment, which averaged around fifteen sessions. Most patients, and particularly the younger ones, reported during follow-up, marked increasing *movement away from* homosexual interest, and growing interest in the opposite sex. Despite obvious difficulties, the therapists tried to achieve a greater than usual approximation between the treatment and real situations. Photographs of real people, both male and female, and provided by the patient, were used for preference. Attention was given to the scheduling of experience, and to the removal of at least some of the emotional obstacles to the development of alternative behaviour.

Feldman and MacCulloch (1971) also compared their aversion

therapy technique with a classical conditioning procedure in which the subjects' behaviour did not affect the presentation of stimuli and with a psychotherapy programme. Both the learning procedures were superior to psychotherapy which in this study produced effectively no improvement. They also showed that behaviour therapy was more effective with 'secondary' homosexuals (those with previous heterosexual experience) than with 'primary' homosexuals who had no prior heterosexual experience.

Two things arise from this. First, it seems important in such cases not merely to reduce the incidence of undesired or deviant behaviour, but also, by increasing social skills and providing the opportunity for their use, to enable patients to engage in heterosexual behaviour. Permanent change probably only comes about when stable heterosexual habits are developed. Second, it reminds us, if we needed reminding, that all patients are different. The advantages of behaviour therapy in stemming from a systematic body of theory should not blind us to individual differences and the resulting need for careful diagnosis in each individual case.

Meyer and Bartlett (1976) have pointed out that 'Therapy aims at bringing about alterations in these (maladaptive) patterns towards greater adaptation and to this end, each and every therapeutic aim must inevitably be individually designed, and hence intrinsically unique, if it is to be most effective'.

## Effectiveness of behaviour therapy techniques

Attempts to evaluate behaviour therapy may take several forms. It can be compared with the 'spontaneous recovery' rate – the proportion of people who seem to get better without any therapeutic intervention – or with other forms of treatment such as psychoanalysis. It could even presumably be evaluated in terms of the soundness of its theoretical basis.

We have already in previous chapters given some attention to the adequacy of learning theories in explaining phenomena for which they were specifically designed and have indicated both that they are continuing to develop and that their application in specific areas is flexible so we will not discuss them further here.

We also cannot attempt here an evaluation of psychoanalytic theories. Certainly therapeutic methods deriving from them, which often involve hundreds of treatment sessions, are time-consuming and expensive when compared with the methods of behaviour therapy.

On the other hand, therapy based on learning theory has been criticized on the basis that it leads to an oversimplified view of neurosis and may lead to an undue emphasis on easily observable behaviour. Nevertheless behaviour therapy has achieved considerable success by its concentration on 'symptoms'. Psychoanalytic approaches, despite their enormous cost in time, have produced entirely unspectacular results, and a more direct attack on symptoms seems wholly justified. Of much greater immediate significance are the success rates of therapists using such techniques as we have described. The figures vary from quite moderate rates to Wolpe's claim of 90 per cent of patients cured or much improved.

One study has shown that 61 per cent of patients receiving behaviour therapy improved compared with 44 per cent of control (spontaneous recovery) subjects showing improvement. Some of this variation may be due to differences in standards of assessment, but what seems fairly clear is that some types of neurotic symptoms respond more to treatment by behaviour therapy than others, and there may be variations in the proportions of these in groups of patients treated by different therapists. In general patients whose symptoms are relatively specific seem to respond best to behaviour therapy. Phobias in particular can be significantly lessened by behaviour therapy, while alcoholism and sexual disorders, among the conditions which would quite frequently be treated by behaviour therapy, seem to respond less satisfactorily; although, as we have seen, some reports suggest that these more complex conditions are also becoming amenable to treatment.

With certain types of cases, then, the success of behaviour

therapy seems quite substantial and this is as much as can be said for any method of treating behaviour disorders. Further improvements might follow a more exact specification of what precisely is learned in neurosis, but this might be dependent on advances in learning theory in general.

# 10. Learning Theory and Education

We began this book by contrasting an idea of learning based on our experience in schools with the psychologist's notion of a very basic and widespread adaptive process, and the specific practical contexts of educational research with the highly simplified and abstract character of most psychological experiments on learning. Should we expect theories that emerge from these psychological preoccupations and methods to have any useful implications for teaching and training? We have certainly come to expect such pay-offs in the natural sciences, where experimental conditions are usually far removed from everyday experience, and results often have no obvious practical relevance – yet they have over the years contributed to a complete change in our way of life, not to say death.

Comparisons between psychology and the natural sciences sometimes lead to the observation that psychology is simply several hundred years behind in its development. While this may well be true, it also carries with it the suggestion that we should expect future development to take place along broadly similar lines – towards global, relatively coherent theories, with increased powers of detailed prediction and control. We believe this view to be mistaken, and its discussion will provide the starting point for the final chapter. For the moment, we simply want to draw attention to one aspect of the impressive practical achievements that we associate with scientific progress – one that is particularly relevant to the utilization of psychological theories.

In the natural sciences, the application of theory to 'real life' nearly always involves the construction of special conditions which permit the 'laws' investigated in the laboratory to produce desired results. Machines and other devices, from radio-sets to nuclear reactors, are specially built parts of the world from which the effects of undesirable variables are excluded and where things are deliberately arranged so that the rest interact according to some plan. It is primarily in such 'artificial islands' that events can be accurately predicted and controlled. Dealing with events 'in the wild' – the weather, say – presents much greater problems; though here too considerable progress is being made, at least as far as prediction is concerned.

## The application of psychological theories

This approach to the application of theory, the creation of highly controlled environments which in many ways mimic the conditions of the experimental laboratory, raises some interesting problems when it comes to theories of learning. We will have to see how far it has been possible to go along this road, towards the development of a *technology of learning*. At the same time, a great deal of learning inevitably goes on in relatively unconstrained and uncontrolled situations, and for the present purpose, we will include 'ordinary' school learning in the latter category. To what extent is it possible to use ideas derived from learning theories in such circumstances – can they, in other words, help people to *teach*, in the more traditional sense of the word?

There is also an aspect of 'application' which does not arise in the natural sciences, and which unavoidably interacts with the approaches already mentioned – the *control* over the learning process, and over the selection of the circumstances in which it occurs, that is exercised by the *learner*. In the present context this means that the theory can be used, not only *on* him, but *by* him. But the issue of control also has general implications for any model of behaviour which traditional learning theories have either denied altogether, or failed to recognize as fundamental.

## A technology of learning

There are two aspects of this idea that need to be distinguished. There is educational technology in the usual sense – the utilization of apparatus and devices, from audio-visual aids to microprocessors. It is the use of a technology based on a variety of *other* disciplines in the service of education. But this is not what is meant by 'technology of learning' in the way that phrase has been used, for example by B. F. Skinner (1956, 1971). He is talking about using *psychological* principles in the construction of an environment which will optimize learning. The use of the term 'technology' is intended to underline his claim that these principles are sufficiently clear, and well established, to be used in a systematic way – much as principles of electronics and logical-circuit design can be used to build a computer.

These two senses of 'technology of learning' do of course often coincide, as when specially designed learning environments use machines of one kind or another for their implementation. One reason for Skinner's considerable influence on early developments in this field is that his analysis of the learning process lent itself relatively easily to mechanization. Another, and perhaps more important, reason was his persistent and articulate conviction that his ideas did in fact provide a comprehensive account of all learning and behaviour. His constant readiness to make prescriptions for reshaping the whole of society and culture, apart from producing widespread irritation and ridicule, also helped to maintain a militant enthusiasm among his followers, which fed into the *programmed learning* and associated *teaching machine* movement.

The great expectations for the potential of programmed learning, shared at the time by the authors, have turned out to be ill-founded. The replacement of teaching machines by computers has not only involved an advance in hardware technology, but has been accompanied by fresh thinking about the processes of learning and of instruction. *Computer Aided Instruction* (CAI), or, with a different emphasis, *Computer Aided Learning* (CAL), at least where this involves the attempt to develop *Intelligent*

*Teaching Systems* (ITS), increasingly relies on an approach to learning based on *Artificial Intelligence* (AI). The programming effort required to achieve relatively modest results has produced a greater realism in the expectations for widespread practical applications, but hopes remain high. Let us trace some of these developments.

## Programmed learning

The inspiration for programmed learning derived primarily from operant conditioning, especially from the procedure called 'shaping', as used in the first instance and with considerable success on animals (but see also the reports of 'misbehaviour' in Chapter 3). To recapitulate this procedure briefly: starting with the existing 'repertoire' of an animal's responses, we select from among these any that constitute a move, however small, towards the behaviour that we are aiming at. Reinforcing these whenever they occur not only increases their relative frequency, but also shifts the whole range of responses surrounding them. Some of these new responses are likely to be even closer to the behavioural goal, and selective reinforcement will produce a further shift towards it. The art of shaping consists in recognizing and choosing, at each stage of the animal's progress, those responses whose reinforcement will edge the behavioural spectrum towards the final desired achievement.

The main features here are the emphasis on behaviour, as the 'handle' available to the trainer for acting on the animal; the prompt use of reinforcement as the medium of communication; and the *very gradual* change in the criteria for reinforcement as training develops, ensuring that reinforcement will in fact be available most of the time.

When we try to translate these features into a human context, a number of important differences become apparent. The availability of language makes it possible to condense much of the 'pointing' function of reinforcement into a few verbal instructions and explanations (remember, however, the limitations of words when dealing with motor skills). When it comes to reinforcement, if we can assume that the learner shares the broad objectives of the trainer, it should be enough to provide confirmation of progress – 'knowledge of results', as discussed in the chapter on skill. Here too, this confirmation could either be provided by the teacher, or preferably things could be arranged so that the learner is able to assess his own performance.

It might be felt that the use of verbal explanation obviates the need for positive action by the learner altogether – i.e. as an integral component of the learning process. Looking at educational practices, there is still quite a lot of emphasis on the purely receptive and passive aspects of learning. The importance of *doing something* is acknowledged as an essential part of learning a motor skill, but not when it is a question of, say, gaining insight into an argument – here it is often supposed that exposition and explanation suffice. One implication of extending the operant conditioning model to human beings is that at all stages of progress the production of *criterion behaviour*, followed by reinforcement, is an important component of learning, irrespective of content.

Let us take the translation of the 'shaping' concept further. Suppose that we try to map out the 'space' between the learner's initial state of knowledge (defined in appropriate behavioural terms), and the state that is to be achieved, in the form of a detailed series of items of information, test questions and learners' responses to those questions. If we follow those responses by 'knowledge of results', this should gently bring the student (or his behaviour) from starting point to goal. The difference between this and a more conventional teaching plan, which, it might be felt, does more or less the same thing, lies in the very great detail of the mapping, and in the inclusion of frequent student responses in the fabric of the program.

There is a snag, of course. If the program is to be prepared in advance, making allowance not only for the student's responses at all the many test points, but also for *reinforcement*, then we need to be able to make some predictions about those responses. If reinforcement is to be provided by a teacher, the problem is much less acute, since he should be able to cope in a flexible way with a whole range of such responses. But is it possible to specify and incorporate this contribution, or at least an essential part of it, from the very beginning?

The approach to this problem most in line with Skinner's ideas aims at ensuring that the learner will make nothing but correct responses throughout the entire learning sequence, and will in consequence get nothing but positive reinforcement. This is achieved by making the steps very small, not to say trivial, and it produces what is called a *linear* program. On the other hand, we can try to allow for one or more categories of wrong responses at some or all stages of the program, by making the instructional path followed by the student at any point depend on the answer he has just given to the preceding question. Thus a wrong answer might lead to an alternative, perhaps more detailed and differently phrased, explanation of the previous stage; this could in turn incorporate further test questions before returning the student to the 'main stream'. Such an arrangement is called a *branching* program, and can be traced back to the ideas behind the multiple-choice teaching and testing devices first introduced by Pressey (1926).

Whatever the structure of the program, a decision must be made about the form of the learner's response. The main division here is between *freely constructed* and *multiple-choice* answers. The latter arrangement, where the program provides a number of alternative answers out of which the learner must choose, can easily be automated – since the number is limited, the choice can be expressed through the selection, say, of a particular key which then determines the next step in the sequence. But for a freely composed answer to have this effect, requires first some kind of 'understanding' or at least 'recognition'. We take it for granted that people can do this, but it has proved to be a type of achievement that is very difficult, even now, to reproduce in machines.

While multiple-choice answers have advantages for machines (and indeed for human assessors), they have disadvantages for the learner. One is that the learner is quite gratuitously introduced to a whole lot of wrong information. To the extent that the wrong alternatives are plausible, this may be quite seriously confusing. If they are not plausible, the achievement in selecting the correct one is insignificant. Furthermore, recognition and spontaneous construction, regarded as responses, are clearly not the same, and it is recognition alone that is being reinforced. The only way, however, at least for the time being, to incorporate truly free responses into an automated sequence is to place the onus for evaluation on the learner – that is, to show him the correct response after he has made his own, and leave him to make the judgement that will determine what will happen next.

## Programmed texts

It is not necessary, of course, to use machines to implement a learning program of the kind we have discussed. The machine simply moves through a sequence of events – the presentation of information, questions, acceptance of answers. Provided the material is available in some orderly form, this step-by-step movement could equally well be carried out by the learner. A *programmed text* is an ordinary printed book organized in a way that directs the reader through a required sequence of informational material, tests based on that material, and answers for comparison with those the learner has produced in the meantime. This has involved some rather unorthodox layouts (e.g. a programmed text on the analysis of behaviour, written by Holland and Skinner in 1961, which uses the ideas being presented in the method of presentation). The main problem is to allow the subject to formulate a response just before being exposed to the correct one.

Programmed learning, both with teaching machines and in the form of texts, enjoyed a vogue during the 1960s, and many studies comparing particular programs with conventional teaching of the same material produced encouraging results. Levels of achievement in tests were similar, usually attained in a substantially shorter time; retention was better; there were also indications that teaching machines were more effective than programmed texts, and that, on the whole, the more able children benefited disproportionately. But evaluations of educational

methods are notoriously difficult. Not only must one try to
disentangle the effect of the method as such from a whole variety
of factors that may be intimately related to it – such as the
subject matter on which it is being used, the impact of novelty
on the learner or the atmosphere of enthusiasm that often sur-
rounds a new project – but there is frequently disagreement
about the appropriateness of criteria to be used, and indeed
about ultimate objectives. One would only be able to provide a
more considered assessment, as we wrote guardedly in our first
edition, once a substantial number of people, part of whose
learning experience had been of the programmed kind, had
passed into the working population.

In the event, despite the enthusiasm in some quarters, programmed learning never really took off. In retrospect it is not
difficult to find reasons. Once one had got over the novelty of
an unfamiliar layout on the page, or of interacting with a
machine, using a program could, paradoxically, be both hard
work and boring. Effort was required because the student was
constantly asked to answer questions before moving on to new
material. The system could of course be beaten by those who
wanted to, easily in the case of texts and with a little ingenuity
in the case of most machines. But those who were both interested
in learning and appreciated the importance of playing by the
rules were also likely to be people who would be frustrated by
the lack of challenge in a linear program. Branching programs,
by making some limited allowance for different student responses, could afford to ask more searching questions; but in
practice, such programs, at least when set up in a book, were
very cumbersome to use.

There were also the difficulties of production. Structuring a
learning program, trying to optimize the order of presentation
of material, finding suitable (optimal) phrasing, both of informational 'frames' and of questions, identifying possible errors
and composing effective remedial frames – all this makes great
demands, not only on knowledge of the subject matter, but on
an aspect of teaching competence about which the theory behind
programmed learning has nothing to say.

It is a significant omission. Earlier we talked about the 'art' of shaping – the ability to select, at any stage of the training sequence, those aspects of current behaviour whose reinforcement would most effectively edge the whole behaviour spectrum towards the desired goal. In the case of most animal training this can probably be done by trial and error, but doing it efficiently involves some (implicit) knowledge about the organization of the relevant behaviour patterns. When it comes to guiding human cognitive learning, it is obvious that a competence, say to solve quadratic equations, cannot be achieved by cobbling together bits of 'criterion behaviour' in some arbitrary order. This means, however, that a well constructed learning program owes its success in large measure to features of the learning process which the underlying analysis does not even acknowledge.

## Computer aided instruction

Computers, with their associated (tele-)Visual Display Units (VDUs), remove many of the difficulties of implementing and using complex programs.* While the problems of devising or changing the structure do of course remain, it becomes much easier to put it into effect – it just has to be typed in. This means also that editorial and more fundamental revisions can be carried out relatively quickly. Above all the computer removes any restrictions on the potential flexibility of the (learning) program. It has been one of the objectives of CAI from the outset to provide a much more *personalized* learning environment, by making greater allowances for individual variations. (Perhaps the most ambitious project in this category is PLATO at the University of Illinois, see Alpert, 1975.)

* The introduction of computers into the discussion means that we will have to distinguish two different uses of the term 'program': a *computer*-program refers to the set of instructions which determines the operation of the computer on any given occasion; a *learning*-program to a prescribed sequence of informational exchanges between a device and a potential user. In order that a computer may take a user through such a *learning*-program, a *computer*-program will have to be written, to provide the underlying control system. We hope that whenever the word 'program' turns up alone, the context will be a sufficient guide to the intended meaning.

Despite its much greater flexibility, this use of the computer still provides us with little more than a glorified teaching machine. If there are any basic flaws in the theory of programmed learning, a more efficient implementation will not remove them. It is true that even in this form CAI gives some individual attention to the student in the form of feedback which, up to a point, is geared to his particular pattern of responses. But does this go far enough? How would such a system compare to a good, personal, *human* tutor?

The most obvious points of discrepancy lie in the interaction between the student's freely composed responses and the tutor's equally freely and *appropriately* formulated replies. We are dealing here with a *conversation* in which each of the participants poses and tries to solve problems as he goes along: the tutor presents information and asks questions in line with some proposed development of the subject-matter, while the student, by his replies, challenges the tutor to probe further into the understanding that has been displayed, or to intuit the source of misunderstanding. It is a continuing attempt by each party to make sense, within his own conceptual framework, of what is being said by the other.

This is a description of an ideal situation, and no doubt most tutors (and students), even when they have the opportunity for such one-to-one exchanges, fail to realize their full potential. But it serves to bring out the essence of what is missing in the interaction between student and learning-program: this kind of program does not really *understand* anything, either about the student's difficulties, or indeed about the subject-matter it is presenting.

Some people might of course feel that this is an obvious and redundant observation: surely 'understanding' is something peculiar to people, and should never have been *expected* to apply to a program, or to a programmed computer? (Skinnerians, in effect, would deny its meaningful application to people as well.)

Not everyone shares this view. The object of work in *Artificial Intelligence*, as the name suggests, is to create and thereby gain insight into systems that can behave intelligently: acquire and use information, solve problems, recognize things and situations including some that have never been met before, apply and indeed discover rules. There has been some progress in this direction – impressive or disappointing depending on your expectations. One thing though has certainly been achieved: a far better appreciation of the complexity involved in even the simplest of human cognitive operations. One important difference between human and machine problem solving is that existing programs only work within severely restricted domains, compared to the way in which people can, at least in principle, tackle anything. Sceptics might claim that this is just an expression of the unbridgeable gap between the purely 'as if' character of artificial understanding, and the real thing. To others the gap does *appear* to be closing, if perhaps rather slowly.

## Intelligent Teaching Systems

The critics of the 'traditional' approach in CAI have come mainly from workers in AI. Rather than organizing a sequential structure of informational 'frames' and tests, their object is to develop 'Intelligent Teaching Systems'. The general idea is to construct computer programs which approximate a little more closely to the tutor we described earlier, both with respect to an understanding of the subject-matter being taught, and to that of the student in his attempt to come to grips with it. This means not only having a record of 'facts' to which the student has been, and is to be, exposed, but being able to 'imagine', to *model*, what the student might be doing with them, what conclusions he might draw or fail to draw. What the student actually *does* can then be interpreted at a deeper cognitive level. Presented in this open-ended way, this is of course a very tall order, and in practice efforts have been made to cope with very limited areas of competence, such as the basic arithmetic operations.

## Knowledge, competence and procedures

One important idea in much of this work is that knowledge must consist of and be represented as the *competence* involved in its use. This applies not only to the human 'knower' but also to the teaching systems aimed at imparting knowledge. In the case of arithmetic this competence–knowledge equivalence is probably more clearly apparent than in some areas where the simple utterance of a statement in reply to a question might be accepted as equivalent to 'knowing' what the statement means. It is a distinction that we express by using the phrase 'knowing how' as compared to 'knowing that'. Knowing how to add is not simply to have access to a store of sums corresponding to pairs of numbers, though it may involve such a store: it is to be able to *apply certain rules* in an open-ended way, and at a somewhat more advanced level, to co-ordinate these rules with those that make up competence in the other arithmetic operations.

But if we look more closely at cases of 'knowing that' – e.g. 'Winston Churchill was Prime Minister of Britain during the second world war' – we find that this kind of knowledge also, to be worthy of the name, must involve some minimum competence to manipulate the statement and its components – Prime Minister, Britain, during, etc. – in a variety of contexts. The ability to produce the sentence about Churchill becomes increasingly significant as a piece of knowledge as it is shown to be part of a complex of related abilities to describe and discuss people and events at that time or indeed within a wider historical setting. It is not simply that someone who can do all this knows *more* – it is that the nature of the 'individual items' themselves is a function of their role within the organization of which they are a part.

Trying to realize such a 'competence model' of knowledge within an artificial system leads to the idea of representing knowledge in the form of *procedures* and *procedural networks*, that is, in the form of sections of program that will enable the computer not only to present information but also to make use of it in some appropriate sense. An Intelligent Teaching System that is to deal with arithmetic operations should thus be able to *perform* them, as well as say something about them.

But we must be clear about what we mean by 'perform' in this context. For the machine to 'know about adding' it is not sufficient that it should be able to arrive at a correct sum, given two numbers. Here it means being able to do so by employing component operations that a human being might be expected to use. It is this requirement which leads to programs of enormous complexity to achieve results which would otherwise need only a few lines.

Let us take as an example a system developed by Brown and Burton (1978) for diagnosing faults in children's basic arithmetic skills. If we analyse such a skill – say subtraction – we find a network of interlocking rules and operations. We produce below their diagram of 'A procedural network for subtraction', simply to give some idea of the surprising complexity involved in the execution of a 'simple' skill. No attempt will be made here to explicate the diagram, except to emphasize that it is not a 'flow diagram', but a representation of procedures (each of which must of course be expressed as a section of program) which can 'call' each other.

Note that the network contains a 'Facts Table' – containing such items as '3 from 8 = 5', etc. (though these too *could* be represented as procedures). If any of the 'facts' are wrong, this will obviously provide a source of error. But there are many such sources. Each sub-procedure in the network can have several erroneous forms; for example, the difference in a column might always be calculated by taking the smaller from the larger digit, no matter which is on top.

In computer jargon, faults in a program are called 'bugs'; often they are obscure errors deep in the structure of the program, and their manifestations in the *output* seldom provide straight-forward clues to their origins. In consequence a great deal of programming time is taken up with 'debugging' – tracking down such errors. The 'bug' concept can provide a useful analogy for thinking about errors in human performance. When a child persistently gets its subtractions wrong, this is likely to be because of one or more basic misconceptions – or bugs – which *underlie* its outward behaviour. Identifying these misconceptions, although it may not be necessary, is likely to facilitate effective remedial action. Knowing about possible 'bugs', and being able to compare their consequences to the actual performance of a child, can in turn facilitate their identification.

The rationale behind this type of approach is that if you have

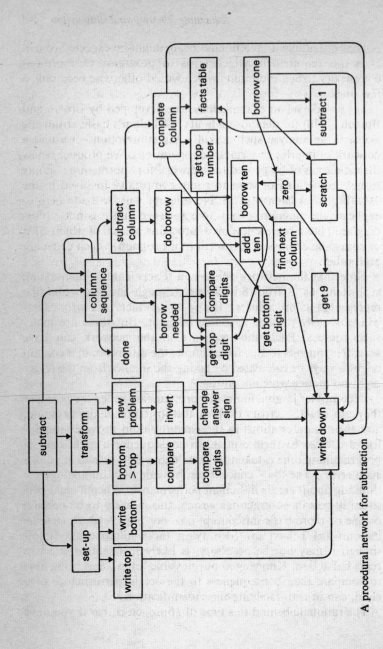

A procedural network for subtraction

a system that can correctly execute some relatively complex skill, that uses the same basic operations or *primitives* that are used by humans, then it should be possible to diagnose any case of faulty human performance *as an identifiable deviation* from the structure embodied in the artificial 'expert'. The Brown–Burton model (appropriately named 'BUGGY') contains from the outset a whole range of such departures representing possible, 'semantically meaningful' misconceptions a child might have about subtraction. By generating a series of problem 'solutions' based on different combinations of such misconceptions, BUGGY has been used with student teachers to heighten their sensitivity to possible types of fault concealed beneath children's 'surface behaviour'. It has also been used more directly to diagnose such faults, given a number of completed subtractions; and the potential clearly exists for combining this diagnosis with appropriate comments, explanations and specially selected practice problems. Brown and Burton also point out that the system may be used for judging the diagnostic value of a test, i.e. the kinds of underlying misunderstandings it is capable of revealing – and hence its use as an aid in test construction. Clearly the number of incorrectly answered test-questions is not necessarily a guide to the magnitude of a student's conceptual difficulties.

There have been a considerable number of projects with similar objectives, if somewhat different rationales – e.g. Jones and Tuggle's HELPERR (1979), aimed at diagnosing and helping to remedy errors in all four basic arithmetic operations; and Howe (1978) has reviewed the contribution of AI thinking to CAI. What is the potential value of this kind of work for education?

Intelligent Teaching Systems, in common with AI programs generally, need relatively large computers to run them, certainly larger than most schools are likely to possess. They are also, for the time being, very limited in scope; all the effort has gone into attaining a measure of *intelligence*, and it has been obtained only at the cost of concentrating on very small knowledge domains. Their use as working systems is thus likely to remain confined to the places where they are being developed for research purposes. Any more widespread impact will come about through a contribution to better *insights* into cognitive learning – by providing a language and a conceptual framework in terms of which cognitive processes can be more effectively analysed.

This situation is not likely to be changed in the immediate future by silicon chips, microcomputers and the associated drop in cost. These systems are still too small, in terms of the available core memory, to handle the sort of programs we have discussed. They can, however, cope quite adequately with the older type of linear or branching learning program, and they do have all the advantages of flexible use. This may seem like 'turning the clock back', as is suggested in the title of a recent review of *microprocessor*-assisted learning (Howe and du Boulay, 1979). But the fact that this sort of presentation has shortcomings, and that its original appearance was accompanied by exaggerated claims, should not be allowed to obscure its usefulness in specific applications, e.g. where a great deal of factual material has to be memorized.

## Writing programs as a way of learning

Thinking of knowledge as consisting of procedures has also lead to another, quite distinct approach to cognitive learning. This suggests that interaction with a computer, and the construction of programs *by the learner* to achieve a variety of goals, can itself, under certain conditions, form an important educational experience – one whose implications go well beyond an increased competence in programming as such.

Suppose that we have a computer language whose elements correspond to a variety of very basic, easily grasped *operations* – for example, various kinds of simple movement, adding things or taking them away, repeating something, etc. Such a language could be used to link these simple operations into more complex procedures, which could then be executed on the computer. We could now see not only the *result* of what had been done, but also the *structure* of the procedure that did it, allowing us to correct it, amplify it, or incorporate it into yet more complex structures. One could think of such a language as providing conceptual building blocks, with the computer making it possible to assemble them in many different ways and display the result – a kind of conceptual 'leggo', permitting the exploration of a potentially unlimited number of 'worlds'.

One such language is LOGO, developed by Seymour Papert and his collaborators at the Massachusetts Institute of Technology. It is a powerful language in the sense that quite sophisticated programs can be written with it; yet it is simple enough for its use to be readily grasped by very young children. As an example, consider the way simple geometrical (or other) drawings can be produced by means of LOGO. Commands can be conveyed to a small moving device (a 'TURTLE') carrying a pen that can be 'down' or 'up' (i.e. in contact with paper, or not; or a drawing can be produced more directly on a T.V.-screen). Commands, apart from PENUP and PENDOWN include FORWARD, BACKWARD (followed by a number which determines how far) and LEFT, RIGHT (followed by a number determining the amount of turn in the given direction). These instructions can be assembled to generate – or with the *intention* that they should generate – triangles, squares, curves, etc. Such a small program can be executed directly, revealing success, or what is more likely to start with, an informative failure (a BUG!). The program can also be used to *define* a new composite operation – say 'TO SQUARE' – which may henceforward be called upon as a whole, to form an element in yet more complex procedures; and so on. There are many other features in the language, and together they provide the user with an opportunity to gain a special kind of *operational* insight into a whole range of concepts which normally either elude people altogether, or come to be understood only tenuously, in a way that is isolated from anything of real significance to them.

In a recent book, Papert (1980) makes some very challenging claims for the potential role of LOGO – and of computing in general – in the education of children. His 'image of a child's relationship with a computer' does not so much go *beyond* what is now common in schools, 'it goes in the opposite direction'. The use of CAI, even when it is an 'intelligent' system, still involves *teaching*; the computer is being used *to program the child*. Papert, by contrast, sees the computer, or rather the computer-plus-appropriate-language, as providing a highly flexible and versatile environment which the child can explore freely, and within which ideas that are usually regarded as abstract and difficult – such as differential analysis in mathematics – are acquired as spontaneously as the native language. It is easy to identify with the TURTLE – to ask, for example 'what would *I* have to do if I wanted to move in a circle?' – and in this way the child establishes a connection between its own movements and that of the TURTLE which illuminates both. Ideas, to become meaningful, must be *used*; by making it possible to use them in a way that is continuous with a child's experience, LOGO (it is claimed) opens up realms of understanding which conventional teaching methods, especially in mathematics, manage to render impenetrable for all but the very gifted.

The inspiration for Papert's ideas on learning and cognitive development comes from Piaget, especially from his 'genetic epistemology'. Epistemology is the inquiry into the nature, basis and conditions of *knowledge*: Piaget's particular contribution has been his emphasis on the intimate and reciprocal relationship between knowledge and its *genesis*. As we saw in Chapter 8, Piaget believes this genesis to take the form of an invariant sequence of developmental stages – the result of an interaction between *given* biological structures and *given* features of the environment. What Papert is suggesting is that the advent of the computer makes possible a fundamentally new kind of environment which allows the child's development to escape from some of the limitations imposed by the old. He shares with Piaget the idea that learning involves an adjustment of 'mental structures' to other, external structures which are inherent in the world – but believes that the course of this adjustment can be facilitated by the creation of 'transitional objects' and 'microworlds' which bridge the gap between what is currently real and meaningful for the child, and the knowledge that is aimed at.

Before you can build a bridge it is of course necessary to know where the banks are – which in this case means analysing the target-knowledge into fundamental 'components' that are comparable to the concepts and operations at the disposal of the child. This can be a difficult undertaking, but it is one that the AI approach to cognition addresses directly.

### 'Piagetian learning' and 'shaping'

We will conclude this section with a brief comparison between the view of learning contained in operant 'shaping' and 'Piagetian learning'. The latter is a term used by Papert to describe the spontaneous, exploratory, and essentially learner-controlled process, exemplified in the acquisition of early motor skills or a first language – a process he wants to extend to a whole range of areas that are currently believed to require formal instruction.

Let us try to describe a child's interaction with a TURTLE in operant terms. The child does various things, and some of these are reinforced by success: the desired drawing appears. To some extent 'failures' are also reinforced, in that the turtle's movements as such, even in response to faulty instructions, are inherently enjoyable. And indeed, after such 'unintended results' – the quotation marks are there because intention does not really have a place in the operant world – the child will frequently go off in a new direction. In the course of a series of such responses and reinforcements, new behaviour patterns emerge, and this includes new thought patterns, if we are prepared to accept thought as a form of internal response. The child's behaviour is seen as being shaped by the existing reinforcement contingencies. To shape it in some other way simply requires a change in these contingencies.

But can one change the *effective* pattern of reinforcement without altering the nature of the learning that is going on? According to reinforcement theories of learning, all reinforcements do the same thing, though they might differ in power: they strengthen responses. Papert, on the other hand, claims a special kind of efficacy for the feedback provided by the TURTLE, arising from the way it *fits* into the child's spontaneous thoughts and actions at the time. One might ask for more evidence of the special effectiveness of learning under these conditions, and particularly of the claim that the experience generalizes to situations and problems that are not straightforwardly represented by the TURTLE and its movements; but at least we can recognize distinctions which a pure reinforcement view does not allow us to make: between goals or interests which 'emerge naturally' out of a learner's cognitive and motivational state, and objectives which are in some way superimposed; between an activity that is carried on essentially 'for its own sake' and one that is a means to some other end. In shaping or teaching one tries to channel the course of learning by introducing information, objectives and reinforcements that lie to some extent outside the 'unconstrained' process of exploration. The view that there *can* be no difference in principle is certainly wrong. How much and what kind of difference it actually makes remains to be investigated further.

### Turtles and teachers

People who have seen the true light tend to overstate their case. In Papert's vision, the school as an institution will wither away, to be bypassed and replaced by universal access to a 'computer-rich environment'. When we think about the various functions of the school within the community, one of which is to provide a relatively stable *context* for learning,* the prospect of teachers being superceded by turtles seems remote. No doubt more and more, and increasingly sophisticated, computers will find their way into the home, but this does not mean that their mind-expanding potential will necessarily be realized. What we must hope for is that they will also find their way into the schools, that they will be befriended and understood by teachers who can then help to set the scene for a fruitful encounter between child and machine.

---

* The only such context suggested by Papert is modelled on a kind of informal, community-based 'dancing school' found in Brazil. See *Mindstorms* for some elaboration of this intriguing idea.

We can also hope that the *ideas* incorporated in the various devices we have discussed will have some direct impact on the way that teaching and learning are thought about. None of them are particularly startling, and in various combinations they undoubtedly already feature in much good teaching. Where the theory, and indeed some of the associated extravagant claims, can help is by throwing into relief ideas that may have been implicit; they can then more easily form the basis of experimental innovations. Trying something out and learning from what happens is a useful procedure on both sides of the educational divide.

### 'Personalized instruction'

One example of such an innovation is a procedure which has come to be known as the 'Personalized System of Instruction' (see for example Kulik, Kulik and Smith, 1976). The basic ideas are very simple: they are essentially those which form the starting point of a machine-operated teaching program, with the control structure somewhat more relaxed and largely under the control of the learner. The most important step is for the teacher to work out in detail what it is that his course is intended to achieve. He then decides on a sequence of 'stages' leading to this objective. The information and materials required for each sub-goal are incorporated into study-packages, and these, together with facilities for self-testing, are made available to the learner. Beyond this, the learner is essentially in control, pacing and testing his own work, asking for advice when needed – though in some versions the testing is done by a member of staff when the student feels ready. The procedure has been tried with considerable success in higher education, as a replacement for teaching based on the formal lecture and timetabled examination.

The PSI approach concentrates the teacher's effort in the specification of the target and the careful preparation of the learning environment, while the student takes charge of his own movement through it. Such control as the teacher exercises in this situation remains relatively unnoticed and undisturbing. As far as the learner is concerned, two things are required for such a system to work. One is that he must at some level *want* to achieve the broad aims for which it has been designed; the other, that he must possess certain basic skills related to the organization of his time, to selecting material, to reading in a way that optimizes assimilation, and so on. The degree and type of skill required will of course depend on the manner in which the learning environment has been prepared and structured in advance. But the idea of 'learning skill' raises an issue of fundamental importance for the objectives of formal education.

## Learning to learn

Almost every day we are reminded that we live in a rapidly changing world. The 'micro-chip revolution' is the latest and potentially largest upheaval brought about by an ever-increasing rate of scientific discovery and technological development. Industries and whole nations benefit or suffer depending on their ability to use the opportunities provided. At all levels there is a need for new knowledge and skills, new ways of thinking, new objectives. By the same token, much of what has been learned previously becomes obsolete.

We must clearly try to ensure that the redundancy of specific skills does not automatically mean the redundancy of people. One thing this will require is a general acceptance that learning is not something confined to school and college years, but should be expected to go on throughout life. It is true that for many people dealing with new material seems to become more difficult with increasing age, but there is no conclusive evidence that, prior to the onset of senility, this is part of some inescapable, maturational process. The conviction that 'old dogs can't learn new tricks' can of course itself create a problem – a belief in the impossibility of success does not provide a good starting point for its achievement. But another source of difficulty may be an inadequate preparation for adult learning during the years of formal education.

It is a common experience in dealing with university students to find that many have difficulty in coping with the greater degree of responsibility which is placed on them for organizing their own learning. Compared to most schools, work at this level involves a much greater dependence on books, articles and relatively unstructured laboratory work, and less detailed guidance by the teaching staff. While students generally welcome this liberating change, they are often ill-prepared for it, having become accustomed to a syllabus that is 'covered' in lessons, to prescribed homework and detailed preparation for examinations – having in general come to regard the teacher and the school as carrying the main responsibility for their own progress.

The lack of preparation for learning as a self-directed activity is a handicap, not only in 'higher education', but in adult learning generally. Most adults do not take kindly to having their studies tightly regulated, even when they are not really equipped for anything else. In any case, most of the learning opportunities that exist *potentially* throughout life are not initially designed for that purpose and depend entirely on the learner for their realization. If this is to become part of normal working life, then clearly one of the most important objectives of formal education must be to enable people to learn *without* detailed guidance, to *extract* whatever is to be gained from situations they find themselves in – whether or not those situations are explicitly labelled 'training' or 'research'. If we recognize that specific knowledge will constantly go out of date, then we must concentrate on developing in each individual the ability to search out and assimilate new knowledge, even in circumstances where it is not already organized and processed.

Education, from this point of view, becomes largely a process of *weaning*, with an increasing emphasis on *learning by the child* rather than on *instruction by the teacher*. In the chapter on skill we suggested that one of the most important functions of a teacher was to provide criteria which the learner could use to assess his own performance. This can now be extended by saying that teaching should be aimed at making the teacher's intervention progressively redundant as a child moves through the educational system.

## Self-regulated learning

How does one go about achieving this? How does one help people to become active learners with the ability to initiate and organize the appropriate activity? or make it easier for them to abandon what has been learned when it becomes obsolete? To some extent it is a question of communicating knowledge and techniques – for example, at a relatively specialized level, of showing people how to make the best use of a library or an abstracting service, or more generally, of helping them to adopt efficient study habits that alternate periods of reading with critical review. But the problem can also be formulated in motivational terms: what can one do to promote an interest in a particular topic or activity, indeed in the activity of learning as such? The importance of 'motivating' students is generally recognized, but we know far too little about what this involves.

Part of the reason for this ignorance is no doubt the oversimplified role that has for so long been assigned to motives and goals in the organization of behaviour by reinforcement theories of learning. It is quite misleading to identify 'high motivation' with behaviour under high-ratio reinforcement schedules. The intense activity generated by such schedules depends on the subject giving priority to the reinforcement being used; and this is ensured, in typical experiments, by maintaining an appropriate level of (food) deprivation, with no distractions or alternative routes for satisfying the need. Short of introducing comparable conditions into the home or classroom, we need to understand more about the *unconstrained* generation of interest in activities, as well as in their more or less direct consequences.

We need to find out much more about the cumulative and generalized effects of early learning experiences. The phenomenon of 'learned helplessness' discussed in the last chapter has an opposite counterpart in a generally positive and confident approach to new, problematic situations. How does this come about? There is no shortage of evidence showing that animals, and especially young primates and humans, will engage in exploratory and manipulative behaviour 'for its own sake', i.e. without any *additional* reinforcing consequences. Such behaviour nevertheless remains susceptible to extraneous rewards or punishments, and we might expect a corresponding increase or decrease in adventurous and inquisitive behaviour. If we accept the latter as broadly indicative of an interest in learning, then a policy of encouraging early acts of exploration *as such* might have the desired effect. The ability to sustain search – or research – depends on an enjoyment of the activity itself, quite apart from the importance attached to its eventual outcome. It could be that the relative emphasis placed on *trying* as distinct from *succeeding* in childhood has far-reaching consequences for the adult's readiness to engage in such activities without the prospect of an immediate and separate pay-off.

The last point also raises the question of a general ability to sustain long-term goals in the presence of more immediate, distracting consequences. To what extent, and in what way, is 'singleness of purpose' a function of early experience? And how are such long-term purposes and aspirations come by at all? We know very little about the aetiology of ambitions, for example about the role played by 'identification' with other people, or about the circumstances that facilitate such identification. Is there some way in which interest generates interest 'directly'? Many people, thinking back over their educational experience, can trace their liking for a particular subject, or sometimes for the whole atmosphere of learning, to the influence of individual teachers, to a kind of contagious transmission of enthusiasm. If we could learn to identify the essential conditions for this effect, they might provide useful objectives for teacher training (or criteria for their selection).

Teachers are not of course the only people that influence children; they co-operate or more often compete with parents, friends both in and out of school, 'heroes' in real life, in literature and on the television screen. A better understanding of the way in which behaviour, interests and values develop would presumably enable them or anybody else – to increase their relative effectiveness. This brings us to the topic for our last chapter: the potential use of psychology to exert influence on others.

# 11. The Application of Psychological Knowledge

Making practical use of knowledge in physics or electronics or chemistry usually involves building a special device or environment that uses established principles to achieve a particular objective. In doing this we may have to take into account the objectives of other people if they are going to be affected by what we are making – the various uses of nuclear energy provide an obvious topical example. We do not, however, have to worry about causing offence to, or meeting any systematic resistance from, the various forces, materials or structures whose properties we exploit in the course of construction or eventual use: atoms have no views on being split or fused, and would as soon be part of a nuclear reactor as of a nuclear protestor. What distinguishes psychology, and in various degrees all the life sciences, is that the objects of study have goals and purposes of their own, expressed both in the form of internal self-regulation and in the directedness of their behaviour. This presents quite distinctive problems for theory, tackled at different levels by psychology, biology and the sciences of artificial systems; it presents practical problems, such as when we want to teach someone things they do not want to learn, and ethical problems, when those very attempts are called into question. We have at various points in this book touched on the theoretical issues involved – in this last chapter we will try to address some of the others.

Anyone who works as a psychologist, or who studies psychology, soon discovers that other people often regard their interest with a mixture of amusement and mild apprehension. The amusement probably derives from some of the more pretentious claims uttered by, or attributed to, members of that largely undifferentiated clan of psychologists/psychiatrists/psychoanalysts; the apprehension from the nagging thought that they just *might* be onto something. In the case of a psychologist, this is taken to mean having some special understanding or insight into the 'workings of the mind', including that of the person he is talking to; it is seen as giving him some potentially 'unfair' advantage, revealing what others cannot see, and providing who knows what skills to override or by-pass the considered wishes of his 'subject'. It may be some reassurance to know that the majority of psychologists are, in their everyday relationships, no better than anybody else at understanding or influencing people – and some are a great deal worse. Yet it is clearly among the aims of the discipline to produce knowledge about people, about how they function – and it is suspicion of the power implied by that knowledge that creates the ambivalence in people's attitude towards psychology.

There are certain professions and associated relationships where the possible exercise of that power becomes explicit: therapy is one, education is another. Many people do of course *seek* therapy, more or less desperately, and many want to learn; presumably they will welcome any help that might be available, as well as any improvements in the methods on which that help is based. The trouble is that these very methods could perhaps also be used, given the inequality of most therapeutic and educational relationships, to bring about changes in practices, attitudes or beliefs which the patient or pupil would not in fact have wanted – or which are in some sense not in their 'real' or 'best' interests, whatever they themselves might say.

We have already touched on some of these objections in the chapter on abnormal behaviour. One version takes the form of portraying the therapist as an agent (conscious or unconscious) of the ruling class, buttressing a sick society by encouraging his patients in their (mistaken) belief that it is *they* who are ill. The practical implication of this claim is presumably that if the pain and anxiety of millions of patients could, instead of being assuaged, be transformed into resentment towards the social order that supposedly produced them, then the day of revolutionary reckoning might be brought that much closer. Similarly, teachers and educators have been cast in the role of 'brainwashing' their helpless and unsuspecting charges into accepting – or, as the case may be, rejecting – the prevailing culture. Leaving aside the more extreme cases of political paranoia, it is certainly true that therapy and education provide considerable opportunities for influence: the problem is to decide what constitutes acceptable, and what *undue* influence.

In Chapter 9 we temporarily dealt with this issue by confining the discussion to 'help on request'; the use of various techniques to achieve 'self-control' provided especially clear-cut examples of therapy under the direction of the 'patient'. Similarly, when talking about education we gave examples of some of the ways in which the student can take charge of his own learning, and suggested that it should be the aim of teaching in a very general sense to make this possible. The taking-over of (at least partial) responsibility by the patient or student not only makes for a more effective therapeutic or educational process, it also goes a long way towards meeting the objection of coercive or undue influence.

It does not, however, get rid of the problem entirely. In the first place, there will be cases where the therapist or educator feels that he cannot relinquish control without at the same time giving up his essential objective. We do on the whole accept that it is possible for a patient to *need* help without recognizing or wanting it; or for children to claim, in the words of the seventies song, that they 'don't need no education' when they manifestly do. But beyond this, even when there is no conflict of goals, it may be felt that we should look more closely at *how* those goals came into being. An important function of a good teacher is to create interest in the subject being taught. A good school somehow manages to *generate* a positive attitude towards learning in general, and a whole variety of intellectual and social values. Successful education depends as much on its motivational as on its cognitive contribution; and this is probably even more true in the case of therapy. So then the question arises, is the *creation* of tastes, interests, values or aspirations in others simply a subtle and devious way of sidetracking their real, intrinsic goals?

Let us first examine this idea of a person's 'real' goals. At one level this could be simply a question of identification, of distinguishing an active commitment from mere lip-service. But if we accept that such a commitment might itself be the result of successful influence, and wish to criticize this on the grounds that it amounts to brainwashing, then we must find some other criterion, one which will allow us to recognize a brain on its truly 'unwashed' course.

The only way to give meaning to such an idea is by appealing to innateness, to 'human nature', to goals that have been 'built in'. It is, however, only in quite primitive species that a significant proportion of identifiable goals in the grown animal can be described in this way, as being relatively independent of environmental influence. In man, apart from a broad pattern of interest in things edible, comfortable or sexual, there is no single desire or aspiration whose object, let alone detailed form, can be separated from the culturally determined environment in which it developed. There is no way in which we can identify a sufficiently detailed, biological 'groundplan', independent of these influences, which could serve as a yard stick for what people are by nature *meant to* want.

Some sociobiologists (e.g. Wilson, 1975) have argued that cultures themselves, being products of creatures subject to natural selection, can be explained and evaluated as responses to evolutionary pressures. But this is hardly tenable. While natural selection undoubtedly imposes some *constraints* on possible cultures – one requiring universal infanticide would not get very far – there is a wide range of variation that is effectively 'decoupled' from biological evolution. We have to study the process of cultural development in its own terms, and cannot expect to explain or judge any particular variety by appealing to evolutionary mechanisms at a lower level.

At one point in time we have a child aged zero, with the usual basic reflexes, dispositions and needs; twenty years later there is an elaborate structure of values, interests, personal and political objectives. In some way that we understand only very imperfectly, the intervening patterns of experience have been instrumental in bringing about this transformation. Parents, teachers, schoolfriends and all sorts of other people have modified and been part of the context of that experience, and had they acted differently, the experience would have been different. Except for those that manage to grow up alone on a desert island, a social environment of some kind is inevitably there, like the weather. Suppose now that we arranged things and behaved *with a view to* influencing the development of another person in some particular direction – would this make it reprehensible? One might argue that since we inevitably affect others, we might as well try to understand what we are doing, and influence them to some purpose.

It is a version of this argument that has been used by Skinner, most recently and explicitly in *Beyond Freedom and Dignity,* and it got him what has been described as 'the worst press since Darwin'. In this book Skinner argued that since all behaviour is controlled by the environment, the entire language of 'inner determination' and autonomy is essentially vacuous: it only serves to conceal our ignorance of the true *external* causes of behaviour, and in consequence obstruct their discovery. Having once traced and unravelled the causal network in sufficient detail, we could then deliberately arrange it so as to generate 'good', mutually compatible patterns of behaviour in everyone, and thereby set us on the road to utopia.

This proposal is absurd from a *psychological* point of view because it uses an inadequate model of people (or indeed of organisms of any kind). While no man is an island in the sense of being completely autonomous, all living things are islands of *relative* autonomy – that is, they maintain internal states and structures, and they act to achieve goals in the face of extensive disturbance from the environment. Certainly the environment will influence the details of behaviour, but that influence depends on the goal state of the individual in question, who will adapt his behaviour in an attempt to attain his current objective in line with prevailing circumstances. In addition, the environment plays a part, not only in the momentary selection of objective but also in shaping the *nature* of an individual's objectives and goals – yet we know relatively little about the mechanics of this influence, especially when we are dealing with creatures that can themselves extensively modify the physical and social environment in which they and their neighbours live.

The concepts of autonomy and of control are closely related. To deny autonomy outright, as Skinner does, attributing all control to the environment, makes nonsense of the very idea of control. It is, paradoxically, only when we recognize the existence of various degrees and kinds of autonomy in all organisms, interacting with each other and forming yet further, superordinate control structures, that it becomes meaningful to talk about an individual, or some part of the system, as exercising (some) control over another.

### The real objection to Skinner

It was not, however, the shortcomings and contradictions of Skinner's underlying model that outraged his critics so much as the thought that to some extent its application might actually *work*. What is strange about this is that Skinner's proposal amounted in effect to a planned and systematic application of methods which we use, haphazardly, all the time, and at least partly in an attempt to influence what people do: we offer rewards and threaten penalties contingent on behaviour. In fact Skinner's emphasis, as we have pointed out, is exclusively on *rewards*, on the grounds that punishments are often not only obnoxious, they are essentially unreliable. One might have thought that a successful regulation of society using only rewards would be an attractive goal, whatever doubts there might be about its practicality. In the event one is left with the feeling that the threat in Skinner's proposal lies in the very idea of an *effective* method. Our current use of rewards and punishments is coupled with the assumption that the individual remains, after all, *free* to avail himself of the rewards, or to risk the punishments – and reassuringly, this assumption keeps being confirmed by the system's frequent failures. Any suggestion that it might be possible to eliminate or significantly reduce such failures immediately arouses the suspicion that freedom is being eroded in some underhand way. The fact that Skinner explicitly rejects freedom as something that does not exist in the first place hardly helps: he is still seen as wanting to *remove* it.

If such anxieties are aroused by a rudimentary model, they are not likely to be removed by the promise of a more comprehensive one. The fundamental concept missing from the operant account of behaviour is that of the *individual's point of view*, both cognitive and motivational. Taking this into account shifts the emphasis away from behaviour and *back* to beliefs and goals. The fact of having a point of view greatly complicates the way in which the environment impinges on the individual, but impinge it does: if psychology can throw light on this process, does it not then inevitably carry with it the threat of effective regulation, albeit of a more indirect and camouflaged kind?

In one sense it probably does, even if it is all still a long way off. To the extent that the directing influence came from the parents or from the schools, the *freely* developed interests and enthusiasms of children might be a little more in line with set objectives than they are now. But should the prospect of greater effectiveness in setting up or passing on values necessarily be seen as a threat? The stability or stable evolution of *any* form of society depends on its success in diffusing some basic set of objectives, of rights and wrongs, among the great majority of its members, and of maintaining a significant overlap between generations. Without such shared values, it can only survive through repression. Clearly those who are fundamentally opposed to the society in question and wish to replace it by another will object to *all* its methods of self-perpetuation. If they cannot point to overt repression, then they will suggest to the population that their basic beliefs and values have been *imposed* on them, that they have been brainwashed or 'mystified' by the establishment, that the very language they learned as children contained the dragon seed of ideological corruption. This is the essential message in the idea of *bourgeois hegemony* as the term has been used by some Marxist writers. It is also an important theme of the feminist movement, that the self image and associated value system of most women has been insinuated into their consciousness through inumerable aspects of a male-dominated society.

The 'charge' that we are all influenced by our social environment is certainly true, and we may not like the results produced in any given case. Provided that criticism remains part of that environment, and especially if a questioning approach is a central objective of the educational system, the society will continue to evolve. But criticisms of the 'social order' frequently contain the misleading implication that the formative influence of one's society is a constraint to be deplored *as such*: and once people have 'reinterpreted' their current condition as one of imprisonment, the space on the far side of the bars is implicitly unbounded. As a result, any changes in the social order that are proposed at the same time, come to look like an absolute liberation. This is itself one example of a 'method', not invented by psychologists, for changing someone's objectives, and should be recognized as such – alongside the whole gamut of persuasive devices contained in the suggestions, comparisons and exhortations to which we are constantly exposed, and which are aimed at getting us to love our neighbour, the party, or the latest sticky drink.

One hegemony is always replaced by another, and new mysteries are set up in the place of those that have just been dispelled. When we object to someone holding, or being converted to, particular values, it is almost invariably because we happen ourselves to favour others. It is not the purpose of this book to promote any particular set of such preferences. What we are trying to stress is that the development of each one of us has inevitably been subject to persuasive and formative influences of *some* kind; that this *by itself* does not make our current freedom-to-choose less genuine or authentic; and that consequently the realization that we have been influenced should not be allowed to undermine whatever confidence we have in our values and beliefs.

Surely this remains true, even if the dynamics of influence become more explicit. If it now turns out that such an improved understanding marginally favours the carriers of the 'established' culture, if it makes teachers more effective in promoting an interest in learning, if it makes therapists better at helping people to live in their particular corner of reality – even if, heaven help us, it makes it easier to maintain law and order by means of constraints that operate from *within* – then this is something to be welcomed in the interests of social continuity. But *that*, of course, *is* an expression of a personal preference.

# References

Adams, J. A. (1971) 'A closed loop theory of motor learning', *Journal of Motor Behavior 3*, 111–49.

Agras, S., and Marshall, C. (1965) 'The application of negative practise to spasmodic torticollis', *American Journal of Psychiatry 122*, 579–82.

Alpert, D. (1975) 'The P L A T O I V system in use: A progress report', in *Computers in Education* ed. O. Lecarne and R. Lewis, North Holland, Amsterdam.

Anderson, R. C., and Bower, G. H. (1973) *Human Associative Memory*, Wiley, New York.

Annett, J. (1970) 'The role of action feedback on the acquisition of simple motor responses', *Journal of Motor Behavior 2*, 217–21.

Auble, P. M., and Franks, J. J. (1978) 'The effects of effort towards comprehension on recall', *Memory and Cognition 6*, 20–25.

Baddeley, A. D. (1976) *The Psychology of Memory*, Harper & Row, New York; (1978) 'The trouble with levels: a re-examination of Craik and Lockart's framework for memory research', *Psychological Review 85*, 139–52.

Baker, B. L., Cohen, D. C., and Saunders, J. T. (1973) 'Self-directed desensitization for acrophobia', *Behaviour Research and Therapy 11*, 79–83.

Bandura, A. (1977) 'Self-efficacy: Towards a unifying theory of behavioural change', *Psychological Review 84*, 191–215; (1977) *Social Learning Theory*, Prentice-Hall, New York.

Barnes, J. M., and Underwood, B. J. (1959) '"Fate" of first-list associations in transfer theory', *Journal of Experimental Psychology 58*, 97–105.

Bartlett, F. C. (1932) *Remembering*, Cambridge University Press.

Bloom, L. (1970) *Language Development: Form and Function in Emerging Grammars*, M.I.T. Press, Cambridge, Mass.

Bolles, R. C. (1979) *Learning Theory*, Holt, Rinehart & Winston.

Bower, T. G. R. (1979) *Human Development*, W. H. Freemantle & Co., San Francisco.

Bower, T. G. R. (1974) *Development in Infancy*, W. H. Freeman, San Francisco.

Bowlby, J. (1971) *Attachment and Loss: Vol. 1 Attachment*, Penguin; (1975) *Attachment and Loss Vol. 11. Separation: Anxiety and Anger*, Penguin.

Braine, M. D. S. (1963) 'The ontogeny of English phrase structure: the first phase', *Language 39*, 1–13.

Breland, K., and Breland, M. (1961) 'The misbehavior of organisms', *American Psychologist 16*, 661–4.

Brown, J. (1976) 'An analysis of recognition and recall, and problems in their comparison', in *Recall and Recognition* ed. J. Brown, Wiley.

Brown, J. (1958) 'Some tests of the decay theory of immediate memory', *Quarterly Journal of Experimental Psychology 10*, 12–21.

Brown, J. S., and Burton, R. R. (1978) 'Diagnostic models for procedural bugs in basic mathematical skills', *Cognitive Science 2*, 155–92.

Brown, R. (1973) *A First Language: The Early Stages*, Harvard University Press, Boston, Mass.

Brown, R., and Hanlon, C. (1970) 'Derivational complexity and order of acquisition in child speech', in *Cognition and the Development of Language* ed. J. R. Hayes, Wiley, New York.

Brown, R., and McNeill, D. (1966) 'The "tip of the tongue" phenomenon', *Journal of Verbal Learning and Behavior 5*, 325–37.

Cellérier, G. (1980) 'Some clarifications on innatism and constructivism', in *Language and Learning* ed. M. Piattelli-Palmarini, Routledge & Kegan Paul.

Chomsky, N. (1980) 'On cognitive structures and their development: A reply to Piaget', in *Language and Learning* ed. M. Piattelli-Palmarini, Routledge & Kegan Paul.

Chomsky, N. (1976) 'On the nature of language', in *Origins and Evolution of Language and Speech* ed. S. R. Harnod, H. D. Steklis and J. Lancaster, *Annual New York Academy of Science 280*, 46–55.

Chomsky, N. (1975) *Reflections on Language*, Pantheon, New York.

Clarke, A. M., and Clarke, A. D. B. (1976) *Early Experience: Myth and Evidence*, Open Books.

Collins, A. M., and Quillian, M. R. (1969) 'Retrieval time from semantic memory', *Journal of Verbal Learning and Verbal Behavior 8*, 240–47.

Craik, F. I. M., and Lockart, R. S. (1972) 'Levels of processing: a framework for memory research', *Journal of Verbal Learning and Verbal Behavior 11*, 671–84.

Cross, T. G. (1977) 'Mother's speech adjustments: the contribution of selected child listener variables', in *Talking to Children: Language Input and Acquisition* ed. C. Ferguson and C. Snow, Cambridge University Press.

Deutsch, J. A. (1960) *The Structural Basis of Behaviour*, Cambridge University Press.

Emmelkamp, P. M. G., Kuipers, A. C. M., and Eggeraat, J. B. (1978) 'Cognitive modification versus prolonged exposure in vivo: A comparison with agoraphobics as subjects', *Behaviour Research and Therapy 16*, 33–41.

Engen, T., and Ross, B. M. (1973) 'Long-term memory of odours with and without verbal descriptions', *Journal of Experimental Psychology 100*, 221–7.

Fagan, J. F. (1976) 'Infants' recognition of invariant features of faces', *Child Development 47*, 627–38.

Fantz, R. L. (1966) 'Pattern discrimination and selective attention as determinants of perceptual development from birth', in *Perceptual Development in Children* ed. A. H. Kidd and J. L. Rivoire, International Universities Press, New York.

Farb, P. (1977) *Word Play*, Coronet Books, Hodder & Stoughton.

Feldman, M. P., and MacCulloch, M. J. (1971) *Homosexual Behaviour: Therapy and Assessment*, Pergamon Press, New York.

Field, T. F. (1979) 'Visual and cardiac responses to animate and inanimate faces by young term and preterm infants', *Child Development 50*, 188–94.

Foss, B. M. (1965) 'Imitation', in *Determinants of Infant Behaviour* vol. III ed. B. M. Foss, Methuen.

Foss, D. J., and Harwood, D. A. (1975) 'Memory for sentences: implications for human associative memory', *Journal of Verbal Learning and Verbal Behavior 14*, 1–16.

Frisch, K. von, (1967) *The Dance Language and Orientation of Bees*, Harvard University Press, Boston, Mass.

Gallistel, C. R. (1980) *The Organization of Action: A New Synthesis*, Lawrence Erlbaum Associates, Hillsdale, New Jersey.

Garcia, K., and Koelling, R. (1966) 'Relation of cue to consequence in avoidance learning', *Psychonomic Science 4*, 123–4.

Gardner, B. T., and Gardner, R. A. (1975) 'Evidence for sentence constituents in the early utterances of child and chimpanzee', *Journal of Experimental Psychology: General 104*, 244–67.

Goren, C. C., Sarty, M. and Wu, P. Y. K. (1975) 'Visual following and pattern discrimination of face-like stimuli by new-born infants', *Pediatrics 56*, 544–9.

Gray, J. A. (1975) *Elements of a Two-Process Theory of Learning*, Academic Press.

Harris, P. (1979) 'Perception and cognition in infancy', in *Psychology Survey No. 2*. ed. K. Connolly, George Allen & Unwin.

Hayes, K. J., and Hayes, C. (1951) 'The intellectual development of a home-raised chimpanzee', *Proceedings of the American Philosophical Society 95*, 105–9.

Hinde, R. A., and Stevenson-Hinde, J. (1973) *Constraints on Learning*, Academic Press.

Howe, J. A. M. (1978) 'Artificial intelligence and computer-assisted learning: ten years on', *Programmed Learning and Educational Technology 15*, 114–25.

Howe, J. A. M., and du Boulay, B. (1979) 'Microprocessor assisted learning: turning the clock back?', *Programmed Learning and Educational Technology 16*, 240–46.

Hull, C. (1952) *A Behavior System*, Yale University Press, New Haven, Conn.; (1943) *Principles of Behavior*, Appleton Century Crofts.

Jones, H. G. (1960) 'Continuation of Yates treatment of a tiqueur', in *Behavior Therapy and the Neuroses* ed. H. J. Eysenck, Pergamon Press.

Jones, M. A., and Tuggle, F. D. (1979) 'Inducing explanations for errors in computer assisted instruction', *International Journal of Man-Machine Studies 11*, 301–24.

Kamin, L. J. (1969) 'Predictability, surprise, attention and conditioning, in *Punishment and Aversive Behavior* ed. R. Church and B. Campbell, Appleton Century Crofts.

Karmel, B. Z. (1969) 'The effect of age, complexity and amount of complexity and amount of contour on pattern preferences in human infants', *Journal of Experimental Child Psychology 7*, 339–54.

Kellog, W. N., and Kellog, L. A. (1933) *The Ape and the Child: A Study of Environmental Influence upon Early Behavior*, McGraw Hill, New York.

Kintsch, W. (1970) 'Models for free recall and recognition', in *Models of Human Memory* ed. D. A. Norman, Academic Press, New York.

Kulik, J. A., Kulik, C. C., and Smith, B. B. (1976) 'Research on the personalized system of instruction', *Journal of Programmed Learning and Educational Technology 13*, 23–30.

Lashley, K. S. (1917) 'The accuracy of movement in the absence of excitation from the moving organ', *American Journal of Physiology 43*, 169–94.

Lorenz, K. (1977) *Behind the Mirror*, Methuen.

McFarland, D. J. (1973) 'Stimulus relevance and homeostasis', in *Constraints on Learning* ed. R. A. Hinde and J. Stevenson-Hinde, Academic Press; (1969) 'Separation of satiating and rewarding consequences of drinking', *Physiology and Behavior 4*, 987–9.

MacIntosh, N. J. (1975) 'A theory of attention: variations in the associability of stimuli with reinforcements', *Psychological Review 82*, 276–98.

McNeill, D. (1966) 'Developmental psycholinguistics', in *The Genesis of Language* ed. F. Smith and G. Miller, M.I.T. Press, Cambridge, Mass.

Marks, I. M., and Gelder, M. G. (1967) 'Transvestism and fetishism: clinical and psychological changes during faradic aversion', *British Journal of Psychiatry 113*, 711–29.

Marks, I. M., Gelder, M. G., and Bancroft, J. (1970) 'Sexual deviants two years after electrical aversion', *British Journal of Psychiatry 11*, 73–85.

Marler, P. (1970) 'A comparative approach to vocal learning: song development in white-crowned sparrows', *Journal of Comparative and Physiological Psychology 71*, 1–25.

Maurer, D, and Salapatek, P. (1976) 'Developmental changes in the scanning of faces by young infants', *Child Development 47*, 523–7.

Meltzoff, A., and Moore, M. K. (1977) 'Imitation of facial and manual gestures by human neonates', *Science 198*, 75–8.

Meyer, V. (1966) 'Modification of expectations in cases with obsessional rituals', *Behaviour Research and Therapy 4*, 273–80.

Meyer, V., and Bartlett, D. (1976) 'Behaviour therapy: technology or psychotherapy?', *Scandinavian Journal of Behaviour Therapy 5*, 1–12.

Miller, N. E. (1969) 'Learning of visceral and glandular responses', *Science 163*, 343–445.

Miller, N. E., and Dollard, J. (1941) *Social Learning and Imitation*, Yale University Press, New Haven, Conn.

Minami, H., and Dallenbach, K. M. (1946) 'The effect of activity upon learning and retention in the cockroach', *American Journal of Psychology 59*, 1–58.

Moore, B. P. (1973) 'The role of directed Pavlovian reactions in simple instrumental learning in the pigeon', in *Constraints on Learning* ed. R. A. Hinde and J. Stevenson-Hinde, Academic Press.

Mowrer, O. H. (1960) *Learning Theory and Behavior*, Wiley, New York; (1947) 'On the dual nature of learning', *Harvard Educational Review 17*, 102–48.

Muir, D., and Field, J. (1979) 'New-born infants orientate to sounds', *Child Development 50*, 431–6.

Mundy-Castle, A. C. (1970) 'The descent of meaning', *Social Psychology Information 9*, 125–41.

Nelson, T. D. (1977) 'Repetition and depth processing', *Journal of Verbal Learning and Verbal Behavior 16*, 151–71.

Oatley, K., and Dickinson, A. (1970) 'Air drinking and the measurement of thirst', *Animal Behavior 18*, 259–69.

Ods, J., and Milner, P. (1954) 'Positive replacement produced by electrical stimulation of septal area and other regions of rat brain', *Journal of Comparative Physiology and Psychology 47*, 419–27.

Olds, J. (1977) *Drives and Reinforcements*, Raven Press.

Omar, M. K. (1973) *The Acquisition of Egyptian Arabic as a Native Language*, Mouton Publishers, The Hague.

Öst, L.-G. (1978) 'Behavioural treatment of thunder and lightning phobias', *Behaviour Research and Therapy 16*, 197–207.

Paivio, A. (1969) 'Mental imagery in associative learning and memory', *Psychological Review 76*, 241–63.

Papert, S. (1980) *Mindstorms*, Harvester Press.

Patterson, F. G. (1978) 'The gesture of a gorilla: language acquisition in another pongid', *Brain and Language 5*, 72–97.

Peterson, L. R., and Peterson, M. J. (1959) 'Short-term retention of individual items', *Journal of Experimental Psychology 58*, 193–8.

Piaget, J. (1979) *Behaviour and Evolution*, Routledge & Kegan Paul.

Plotkin, H. C., and Odling-Smee, J. (1979) 'Learning, change and evolution', *Advances in the Study of Behaviour 10*, 1–41.

Postman, L. (1976) 'Interference theory revisited', in *Recall and Recognition* ed. J. Brown, Wiley.

Powers, W. T. (1978) 'Quantitative analysis of purposive systems: some spadework at the foundations of scientific psychology', *Psychological Review 85*, 417–35.

Premack, D. (1978) 'On the abstractness of human concepts: why it would be difficult to talk to a pigeon', in *Cognitive Processes in Animal Behavior* ed. S. H. Hulse, H. Fowler and W. K. Honig, Lawrence Erlbaum Associates, Hillsdale, New Jersey; (1976) *Intelligence in Ape and Man*, Lawrence Erlbaum Associates; (1965) 'Reinforcement theory', in *Nebraska Symposium on Motivation* ed. D. Levine, University of Nebraska Press.

Pressey, S. L. (1926) 'A single apparatus which gives tests and scores – and teaches', *School and Society 23*, 373–6.

Rachman, S. J. (1978) *Fear and Courage*, W. H. Freeman.

Rescorla, R. A. (1980) *Pavlovian Second-Order Conditioning: Studies in Associative Learning*. Lawrence Erlbaum Associates, Hillsdale, New Jersey.

Rescorla, R. A., and Wagner, A. R. (1972) 'A theory of Pavlovian conditioning: variations in the effectiveness of reinforcement and non-reinforcement', in *Classical Conditioning II: Current Research and Theory*, ed. A. H. Black and W. F. Prokasy, Appleton Century Crofts.

Richter, C. (1957) 'On the phenomenon of sudden death in animals and men', *Psychosomatic Medicine 19*, 191–8.

Rippere, V. (1977) 'Comments on Seligman's theory of helplessness', *Behavior Research and Therapy 15*, 207–9.

Rips, L. J., Shoben, E. J., and Smith, E. E. (1973) 'Semantic distance and the verification of semantic relations', *Journal of Verbal Learning and Verbal Behaviour 12*, 1–20.

Schmidt, R. A. (1975) 'A schema theory of discrete motor skill learning', *Psychological Review 82*, 225–60.

Seligman, M. E. P. (1975) *Helplessness: On Depression, Development and Death*, W. H. Freeman.

Seligman, M. E. P., and Hager, L. (eds.) (1972) *Biological Boundaries of Learning*, Appleton Century Crofts.

Siqueland, E. R., and Lipsitt, L. P. (1966) 'Conditioned head-turning in human new-borns', *Journal of Experimental Child Psychology 3*, 356–76.

Skinner, B. F. (1971) *Beyond Freedom and Dignity*, Knopf; (1956) 'A case history in scientific method', *American Psychologist 11*, 221–33.

Slobin, D. I. (1973) 'Cognitive prerequisites of the development of grammar', in *Studies in Child Language Development* ed. C. A. Ferguson and D. I. Slobin, Holt, Rinehart & Winston, New York.

Sokolov, E. N. (1963) 'Higher nervous functioning: the orienting reflex', *Annual Review of Physiology 25*, 545–80.

Sperling, G. (1960) 'The information available in brief visual presentations', *Psychological Monographs 74*, No. 498.

Spiker, C. C., Gerjouy, I. R., and Shepard, W. O. (1956) 'Children's concept of middle-sizedness and performance on the intermediate size problem', *Journal of Comparative and Physiological Psychology 49*, 416–9.

Stern, R., and Marks, I. (1973) 'Brief and prolonged flooding', *Archives of General Psychiatry 28*, 270–76.

Szasz, T. (1972) *The Myth of Mental Illness*, Secker & Warburg.

Terrace, H. S., Petitto, L. A., Sanders, R. J., and Bever, T. G. (1979) 'Can an ape create a sentence?', *Science 206*, 891–902.

Tolman, E. C. (1959) 'Principles of purposive behavior', in *Psychology: A Study of a Science*, Vol. 2, ed. S. Koch, McGraw-Hill; (1932) *Purposive Behavior in Animals and Men*, Appleton Century Crofts.

Turvey, M. T., and Kravetz, S. (1970) 'Retrieval from iconic memory with shape as the selection criterion', *Perception and Psychophysics 8*, 171–2.

Waddington, C. H. (1975) *The Evolution of an Evolutionist*, Edinburgh University Press.

Warrington, E. K., and Shallice, T. (1969) 'The selective impairment of auditory verbal short-term memory', *Brain 92*, 885–96.

Watson, J. B. (1919) *Psychology from the Standpoint of a Behaviorist*, J. B. Lippincot.

Weiss, P. (1969) 'The living system: determinism stratified', in *Beyond Reductionism* ed. A. Koestler and J. R. Smythies, Hutchinson; (1941)

'Self-differentiation of the basic patterns of coordination', *Comparative Psychology Monographs 17*, No. 4.

Welford, A.T. (1976) *Skilled Performance*, Scott, Foresman & Co.

Wilcoxon, H.C., Dragoin, W.B., and Kral, P.A. (1971) 'Illness-induced aversions in rat and quail: relative salience of visual and gustatory cues', *Science 171*, 826–8.

Williams, D.R., and Williams, H. (1969) 'Auto-maintenance in the pigeon: sustained pecking despite contingent non-reinforcement', *Journal for the Experimental Analysis of Behavior 12*, 511–20.

Williams, G.C. (1975) *Sex and Evolution*, Princeton University Press, Princeton, N.J.

Wilson, E.O. (1975) *Sociobiology: The New Synthesis*, Belknap Press.

Wishart, J.G., Bower, T.G.R., and Dunkeld, J. (1978) 'Reaching in the dark', *Perception 7*, 507–12.

Wolpe, J. (1958) *Psychotherapy by Reciprocal Inhibition*, Stanford University Press, California.

Wright, J.M. von, (1957) 'A note on the role of "guidance" in learning', *British Journal of Psychology 48*, 133–7.

Yates, A.J. (1960) 'The application of learning theory to the treatment of tics', in *Behaviour Theory and the Neuroses* ed. H.J. Eysenck, Pergamon Press.

# Further Reading

Baddeley, A. D. (1976) *The Psychology of Memory*, Harper & Row, New York.

Blackman, D. (1974) *Operant Conditioning: An Experimental Analysis of Behaviour*, Methuen.

Bolles, R. C. (1979) *Learning Theory* (2nd edn.). Holt, Rinehart & Winston.

Bower, T. G. R. (1979) *Human Development*, W. H. Freeman & Co.

Eysenck, M. W. (1977) *Human Memory: Theory, Research and Individual Differences*, Pergamon Press.

Holding, D. H. (1981) *Human Skills*, John Wiley.

Meyer, V., and Chesser, E. S. (1970), *Behaviour Therapy in Clinical Psychiatry*, Penguin Books.

Milunsky, A. (1980) *Know Your Genes*, Pelican Books.

Piattelli-Palmarini, M. (ed.) (1980), *Language and Learning*, Routledge & Kegan Paul.

Seligman, M. E. P., and Hager, L. (eds.) (1972) *Biological Boundaries of Learning*, Appleton Century Crofts.

# Index

accommodation 189
Adams, J. A. 179, 180
adaptation 56, 57
Agras, S. 219
alcoholism 224, 225, 229
Alpert, D. 239
amnesia 145
Anderson, R. C. 137, 138
Annett, J. 170
anxiety 209–17 *passim*
aphasia 121
Artificial Intelligence 234, 240
assimilation 189
Auble, P. M. 155
aversion 53

Baddeley, A. D. 136, 154
Baker, B. L. 215
Bancroft, J. 226
Bandura, A. 199
Bartlett, D. 228
Bartlett, Sir F. C. 133–5
behaviour therapy 205–30
 and aversion 225–8
 cognitive restructuring in 216, 217
 desensitization 213
 effectiveness of 228–30
 flooding 217
 intermittent reinforcement in 227
 negative practice 218, 221
 positive reinforcement in 219–21
 reciprocal inhibition 212–18
 and symptom substitution 215, 219
 token economy 220
behavioural repertoire 41
behaviourism 16
binocular vision 184, 185, 197
blocking 98, 99
Bloom, L. 118
body-image 161, 162
Bolles, R. C. 101
Boulay, B. du 245
Bower, G. H. 137, 138
Bower, T. G. R. 192, 193, 198

Braine, M. D. S. 115
brainwashing 258, 259, 262
Breland, K. 55
Brown J. 143, 152
Brown J. S. 243, 244
Brown, R. 107, 115, 119, 153
'bugs' 244, 247
Burton, R. R. 243, 244

Cellerier, G. 185
Chomsky, N. 112–14, 186, 191
chromosome 57–60
claustrophobia 220
closed loop 179, 180
Cohen, D. C. 215
Collins, A. M. 136
competence and performance 17
compulsive behaviour 217
Computer Aided Instruction 233, 239–41
conditioning
 classical 23–48, 49, 80–82, 209, 228
 conditioned inhibition 219
 instrumental, operant 25–48, 54, 55, 56, 80–82, 103, 235
 timing 32
contingency 26, 29, 30, 46
Craik, F. I. M. 154
 crime, control of 47
Cross, T. G. 107

Dallenbach, K. M. 146
depression 221–4
Deutsch, J. A. 103
development, human 184–204
 constant order of 190
 critical periods in 186, 187
 experience and 185, 191
 identification and 201
 imitation and 198–201
 innate factors in 191
 perceptual 194–8
 phases of 187, 188
 role of conflict in 192, 193

development *contd*
  social 198–204
Dickinson, A. 89
DNA 57
Dollard, J. 86
Dragoin, W. B. 50
drive 85–90
  enhancement 88, 89
  reduction 86–9
drug addiction 224
Dunkeld, J. 198

Eggeraat, J. B. 216
Emmelkamp, T. M. G. 216
Engen, T. 139
epigenesis 184
ethology 52, 62
expectation 23, 78, 79, 102
extinction 34, 35, 40, 44, 149, 219
  of fear responses 211

Fagan, J. F. 196
Fantz, R. L. 194
Farb, P. 106
feedback 84, 85, 93–7, 170, 179–83
feed-forward 179
Feldman, M. P. 226, 227
fetishism 225, 226
Field, J. 196, 197
Foss, B. J. 138
Foss, B. M. 191
Franks, J. J. 155
Frisch, K. von 108
frustration 46

Gallistel, C. R. 103
Garcia, K. 49
Gardner, B. T. 110
Gelder, M. G. 225, 226
gene 57–61, 69
gene-pool 61
genetic recombination 59, 60, 61
genotype 58, 79
Gerjouy, I. R. 128

goal (target) 63, 65, 73, 79, 87–95
  *passim*, 103, 258, 259, 262
Goren, C. C. 196
Gray, J. A. 96, 97, 99

habituation 99, 100
Hager, L. 52
Hanlon, C. 107
Harris, P. 195
Harwood, D. A. 138
Hayes, K. J. 110
helplessness, learned 46, 221–3, 254
Hinde, R. A. 52
homeostasis 84, 85, 92
homosexuality 226, 227
Howe, J. A. M. 245
Hull, C. 85, 86, 125, 219

imprinting 66, 68, 187
information
  gain of 61, 62
innateness 19, 68–71, 113
institutionalization 220, 221
Intelligent Teaching Systems 233, 241,
  242, 245

Jones, H. G. 218, 219
Jones, M. A. 245

Kamin, L. J. 98, 100
Karmel, B. Z. 196
Kellog, W. N. 109
Kintsch, W. 152
knowledge of results 168–72, 235
  and motivation 176, 177
Koelling, R. 49
Korsakov syndrome 145
Kral, P. A. 50
Kravetz, S. 141
Kuipers, A. C. M 216

Lamarck 72
language 104–30
  acquisition of 112, 114

American sign 110, 111
of animals 108–12
of apes 106–12 *passim*
of bees 108, 109
behaviour and 122
of bilingual children 120, 121
early 114
Hopi 117
innateness of 113–16
grammatical rules of 106, 107, 113, 114
structure of 105, 106, 117, 118
Lashley, K. S. 181n.
Law of Effect 25, 26, 42
learning
avoidance 44, 45, 46, 55, 209–12, 219, 222
capacity for 19
cognitive 101, 102
definition of 10
escape 44
and goal-directed behaviour 92
maladaptive 208, 209
and maturation 18, 19
observational 199, 200
predispositions 50
programmed 41, 233–9
self-regulated 253
technology of 232–4
theory 75–103
Lipsitt, L. P. 197
'Little Albert' 49
Lockart, R. S. 154
LOGO 247–50
Lorenz, K. 52, 63
Luria, S. E. 123, 124

MacCulloch, M. J. 226, 227
McFarland, D. J. 88, 89
MacIntosh, N. J. 101
McNeill, D. 114, 115
Marks, I. M. 217, 225, 226
Marler, P. 64
Marshall, C. 219

Maurer, D. 196
memory 131–55
brain damage and 144, 145
depth of processing and 153, 154
encoding and 131, 132, 144, 153–5
and forgetting 142, 146
iconic 141
imagery and 154
interference in 139, 143, 146–50
long-term 133, 140, 142–6, 177
motor 178
perceptual 138–41
qualitative changes in 134
recall and 131, 132, 145, 150–52
recognition and 131, 139, 150–52
rehearsal and 142, 143
retroactive inhibition 147, 148
semantic 122, 135, 136, 139
sensory storage in 140, 144, 145
short term 140–47
two-stage theory of 152
Meyer, V. 217, 218, 228
Miller, N. E. 81, 86
Milner, P. 89
Minami, H. 147
Moore, B. P. 55
motivation 82–8
incentive 88
Mowrer, O. H. 44
Muir, D. 197
Mundy-Castle, A. C. 193
mutation 59, 61, 72

natural selection 57–62, 68, 73, 79, 259
nature and nurture 68–71, 185
Neisser, U. 141
Nelson, T. D. 154
neuron 75–7

Oatley, K. 89
Odling-Smee, J. 61, 62
Olds, J. 89, 90
Omar, M. K. 121

Ost, L.-G. 213, 214
overshadowing 99
orienting response 99, 100

Paivio, A. 154
Papert, S. 246–50
Patterson, F. G. 110
Pavlov, I. P. 23, 24, 30, 32, 97, 99
Personalized Instruction 250, 251
Peterson, L. R. 143
phenotype 58, 60
phobia 49, 209–16 *passim*, 224, 229
Piaget, J. 72, 73, 112, 113, 187–94, 247–9
Plotkin, H. C. 61, 62
Postman, L. 150
Powers, W. T. 94n.
prediction 78
Premack, D. 91, 92, 110, 129, 220
preparedness 53, 57, 67–71, 82, 207, 222
Pressey, S. L. 236
procedural network 242
psychoanalysis 228, 229
psychotherapy 208, 228
punishment 43, 46, 91, 170, 224, 225, 261

Quillian, M. R. 136

reaction time 163, 164
reinforcement 26–30, 38, 41, 47, 55, 63, 80–91, 96, 168–70
  as factor in development 192, 193
  continuous and partial 35, 40
  negative 43, 44
  primary and secondary 33, 39
  schedules of 35, 36, 39
  in social learning 201
Rescorla, R. A. 100, 101
reward 44, 46
Rippere, V. 224
Rips, L. J. 136
Ross, B. M. 139

Salapatek, P. 196
Sapir, E. 116
Sarty, M. 196
Saunders, J. T. 215
Schmidt, R. A. 182, 183
self-stimulation 90
Seligman, M. E. P. 46, 52, 53, 54, 221–3
Shallice, T. 145
shaping 39–41, 55, 234, 235, 239, 248, 249
  auto-shaping 54
Shepard, W. O. 128
Shoben, E. J. 136
Siqueland, E. R. 197
skill 156–204
  arithmetic 243, 245
  and demonstration 167
  display–control relationship 162
  and motor programs 180–82
  perceptual organization 165
  theories of 178, 179
  and timing 163
  and verbal instruction 167
Skinner, B. F. 25–42 *passim*, 51, 52, 78, 112, 233, 236, 237, 260
Skinner box 25, 30, 37
Slobin, D. I. 121
Smith, E. E. 136
Smoke, K. L. 126
Sokolov, E. N. 99, 100
Sperling, G. 141
Spiker, C. C. 128
spontaneous recovery 34, 228, 229
Stern, R. 217
stimulus
  aversive, painful 41–8, 90
  control 38, 39
  discrimination 36, 37, 38
  generalization 36, 37, 38
  substitution 97
synapse 76
Szasz, T. 206

Terrace, H. S. 110

Thorndike, E. L. 25, 42, 54
Tinbergen, N. 52
Tolman, E. C. 101, 102
training, transfer of 173–6
Tuggle, F. D. 245
Turvey, M. T. 141

understanding 15, 16, 17, 18, 240

Waddington, C. H. 73
Wagner, A. R. 100, 101
Warrington, E. K. 145
Watson, J. B. 49

Weiss, P. 72, 95
Whorf, B. L. 116, 118
Wilcoxon, H. C. 50
Williams, D. R. 81
Williams, G. C. 73
Wilson, E. O. 259
Wishart, J. G. 198
Wolpe, J. 212, 213
Wright, J. von 171, 172
Wu, P. Y. K. 196

Yates, A. J. 218, 219

*Books on Psychology and Psychiatry by*
*D. W. Winnicott*

## THE CHILD, THE FAMILY, AND THE OUTSIDE WORLD

Beginning with the natural bond between mother and child – the key to personality, which we call love – Dr Winnicott deals in turn in this volume with the phases of mother/infant, parent/child and child/school relationships. From the minor problems of feeding, weaning and innate morality in babies he ranges to the very real difficulties of only children, of stealing and lying, and of the first experiments in independence. Shyness, sex education in schools, and the roots of aggression are among the many other topics he covers in this sympathetic and indispensable book.

## PLAYING AND REALITY

Dreaming, playing, creativity, cultural experience and the often hidden rivalry between a male and a female element in the individual are among the apparently random topics discussed by Dr Winnicott in this study. The connection, however, lies in what are termed 'transitional objects' and phenomena – the rags, dolls and teddy-bears which provide a child's first 'not-me' experience.

With its case-histories, its comments on the motivation of artists and its tentative and attractive manner of thinking aloud, Dr Winnicott's last book makes a fitting epilogue to his famous books on childhood. It exposes the roots of that *joie de vivre* he frequently awakened in others – children and adults alike.

'His style is lucid, his manner friendly, and his years of experience provide much wise insight into child behaviour and parental attitudes' – *British Journal of Psychology*

*Also published in Penguins*

## THE MYTH OF THE HYPERACTIVE CHILD
And Other Means of Child Control

*Peter Schrag and Diane Divoky*

'A well-researched and thoughtfully argued brief intended to stimulate action against the widespread use of drugs, psychological testing, and behaviour modification used by agents of the state to control children's lives and undermine their rights' – *The New York Times Book Review*

## CHILD CARE AND THE GROWTH OF LOVE

*John Bowlby*

In 1951, under the auspices of the World Health Organization, Dr John Bowlby wrote a report on *Maternal Care and Mental Health* which collated expert world opinion on the subject and the issues arising from it – the prevention of juvenile and adult delinquency, the problem of the 'unwanted child', the training of women for motherhood, and the best ways of supplying the needs of children deprived of their natural mothers. This Pelican is a summary of Dr Bowlby's report, freed from many of its technicalities and prepared for the general reader.

This revised edition contains chapters based on an article by Dr Mary Salter Ainsworth, written in 1962 also for the World Health Organization when it once again made an important study of child care.

*Also published in Penguins*

## HOW CHILDREN FAIL
*John Holt*

Most children fail to develop more than a small part of their capacity for learning and creating. Afraid, bored, or confused, they fall short; and their failure is sometimes not even noticed. This book records a teacher's search for the beginnings of an answer to the question why children fail.

'It is possibly the most penetrating, and probably the most eloquent book on education to be published in recent years. To anyone who deals with children and cares about children, it cannot be too highly recommended' – *New York Times*

'John Holt has done a good and necessary job. A very good book indeed' – A. S. Neill

## SUCCESS AND FAILURE IN LEARNING TO READ
*Ronald Morris*

No educational issue has given rise to such a mountain of research and argument as the teaching of reading. The debates, the texts, the hypotheses continue to appear, and unlike many complex educational issues they very largely appear in public. For reading is perhaps the major ground on which the public at large chooses to question and challenge the teaching profession. Is Johnny reading or not? And it not, why not?

# CHILDMINDER

*Brian Jackson and Sonia Jackson*

'Who minds the child?' is a basic question for working-class communities and for families struggling to establish themselves. But it is also the crunch for middle-class parents, when both of them *choose* to work, and for many more.

*Childminder* – 'a rare piece of research, a vivid, warm and often harrowing book' (*Social Work Today*) – 'raised questions and faced answers that are hard to ignore' (*Guardian*) in a way that 'reads more like a novel than a research report' (*New Society*).

But Brian and Sonia Jackson go beyond revealing the best and the most horrendous, further even than 'a plethora of suggestions, practical and positive' (*Guardian*) to argue for a change in the whole status of childminding in the community.

And happily, beyond the news stories, the reviews and the TV programmes that publication generated, *Childminder* did indeed, as the *Daily Telegraph* prophesied, 'change official attitudes to children'.

# NURSERIES NOW
## A Fair Deal for Parents and Children
*Hughes, Mayall, Perry, Petrie and Pinkerton*

The need for nurseries is greater in Britain now than ever before. *Nurseries Now* combines a consumer's guide to what nurseries are available with a sensible critique of the gaps and anomalies in the present system. The authors emphasize the importance of equal opportunities, of more choice for parents in child-care, and of a greater involvement by men in their children's upbringing. Nurseries alone cannot achieve these aims, and the book also looks at some of the other measures needed, including radical changes in the employment patterns of both sexes.